OPERATION SEALION

OPERATION SEALION

The Invasion of England 1940

PETER SCHENK

Foreword
by

Sönke Neitzel

Greenhill Books

Operation Sealion:
The Invasion of England 1940
This edition published in 2019 by
Greenhill Books,
c/o Pen & Sword Books Ltd,
47 Church Street, Barnsley,
S. Yorkshire, S70 2AS

www.greenhillbooks.com
contact@greenhillbooks.com

ISBN: 978–1–78438–394–7

First published in Germany in 1987 as
Landung in England
by Oberbaum Verlag, Berlin

First published in English as
Invasion of England 1940: The Planning of Operation Sealion
by Conway Maritime Press, 1990

CIP data records for this title are available from the British Library

Designed and typeset by Donald Sommerville

Printed and bound in the UK by TJ International Ltd, Padstow

Typeset in 11/14 pt Arno Pro Small Text

Contents

Preface

AFTER THE FALL OF FRANCE in June 1940 Hitler was near the height of his power. Only one enemy remained – Great Britain – which he did not wish to fight with but which would not give in. His real aims were in the east. If he started an eastern campaign without overwhelming Britain first he ran the risk of a two-front war, especially if Britain was supported by the USA. So an air battle was started and an invasion across the Channel prepared. When the air war did not achieve the desired result the invasion was not considered any longer. This became the turning point of the war, the abandoning of Operation Sealion, the planned invasion of Great Britain.

Though the preparations were significant for this reason, they were also important because they heralded a new aspect of modern warfare, amphibious operations. For the first time, a modern army, with its vehicles and equipment, was to be landed on a defended coast, far from any harbour. A new class of warship, landing craft, was developed, and troops with specialised equipment were brought into existence. This book concentrates on these less familiar aspects of the preparations for Operation Sealion.

May I take this opportunity to thank Dr Dieter Jung, without whose help and active support this book would not have been completed.

I would also like to express my gratitude to Lt Colonel (Retd) Randolf Kugler, who provided many of the technical details for the book. Messrs Arno Abendroth and Norbert Kelling, colleagues in the Erich Gröner Study Group, were of great assistance in selecting and retouching photographs. Thanks are also due to the Director of Archives, Dr H. Maierhöfer and Mr Meyer, Curator of the Military Archives of the Federal German Archives (Bundesarchiv), who were most helpful in searching out the files on which this work was based. The Historical Archives of Friedrich Krupp GmbH also provided documents which helped to complete the picture of some of the technical developments. The following also provided information for this book: R. L. Bridges; Colonel (Retd) E. Dennerlein, who played a major part in the development of Siebel ferries and gave details of Engineer Battalion 47; L. Frädrich, A. Gibbons; Lt Colonel (Retd) Haussmann;

R. Kramer; W. Kähling; G. Freiherr von Ledebur; C. Partridge; Lt Colonel (Retd) Rudloff; Vice-Admiral (Retd) F. Ruge (deceased); Captain (Retd) E. Röseke; Commander (Retd) G. Strempel and B. Wenzel. I would like to express my gratitude to them, as well as to Mrs M. Suykerbuyk.

Photographs were provided by the Bibliothek für Zeitgeschichte, Stuttgart; the Bundesarchiv, Koblenz; the Historical Collection of the Naval School at Mürwik; the Imperial War Museum, London; and Messrs H. Christiansen, Colonel (Retd) E. Dennerlein, L. Frädrich, F. Hausen, H. Hildebrand, Dr D. Jung, G. Rehwald, H. Rindt, Captain (Retd) E. Röseke, F. Selinger, T. Siersdorfer and K. Tough.

Mrs M. Schenk-Lovison helped in countless ways producing this book, and deserves my special thanks.

Mr E. Mahlo was kind enough to read the manuscript.

Lack of space meant a list of the ships prepared for the operation could not be included, but lists of them are to be found in Volume 6 and 7 of Gröner, *Die Deutschen Kriegsschiffe 1815–1945*, Koblenz, 1989 and 1990.

Peter Schenk
Berlin, 1990

Preface to the Second Edition

ALTHOUGH ALMOST THIRTY YEARS have passed since the first publishing of my book, it can be stated that no new sources have turned up in these years to change fundamentally the arguments of this work. Most of the later books have drawn on this work. What has changed over the years is my personal view on the German efforts and their meaning for the outcome of the war. Being more optimistic for the chances of the operation when reading all the enormous efforts made by the German side in the preserved files in the archives, I am nowadays inclined to follow the view of Admiral Karlgeorg Schuster, who in 1940 as Commanding Admiral France had been the head of the landing preparations. In his recollections, written in April 1952, he concluded that for the 'jump' of 'Sealion' the shield was missing, a sufficient fleet to counter the British Navy.

The photos are from the my own collection if not otherwise stated.

I would like to thank Prof Dr Sönke Neitzel for the preface to this second edition.

Peter Schenk
Berlin, 2019

Foreword

ON 22 JUNE 1940, IT SEEMED that Hitler had won the war. France had surrendered and the British Expeditionary Force had been driven from the continent. No one had previously allowed that the Wehrmacht would be capable of defeating the Western military alliance within six weeks. Even the Germans had not really reckoned with such success: on the contrary, their generals had urgently warned against attacking France, their nemesis. A military campaign devised by Erich von Manstein, which completely surprised the Allies, provided the foundation for the Germans' unexpected victory. There was also the additional fact that, beginning on 10 May 1940, the Belgians, French and British did pretty much everything wrong that they could.

The fact that Great Britain continued fighting after the shock of defeat in the summer of 1940, and did not seek an arrangement with the German Reich, rightly qualifies as one of the most important milestones of the Second World War. On the German side, there was no consensus about how the war should be brought to an end. The Luftwaffe believed that the UK could be bombed into a peace settlement; the Navy bet on a long-term blockade; and the Army was the only branch of the armed forces that advocated an invasion. The Luftwaffe was forced to recognise the limits of its options in August and September of 1940; the Navy's capabilities were very limited in any case in 1940; and the rejection of a landing on the southern coast of England on 17 September 1940 rendered the Army's considerations obsolete.

Although Operation Sealion never too place, Peter Schenk's lucid analysis shows how rewarding it is to take a more intensive look at the German preparations for a landing in England. He convincingly demonstrates how Hitler had not planned actually to implement plans for the operation. Sealion was in the final analysis never more than a means of applying pressure to force Great Britain into a settlement with Germany. Only the Army really took the planning seriously, while Hitler allowed the Luftwaffe and the Navy to maintain a half-hearted attitude. The German plans for the attacks on Norway and France could scarcely have been more different; if we look at the plans for Operation Sealion, we seek in vain for clear orders, innovation, and the dedication of branches of the armed forces. *This* plan would obviously never have worked. However, this should not lead historians to the premature conclusion that a German landing in England in the late summer of 1940 would have been condemned *per se* to failure, and Peter Schenk is right to point this out.

His book, however, does not just illustrate the dilemma of Germany's military leadership in its attempt to adjust quickly to an unexpected situation in the summer of 1940 and to agree on an operational concept. His work also illuminates, on the basis of a broad foundation of sources, how the lower ranks of the Army, Luftwaffe and especially the Navy, working under immense time pressure and without any experience, conjured a landing fleet out of thin air, in the process developing numerous technical concepts that pointed to the future. The fact that pioneering technical achievements were developed in a short period of time often receives too little attention in analyses of Operation Sealion. The Germans designed landing boats, amphibious tanks and artificial ports for the first time during this period. In certain ways, the innovation and improvisational prowess of the lower ranks stood in stark contrast to the narrow-mindedness of the highest echelons of the military.

Those who would like to delve into the German perspective on the plans for Operation Sealion will find Peter Schenk's book, which combines in exemplary fashion the history of technology and military history, an indispensable work.

Sönke Neitzel

Introduction

IN JUNE 1940 THE SWASTIKA waved over the coast of the entire European continent, from Biarritz to Hammerfest. The September 1939 invasion of Poland, which led France and Great Britain to declare war against Germany, had been followed scarcely a month later by the crushing of the last remnants of Polish resistance. Hitler was able to secure supplies of ore and important strategic positions through the rapid occupation of Denmark and Norway in 1940. One month later he launched the Western offensive, which ended after only a few weeks with the defeat of the armed forces of France, the Netherlands, Belgium and Luxembourg. France, the last bastion against the German advance on the European mainland, had fallen. Great Britain alone remained, separated from the Continent by the English Channel, only 21 miles wide at its narrowest point. German troops peered through telescopes at British ships in convoy passing the White Cliffs of Dover. It was clear that Germany could achieve a quick military victory simply by crossing the Channel and landing in England.

On 10 August 1940, the first General Staff Officer of the 12th Infantry Division, Major (iG) Teske, sent a letter to his regimental and detachment commanders which stated, 'Due to the lack of useful precedents, the following report of 55 BC is submitted,' followed by a translation of Caesar's *De Bello Gallico* describing the crossing of Roman troops from Boulogne to Britain, and the subsequent defeat of the native Britons.

This might surprise the present-day reader, who is familiar with the massive Allied landing operations during the Second World War: in early summer 1940, however, Germany lacked the know-how and experience to land large numbers of troops, their combat vehicles and heavy equipment on an open coastline. There had been small-scale landing operations during the First World War: in Europe only the ill-fated attempt by the British to land at Gallipoli, and the German invasion of the Russian island of Ösel in the Baltic. Specially developed landing boats were used during these operations, though not many of them were powered, nor were they suitable for transporting motorised vehicles. Further development of these craft took place only on a small scale after the First World War, but the Germans were able to use warships to capture the weakly defended harbours of Norway in the spring of 1940 so that transports could unload there directly. Nonetheless, it was abundantly clear that such a method would never prove successful against Great Britain, which was strongly defended. A landing, if it were to succeed at all, would have to be attempted on an open coast.

When Caesar invaded Britain in 55 BC with two legions and mounted troops in ninety-eight requisitioned transport ships and a number of warships, he had one great advantage: the Britons did not engage him at sea. In the centuries after the Romans withdrew from Britain, in the wake of invasions of the Saxons, Angles and Normans, the inhabitants of the island recognised that their land was best defended at sea. Thus William the Conqueror was fortunate to have the help of Harald Hardrada, the King of Norway, at the time of his invasion. The Norwegian king landed on the east coast and diverted the Anglo-Saxon forces of King Harold so that William was able to cross the Channel and land unchallenged at Pevensey in 1066 in 400 large and 1,000 small ships. The Battle of Hastings, which resulted in Harold's death and the crown for William, took place several weeks later. It was the last completely successful invasion of England. It should be noted that the Germans planned a similar diversion off the east coast as part of Operation Sealion in 1940.

The Spanish Armada encountered such bitter resistance from the English fleet in 1588 that the Duke of Parma's Spanish army in the Netherlands never set foot on English soil. The landing fleet which Napoleon assembled in Boulogne in 1805 also never sailed: the Spanish and French ships-of-the-line were blockaded by the Royal Navy, and then defeated by Nelson in the Battle of Trafalgar in the autumn of the same year.

In July 1940, soldiers again stood on the heights at Calais. This time it was German troops who gazed over at the White Cliffs of Dover and German bombers which crossed over them on their northward course. Air power, especially naval air power, was a new and relatively untested element. Would it be able to neutralise the vastly superior British fleet?

Caesar, William the Conqueror, the Duke of Parma and Napoleon were able to use shallow-draught sailing ships to transport men and horses, but a modern army needed specialised landing craft, which were still under development in 1940, not only in Germany, but in all other countries as well.

In his excellent book *Hitler Confronts England* American author Walter Ansel stated that development of amphibious craft was still in its infancy in the USA and Great Britain in 1940. Having reached the English Channel in 1940, the Germans urgently needed an amphibious fleet if they were to prosecute the war further to the west. German preparations in the summer and autumn of 1940 for Operation Sealion forged the way in amphibious technology, even though it was the Allies who fully developed and employed amphibious operations much later in the war. And even their achievements were somewhat eclipsed by Japan which built the first specialised 'mother ship' for landing operations, the *Shinshu Maru*, in 1934–5.

For the Gallipoli landings in 1915 the British very quickly built 200 motor lighters. A number of developments in the First World War such as the Russian *Elpidifor* type infantry landing ship or the *Russud* type motor lighter, or other designs which originated in the Austro-Hungarian Empire, Great Britain and Germany, did not meet the requirements of a modern, mechanised army. Operation Sealion stands alone as the first planned, large-scale amphibious operation, and it is the subject of this book.

Prelude to a Landing

THE POLITICAL AND STRATEGIC BACKGROUNDS to Operation Sealion have been described in many works and the events can be quickly summarised.

On 13 March 1936, Commander Meendsen-Bohlken gave a lecture on Combined Land and Naval Operations at the Wehrmacht Academy, considering the advantages of landing operations and establishing their requirements, based on Gallipoli in 1915 and Ösel in 1917:

- clearly defined operational concept
- no improvisation of combined (amphibious) operations
- unified supreme command
- surprise (crucial)
- sea control the most important prerequisite, either in general or for as long as the operation required

Expanding on the second point, Meendsen-Bohlken proposed a tri-service study group, which would formulate the technical and tactical requirements, testing them in exercises.

The course of many landing operations in the Second World War would prove these requirements essentially correct.

Although the German Army and Navy had held a few joint landing exercises before the Second World War, the experience gained during the landing on Ösel in 1917 was exploited as far as limited funding would allow, though only by the Army Engineers, specifically Pionierbataillon 2 (Engineer Battalion 2) in Stettin. This unit held annual landing exercises starting in 1925 on the Baltic coast and on the island of Piepenwerder in the estuary at Stettin. The battalion used some ship's boats and First World War horse barges and later two lighters and seven motorboats. Development of powered landing craft was begun in 1935, though the first prototype, produced in 1938, was disappointing, and it was only the war which spurred development.

Before the Second World War Germany had never seriously considered invading Britain. Official policy in the Nazi era, at least at first, was pro-British, and this was

Forerunners of Germany's Second World War assault craft, a pair of unpowered
First World War horse boats. (*Jung Collection*)

backed by the German Navy, which had tended to co-operate with the British
since the naval treaty of 18 June 1935. Aware of this position, Meendsen-Bohlken
confined his comments to an amphibious operation in the enemy's rear on the
French Atlantic coast in a future wartime scenario, during which the French alone
were to be engaged. This posture persisted until 1938, when the German Navy,
faced with Britain as a potential enemy, proposed a huge battlefleet in the Z Plan.
Its implementation would have been problematical.

An amphibious assault against England was not considered until the
preparations for the Western offensive in the winter of 1939–40. Speaking at an
internal meeting in Kiel, Grand Admiral Raeder, the Commander-in-Chief of the
German Navy (*Oberbefehlshaber der Kriegsmarine*), stated that he had considered a
landing operation in England during the planning for the occupation of Norway
in November 1939. After consultation with Admiral Saalwächter, who was
Commander-in-Chief of Naval Group West (*Marinegruppen-kommando West*), he
tasked Rear-Admiral Fricke, Chief of the Operations Division, with undertaking
a feasibility study. This study was based on Hitler's Directive No. 6 of 9 October
1939 which stated that the objective of the Western offensive would be to capture
sections of the Dutch, Belgian and French coast. The resulting report of November
1939 by Commander Reinicke concluded that if all the conditions for a landing in
Britain could be set up, the British would be so demoralised that an assault would
be unnecessary. Curiously, in view of later developments, a landing from the North

Sea on the east coast of England was favoured over an assault via the Channel, though a landing on an open coast was considered to be less advantageous than capturing harbours. If this study does indeed represent an initial attempt to tackle the problem, then mistakes were made already at this stage which later crept into the planning for Sealion. Meendsen-Bohlken's ideas were disregarded: there was no unified command and no timely provision of amphibious equipment.

Walter Ansel concluded in 1960 that the Navy's east coast objective had caused them to persist in their ship-to-shore concept; the Channel as an invasion zone with the chance for coast-to-coast movement was not appreciated early enough. In the face of such a massive transport operation required by the ship-to-shore concept, the Navy balked at having to provide cover for a landing as well, and thus immediately rejected the idea of a landing operation outright. The idea of a landing force having to reach the coast by overcoming enemy naval forces had never been considered.

The prevailing concept of control at sea played a role in the planning for Sealion. According to this view, the superior force controlled the sea, and had to be suppressed before a landing operation on an enemy coast could be undertaken.

As the Second World War unfolded it became apparent that it was better to have control of the sea for a limited time and area for particular operations.

A conference held in January 1940 during an inspection of the engineers for the Western offensive reported that a landing in England could be considered after a successful Western campaign, and recommended that the establishment of an amphibious engineer brigade as well as procurement of landing craft be given the highest priority. The authors of the report did not consider the operational aspects. The proceedings were submitted to both the Army and Navy High Command (*Oberkommando des Heeres* [OKH] and *Oberkommando der Marine* [OKM]). The only result was that the Amphibious Landing Craft Study Group of the Navy, which had existed since November 1939, was joined by representatives from the Army Ordnance Department (*Heereswaffenamt*), Department WaPrüf5, which was responsible for engineering equipment.

In late April 1940, the First General Officer of the Staff of the Engineers, Lieutenant Colonel von Ahlfen, asked the Chief of the Operations Branch of the Army High Command, Major General von Greiffenberg, whether any conclusions had been drawn from the report. Greiffenberg replied that the only landing operation of the war, in Norway, had been implemented without amphibious engineers (*Landungspioniere*), and that no further landings were to be expected.

One month later, German tanks were at the Channel, blocking the withdrawal westward of the bulk of the British Expeditionary Force. The German tanks could have occupied the Channel coast in a few days and completely surrounded the British forces. However, Hitler issued an order to halt the advance and took the advice of the Commander-in-Chief of the Luftwaffe, Field Marshal Göring, to destroy the enemy from the air. The end of the story is well known: by abandoning all their equipment, the British forces were able to withdraw from Dunkirk despite the heavy German air strikes.

The reasons for Hitler's decision, with its sweeping ramifications, are difficult to fathom. Perhaps it is closest to the truth that Hitler had never wanted to attack Britain specifically, but had wanted to achieve diverse spheres of influence and tolerance of German ambitions on the Continent. This policy also held sway in the weeks after France capitulated. Nonetheless, Churchill's speeches to Parliament on 4 June 1940 and on the radio on 17 June, as well as his actions against the French fleet at the beginning of July attest to the fact that Britain had not given up. The successful evacuation from Dunkirk had given the country enough troops to defend itself effectively; at the same time Britain hoped for support from the United States, and for a conflict of interests between Germany and the Soviet Union.

Admiral Raeder first mentioned the possibility of a landing to Hitler at the Führer conference of 20 June. Hitler seemed indifferent, and Raeder assumed that the subject was not of current interest. Despite this, the concept was still being pursued at lower levels: Rear-Admiral Fricke prepared a study on Britain and Captain Reinicke revised his study of November 1939. Preparations were also continued by the Army General Staff and the Wehrmacht High Command (OKW – *Oberkommando der Wehrmacht*), though these were not intensively pursued until after France surrendered. On 30 June, General Jodl, Chief of the Wehrmacht

Hitler and his War Minister up to 1938, Field Marshal Werner von Blomberg, on board a naval vessel.

Operations Staff, produced a study on 'Continuation of the War against England'. It viewed a sea strike against Britain as a last resort, preparations for which, however, should be made to exert political pressure on Britain to remain inactive. Hitler approved these plans, and on 2 July the armed forces were informed that landing operations would be considered under certain conditions, the most important of which was German air superiority. These ideas were formalised in Hitler's Directive No. 16.

At this point the various conflicts of interest began to surface. Hitler, as well as Jodl, considered Britain to be defeated *de facto*, and thought that an invasion scare would keep the country in line. Hitler was increasingly looking eastward, where the Soviet Union had begun to make threatening moves against Romania, a supplier of vital oil supplies to Germany. A pre-emptive strike seemed like a good solution to Hitler;

Chief of the General Staff General Franz Halder (*left*) and Commander-in-Chief of the Army Field Marshal Walther von Brauchitsch. (*Bundesarchiv*)

it would also weaken British resolve and gain Germany the territory it desired. The Army viewed the plan coolly, and the Chief of the Army General Staff (*Chef des Generalstabs des Heeres*), Colonel-General Halder, found himself allied with the Chief of the Wehrmacht Operations Staff, Operations Branch (*Chef der Abteilung Landesverteidigung des OKW*), Colonel Warlimont, and later with the Commander-in-Chief of the Army (*Oberbefehlshaber des Heeres*), Field Marshal von Brauchitsch, in supporting an assault against Britain to divert Hitler from his plans for the east and to keep the initiative in the current war. On the other hand, the Navy felt itself circumvented by the sudden reversal and rejected a landing. The Navy viewed the venture as so risky that it set impossible preconditions, such as the achievement of absolute air superiority. Independently, the Luftwaffe had also begun considering a landing; in early May, Colonel-General Milch had contemplated using the newly established airborne division, but attention was then being focused on Göring's strategy of bombing Britain into submission in an all-out air war. This was to be achieved, not through cutting off supply lines, as the Navy had wanted, but by direct air strikes.

On 1 July Halder met the Chief of the Naval War Staff (*Chef des Stabs der Seekriegsleitung*), Admiral Schniewind, in Berlin, in order to discuss details of a

Commander-in-Chief of the Navy General Admiral Raeder (*centre*) and Admiral Saalwächter, commander of Naval Group West (*right*).

landing operation. It was Halder's impression from the discussion that a landing was feasible, but this is not what Schniewind intended. Both services then began planning the operation independently. There was no joint staff formed which could have quickly ironed out the problems and requirements of each service. Correspondence between the OKH, which had been transferred to Fontainebleau in France, and the OKM in Berlin took a long time and led to misunderstandings. A sufficiently empowered joint commander-in-chief for this operation, which Meendsen-Bohlken had called for, would have simplified this planning and himself made it more dynamic. Hitler, however, was not interested in this.

It was not until July that it became apparent that the Army and Navy had been working from different angles on the so called 'Basis Plan'. The Army had regarded the operation from a ground force's strategic viewpoint and had as its objective the widest possible front in order to split the enemy's strength. The Navy, on the other hand, believed it could secure only a narrow corridor west of the Channel narrows. The Navy failed to communicate its premise to the Army on time, and the Army assumed a full-scale naval assault with no appreciation of the Navy's problems. It postulated a defensive force of twenty divisions, and thus planned for an offensive force of thirty divisions. The three main assault groups were designated according to their embarkation points.

- The Calais assault group against the English coast between Margate and Hastings (Sixteenth Army, Army Group A).
- The Le Havre assault group against the English coast between Brighton and Portsmouth (Ninth Army, Army Group A)
- The Cherbourg group against both sides of Weymouth, east of Lyme Bay (Sixth Army, Army Group B)

In each phase of the operation, the First Wave would be infantry divisions which would establish bridgeheads. The Second Wave of mobile forces would consist of two armoured divisions and a motorised infantry division for each group. These were to be an armoured shock force which would force a decision on the battlefield. The infantry divisions of the Third Wave were reserve forces.

The forces were divided as follows:

First Wave

Calais	VII Corps	
		7th Infantry Division
		1st Mountain Division
	XIII Corps	
		17th Infantry Division
		35th Infantry Division
	XXXVIII Corps	
		26th Infantry Division
		34th Infantry Division
Le Havre	VIII Corps	
		8th Infantry Division
		28th Infantry Division
	X Corps	
		30th Infantry Division
		6th Mountain Division
Cherbourg	II Corps	
		12th InfantryDivision
		31st InfantryDivision
		32nd Infantry Division

Second Wave

Calais	XLI Corps	
		3rd Panzer Division
		10th Panzer Division
		29th Infantry Division (motorised)

Le Havre	XV Corps	
	7th Panzer Division	
	8th Panzer Division	
	20th Infantry Division (motorised)	
Cherbourg	XXII Corps	
	1st Panzer Division	
	4th Panzer Division	
	SS-Division *Totenkopf*	

Third Wave

Calais	IV Corps	
	24th Infantry Division	
	58th Infantry Division	
	XLII Corps	
	45th Infantry Division	
	164th Infantry Division	
Le Havre	XXIV Corps	
	15th Infantry Division	
	78th Infantry Division	
Cherbourg	IX Corps	
	6th Infantry Division	
	87th Infantry Division	
	256th Infantry Division	

Acting on the initial planning which resulted from this Army draft, the Navy earmarked tow groups, each with three and later two converted river barges for the Calais group, which was crossing at the narrowest point. Off the coast, these barges would be taken in tow by motorboats and landed. The same procedure was not feasible for the Le Havre and Cherbourg groups due to the rougher seas in the western part of the Channel. For this reason, transports were to be used which would tow barges that could then be used to unload the transports on the open coastline.

The chart on page 13 shows further details of the Navy planning based on the Army concept. The harbour at Dunkirk was still not in service by early summer, and so it did not appear in the planning. Since there was insufficient shipping capacity to transport the First Wave together, it was broken down into a first and second echelon. Each infantry division of the First Wave was divided into a first echelon, containing two reinforced infantry regiments, and a second echelon, containing the remaining regiment and the rest of the division.

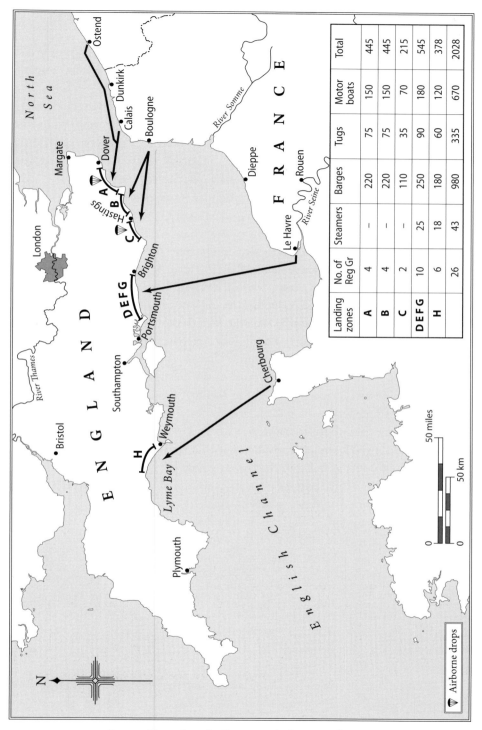

Landing zones	No. of Reg Gr	Steamers	Barges	Tugs	Motor boats	Total
A	4	–	220	75	150	445
B	4	–	220	75	150	445
C	2	–	110	35	70	215
DEFG	10	25	250	90	180	545
H	6	18	180	60	120	378
	26	43	980	335	670	2028

German Navy plans for Operation Sealion, 17 July 1940.

The inset table gives the approximate transport capacity estimated for the First Wave. It should be noted that at the time of the planning there was no reliable documentation on the transport capacity potentially available.

It was not until July that the Navy took issue with the Basis Plan, completely rejecting landings in Lyme Bay and Brighton Bay, since neither an assault nor logistical support could be ensured. A continuous wave of transports could only be guaranteed in and on both sides of the Dover Straits, which would have shrunk the landing front to between Eastbourne and Folkestone.

A meeting designed to reach a compromise took place between Admiral Schniewind, Vice-Admiral Fricke, Fregattenkapitän Reinicke and Colonel-General Halder on 7 August on a train to the Channel. The Chief of Naval War Staff had not seen the Chief of the Army General Staff for a month. Halder called for flanking landings on both sides of the Beachy Head–Folkestone front proposed by the Navy, since the landing troops would not be able to attack the high ground held by the British due to its marshy terrain. He insisted on a landing at Brighton Bay, since the ground was suitable for a flanking armoured offensive to the east; for the same reason he supported a landing between Ramsgate and Deal. The Navy spokesmen objected on the grounds that Deal could be approached only via the Downs, a shipping channel parallel to the coast, which would be exposed to British coastal artillery, while Brighton Bay had a greater likelihood of rough seas, and was threatened by the British naval base at Portsmouth. Halder retorted: 'I strongly reject the proposal of the Navy for a landing on the narrow front of Folkestone–Beachy Head and consider that this would be complete suicide for the Army. I might just as well put the troops which have landed straight through a sausage machine.' The Navy contingent maintained just as adamantly that a broader landing front would be equally suicidal.

After much discussion, accord was finally reached in late August through the mediation of Colonel Warlimont of the Wehrmacht Operations Branch. The compromise foresaw a flanking manoeuvre through an airborne assault and the landing of a lightly armed shock force of about 7,000–8,000 men at Brighton Bay using a large number of small motor fishing vessels. Reinforcements and heavy equipment would then be landed either in the sector just to the east, or directly in Brighton Bay under favourable conditions. The Navy was prepared to dedicate fifty transports to this purpose. The Army cut the left flank by one division, reducing the First Wave to only nine.

An additional and vexing problem was how long the operation would take. The Army had originally foreseen that the thirteen divisions of the First Wave which had been planned for the broad-based operation should be landed within two to three days. The Navy's initial estimates in July were sobering, however: ten days for transport of the First Wave. Jodl had calculated ten divisions in four days and a further three divisions in four days thereafter as a minimum to ensure a successful narrow-front landing.

In late August, the Army was forced to acquiesce to the Navy, which maintained that with the hastily assembled, improvised landing fleet, the operation could not be accomplished any faster. The Army began to lose hope of conquering Britain by sea, and came to regard such an operation only as a last blow against an already weakened adversary.

The final operational plan, as of mid-September, assigned the following Army forces to the landing:

Sixteenth Army

First Wave
XIII Corps
    17th Infantry Division
    35th Infantry Division
VII Corps
    7th Infantry Division
    1st Mountain Division

Second Wave
V Corps
    30th Infantry Division
    12th Infantry Division
XLI Corps
    8th Panzer Division
    10th Panzer Division
    29th Infantry Div. (motorised)
    Infantry Regiment
        Großdeutschland
    SS-Leibstandarte Adolf Hitler

Third Wave
XLII Corps
    45th Infantry Division
    164th Infantry Division
IV Corps
    24th Infantry Division
    58th Infantry Division

Ninth Army

First Wave
XXXVII Corps
    26th Infantry Division
    34th Infantry Division
VIII Corps
    8th Infantry Division
    28th Infantry Division
    6th Mountain Division
X Corps

Second Wave
XV Corps
    4th Panzer Division
    7th Panzer Division
    20th Infantry Div. (motorised)

Third Wave
XXIV Corps
    15th Infantry Division
    78th Infantry Division

Thus only Army Group A was assigned to the landing, while Army Group B held the Sixth Army in reserve. The nine divisions of the First Wave were augmented by the airborne troops of the 7th Fliegerdivision, with a strength of about 10,000 men. An infantry division comprised about 19,000 men. The deployment of the 22nd Airborne Division (*Luftlandedivision*) can only be surmised due to missing files. Shipping capacity could not be divided equally between the Ninth Army in the west and the Sixteenth Army in the east, due to the unfavourable situation in the west of the embarkation zone and the threat to the western flank of the transport fleet, which the Navy had to take into consideration. This meant a longer crossing time for the Ninth Army. The Sixteenth Army believed they would be able to transport at least the fighting arm of the landing divisions and part of the corps troops in the First Wave; the Ninth Army had to contend with transporting the bulk of the second echelon of assault troops in stages, this being due to the original Army plan for a broad-based landing operation. With the diminished transport capacity in the west, there were now five divisions and only four divisions in the east for the First Wave. It should be noted. however, that the Sixteenth Army had foreseen six divisions in the east for the First Wave, then altered this figure to four divisions, though these were to be almost at full strength in the first echelon.

The 'narrow front' plan comprised four landing zones which were designated 'B', 'C', 'D' and 'E' from east to west (see map p. 13). Zone 'A' was originally supposed to be at Deal. but was deleted for the reasons cited earlier. The Navy assigned one transport fleet, giving them the same designations, to each of the zones; with the exception of Transport Fleet D, these comprised several parts: the first echelon was to be sea-lifted in formations of tugs and barges. In the controversial Landing Zone E at Brighton Bay, the advance detachments of the first echelon would have to be landed in motor fishing vessels. The remainder of the first and a small part of the second echelon were to be carried on the transports which were to arrive shortly after the fishing craft and unload. The bulk of the second echelon for Zones B and C would be in convoys of transports which would also arrive shortly after the tows and begin unloading.

It was not possible to provide transport for simultaneous crossing of the second echelon to Zone D.

The landing force comprised:

> *Transport Fleet B*
>> Tow Formation 1 from Dunkirk, 75 tows
>> Tow Formation 2 from Ostend, 25 tows
>> Convoy 1 from Ostend, 8 transports
>> Convoy 2 from Rotterdam, 49 transports, 98 barges

Transport Fleet C

    From Calais, 100 tows

    Convoy 3 from Antwerp, 57 transports, 114 barges,
    14 pusher boats

Transport Fleet D

    From Boulogne, 165 tows

Transport Fleet E

    From Le Havre, 100 coasters, 200 motor fishing vessels

    Convoy 4 from Le Havre, 25 steamers

    Convoy 5 from Le Havre, 25 steamers

This was the extent of the Navy's transports, aside from the reserve barges, for which there were no more tugs available. Everything which could not be loaded into these craft was to be brought by the transports on the return trip. While Transport Fleet D was to return to its embarkation port of Boulogne and reload, the other escort fleets and formations were to be disbanded after the landing. Some of the barges were to remain in the landing zones to offload the transports which followed; the others were to be grouped into small formations to carry the remainder of the first and following waves, along with the transport groups.

This mission stretched the Navy to its limits in terms of materiel and personnel. The most critical issue was transport. The Luftwaffe was to defend the transport fleet against British naval attacks. In view of its reduced capacity, the Navy had wanted to confine its own tasks to minelaying, deployment of a small defensive force and submarines, and an extensive decoy operation in the North Sea code-named Autumn Journey (*Herbstreise*). Coastal artillery emplacements were quickly set up at the narrowest part of the Channel. None of these measures would provide sufficient protection, and, instead of weakening the adversary's fleet, the Luftwaffe concentrated on a different objective: bringing Britain to its knees by itself. By September, the Luftwaffe had to admit that this was impossible, and finally began to consider air support for Operation Sealion.

While the High Commands were still unable to reach agreement on the operation, the lower ranks of all three services were well on their way toward performing a herculean task: improvising a modern landing fleet, the like of which had never been seen before.

The Invasion Fleet

The directive to prepare a landing operation in England caught those authorities which were to be responsible for its implementation largely unprepared. The Merchant Shipping Division (*Schiffahrtsabteilung*) of the Naval High Command started by calculating the strength of the merchant fleet which was available and suitable for this purpose. In 1939 Germany had a total of 3,500,000 gross register tons (grt) of blue-water and coastal vessels, but 1,000,000 grt of it was inaccessible, having been blockaded in neutral harbours at the onset of the war. An additional 350,000 grt had been lost while trying to run the British blockade. Discounting other merchant ships which had been lost during the war, as well as those fishing vessels, tankers and freighters which had been converted to auxiliary cruisers or other auxiliary warships, plus those which were vital to the Scandinavian route, then only 550,000 grt could be diverted to Operation Sealion; a further 200,000 grt of freighter capacity had been captured in the Netherlands, Belgium and France, making a total of 750,000 grt in ocean-going ships.

The British author Grinnell-Milne has correctly observed that if the freighters blockaded in foreign ports are taken into account, there would have been enough to lift thirteen German Army divisions. Here Hitler's short-sightedness, which failed to anticipate British opposition, is amply demonstrated.

The next problem concerned the landing of troops and their equipment and vehicles, including tanks, since the Germans could hardly count on capturing harbours intact. The solutions proposed were imaginative, to say the least. A State Secretary in the Ministry of Economics, Gottfried Feder, having considered a landing in England in April 1940, suggested floating bunkers with powered caterpillar tracks which could climb beaches and land troops and vehicles.

Feder believed that series production of these vessels would be simple, since 10,000 bunkers had been finished in only a few months for the Western Wall. The ability to float was only a function of the size of the enclosed space, he believed. This project was considered seriously by the Navy all the way up to Admiral Schniewind and Grossadmiral Raeder, until the Naval Ordnance Bureau's (*Marinewaffenamt*) objections about design difficulties prevailed.

The *Schell I* in the Sachsenberg yard in 1941.

One quite forward-thinking project involved using hydrofoils for troop transport. A vessel of this type was ordered by General Schell of the Army Engineers for construction by the Sachsenberg Yard in Rosslau, which had already experimented with the hydrofoil principle in motorboats. The requirements specified a maximum payload of 6 tons and a speed of 80 km/h. Since the correspondence on this project was dated June 1940, it seems reasonable to assume that General Schell had planned this type of craft for the landing in England. But Rear-Admiral Fuchs, the Chief of the Main Bureau for Naval Shipbuilding (*Chef des Hauptamtes Kriegsschiffbau*), doubted the seaworthiness of the craft in open waters and development was halted. However, the Navy took over the Army contract and a test craft, the *VS 8* (ex *Schell I*) was completed in 1943. Additional requirements were the capability to transport a 26-ton tank and the ability to land on an open coast using a special landing pontoon with an auxiliary engine. Test results were disappointing, however. The hydrofoil's complex design could not accommodate both a high speed and a heavy-load capacity. Perhaps the project was engendered by the special conditions for a landing in England: the relatively calm waters of the Channel at its narrowest point, and the inferiority of the German fleet at sea. Obviously, the idea was to use high speed help to avoid a confrontation with the British fleet.

Both the hydrofoil and the bunkers were mentioned by Admiral Raeder at the Führer conference of 21 May 1940. It must have been patently obvious to the

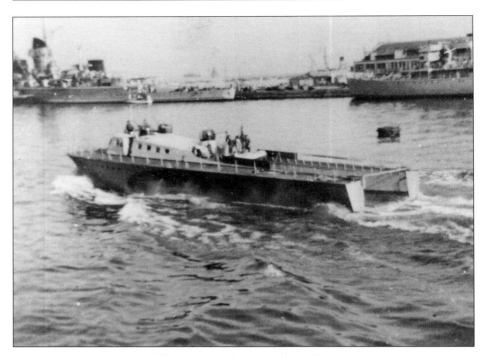

Schell I with the dock space visible at the rear.

officers, however, that the landing fleet could only be assembled in the allotted time-frame by using merchant vessels, and undoubtedly they consulted the Maritime Transport Regulations, which had existed since 1930 as Naval Order No. 406 and were based on the Maritime Transport Regulations of 1907. An updated version of these had been published in 1939. In addition to covering organisational matters, certain practical experience, which had been gained in joint manoeuvres between the Navy and Engineer Battalion 2 in the Baltic with amphibious craft, had contributed. Unpowered craft such as ship's boats on merchant vessels were proposed for landing troops and light equipment. The section on 'Other Equipment' covered the construction of large seagoing lighters for use as auxiliary landing vessels, specifying a longitudinal ramp running up to the bow from the hold. The surface of the ramp was to be covered with planks with trackways left for the wheels of vehicles (see Fig. 2 in sketch opposite).

A secondary ramp would be attached to the barge for unloading horses and vehicles.

In view of this scanty description it is no surprise that Captain Kiderlen, Chief of the Department for Military Matters (*Abteilung militärische Fragen K III M*), stated at a first meeting at the Main Bureau for Naval Shipbuilding (*Hauptamt Kriegsschiffbau*) that barges would be capable of transporting lightly equipped

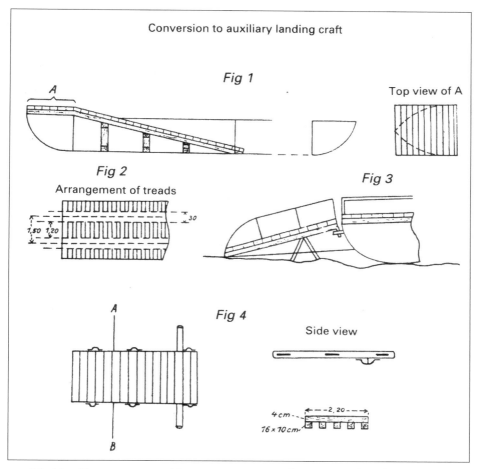

Maritime Transport proposal for converting seagoing barges to auxiliary landing craft.

infantry only. Provision of ferry barges (*Fährprähme*) for transporting tanks and heavy weapons was still at the concept stage.

Army design engineer Speidel from the Army Ordnance Department (*Heereswaffenamt*), Department WaPrüf 5 (Engineers) which was responsible for testing, rejected this contention and was able to add fuel to the argument. He had brought along information on the engineer landing craft being planned or built, which so impressed Captain Kiderlen that he promptly called a large meeting. The Army representative reported that Engineer Battalion 2 had been testing proposals for some time. The small lighter *Louise* had been assigned to the Stettin battalion fleet in 1924. This was used to practise landing operations on the Baltic coast, later in conjunction with the lighter *Podejuch* which was capable of carrying 600 tons and which was built in 1938 at the Oder Yard at Stettin. A number of proposals for provisional conversion of barges into landing craft had been prepared, but were not completed before the outbreak of the war. Barges seemed to be the solution to the problem of landing tanks and heavy equipment on an open coastline. The Merchant Shipping Division had sufficient barges in Germany and requisitioned in occupied countries and their conversion into landing craft presented no technical difficulties. The technical concept for the conversion of river barges to auxiliary landing boats had been found finally. Since time was short, the work on these barges was quickly authorised, which put a tremendous strain on the economy and the engineer construction troops (*Pionierbautrupps*) as almost 2,000 barges were supposed to be converted in a month. Furthermore, these landing boats had not been proven as workable.

It is perhaps useful to digress here and look at the achievements of the Army and Navy in amphibious warfare before the war. The Merchant Shipping Division (*Schiffahrtsabteilung*) stated in a report of 5 July 1941:

> Aside from the operation on Ösel in the [First] World War. in which the Navy successfully co-operated with the engineer amphibious troops in a large-scale landing on an open coast. several such landings were undertaken on training exercises. On the basis of this experience the loading equipment and auxiliary craft were designed to be carried by the transports but had to be constantly modified, due to the increasing mechanisation of the Army. While the design of fittings such as horse boxes and gear for loading vehicles was able to keep pace with these developments, the construction of auxiliary craft (horse boats and landing craft) meant a substantial investment, for which there was no funding after the World War. Nevertheless, the Merchant Shipping Division had seagoing lighters and barges tested for their suitability as landing craft already available in harbours; these could be converted using ramps and connecting ramps – see Maritime Transport Regulations, Annex 21. Most of the auxiliary vessels could not be carried on board the transport ships due to their weight. Furthermore, since most of these auxiliary vessels were unpowered, they had to be towed by seagoing tugs to the landing zone. In view of these circumstances, the Maritime Transport Regulations, Part III (Landing and Embarkation on Open Coast), in accordance with the OKH General Staff. Division 5 are applicable.
>
> At the outbreak of the current war, and on the order of Ski QuA IV, thirty-eight flat-bottomed pontoons, each with a capacity of 25 tonnes, which is sufficient for the heaviest tanks, were produced and allocated to various ships preparatory to landing operations on open coastlines; the auxiliary craft were again carried on board the transports, since the distance to the landing areas could be too great. These pontoons proved successful for transferring

Horse-landing boat of the engineers at the Baltic landing in 1917 on a transport.

troops from MS *Ulanga*, which had run aground, to the reserve ships *Muansa* and *Malgache* on 13–15 June 1941. Some of the pontoons have been used for several months by the Army for training at the Antwerp Naval Headquarters [*Kriegsmarinedienststelle*, KMD]. The disadvantage of these pontoons is that they are unpowered, which has been compensated for by using powered ships' lifeboats which were especially fitted for towing. Trials with outboard engines have not yet been completed.

Preparations which had been ordered in summer 1940 for Operation Sealion caused Ski Qu A VI quickly to solve the problem of fitting out existing craft for a landing mission in accordance with K [*Hauptamt Kriegsschiffbau*].

These retrospective statements from the Merchant Shipping Division conflict with the file notes from the time a landing in England was first being considered. A letter from the Merchant Shipping Division to the Naval High Command dated 13 June 1940 concerning the status of transports stated: 'Rhine ships can be available in fourteen days to three weeks. Ten motor passenger vessels, 200 motor tugs, 85 powered barges, 12 motor tankers, 2,000 barges. Rhine vessels are not considered very suitable for transport of troops and equipment due to their lack of seaworthiness and low longitudinal strength.'

It seems evident from this that the Navy's capability, at least in this type of operation, was not very well developed. Furthermore, it should be noted that the

A PiLb 39 engineer landing craft during exercises.

pontoons described were not ordered until June 1940, and not, as was stated, at the beginning of the war (see page 39).

Regrettably, no records from before the war on testing of vessels have survived from Engineer Battalion 2 and Department WaPrüf 5; the only evidence of testing is derived from letters or interviews with Major General (Retd) von Ahlfen and Dipl-Ing Speidel and indicate that WaPrüf 5 began development of a powered landing boat in 1937. The first prototype of an engineer landing boat (*Pionierlandungsboot 39 – PiLb 39*) was already being built when the war broke out. In October 1939, Colonel Braunig, Director of WaPrüf 5, ordered construction of twenty of these boats and it was not until the following June that the Navy placed an order for the thirty-eight unpowered pontoons.

It is not difficult to see who played the largest part in the development of amphibious techniques. Leaving aside the question of whether the Shipping Division's plans for the conversion of barges were entirely their own work as claimed, it is a fact that later Sealion barge conversions were much more sophisticated.

*

Even though the Army and Navy started from different assumptions, both approaches fell very far short of what was needed. The wartime Army, Navy and Luftwaffe team which had to come up with the 'how' of the projected landing operation in the shortest possible time was fully aware of this, and co-operated in an unbureaucratic and effective way. They were the true pioneers.

Trials staff R (*Versuchsstab R*) during an inspection on Memmertsand near Emden. General Georg-Hans Reinhardt is seen in the middle.

Various test commands were established in mid-July 1940. On 10 July, General of Panzer Troops Reinhardt visited Admiral Schniewind to discuss co-operation between the armoured forces and the Navy. Five days later, Trials Staff R (*Versuchsstab R*) began work. The staff reported to XLI Corps and co-operated not only with the armoured forces, but also with units of Engineer Training Battalion 1 (*Pionierlehrbataillon 1*). Initially trials were conducted at Westerland on the island of Sylt with the installation of field guns on small seagoing craft. These were followed by tests with submersible tanks in conjunction with the Army Ordnance Department and the Navy. Trials also included launching assault boats from transports and the construction of landing bridges on shore. As soon as they received the first modified barges from the yards, the staff ordered landing and unloading trials. Ramp design and the beaching of the unpowered barges posed particular problems. The results of these trials were documented in a number of memoranda and regulations submitted to the armed forces assigned to the landing operation. On 22 August the Westerland Trials Command, as it had become known, was disbanded, since the troops could now carry out practical tests themselves.

A tri-service test centre was established at Emden. The Army was represented by sections of Engineer Training Battalion 1, which had test facilities at Husum as well as on Sylt. This unit was commanded by Lieutenant-Colonel Henke, who had served in Engineer Battalion 2 and was considered the leading authority in the amphibious engineers. The Trials Command of the Merchant Shipping Division was headed by Captain Bartels. A special command in the Luftwaffe under Major Siebel tested ferries, which were essentially bridge pontoons propelled by airscrews. Heavy-duty transports such as barges and various ramp designs were tested in Emden – at first in Pettkummer Siel and later in Memmertsand, both located on the Ems estuary. Lieutenant Colonel Henke headed the training staff for assault boats with Major Gantke, who ran a training course from 25 July to 5 September for approximately 1,000 assault boat coxswains in Emden-Borssum. During the winter of 1940/41 these formed Assault Boat Commandos 901–906.

Unlike Battalion 1, which tested heavy transports, Engineer Battalion 47 built light transports in its capacity as a 'Trials Battalion of the OKH for the Construction of Seagoing Ferries from Auxiliary and Bridging Equipment, and Local Command Resources'. Part of the battalion was quartered in Bray sur Somme, and later moved on 27 July with the remainder of the battalion to Carteret on the west coast of the Cotentin peninsula. Anything in this area which would float was commandeered to be converted into rafts: wine barrels, petrol drums, aircraft floats and tanks (see pages 97–8). As these methods proved disappointing, the battalion began building ferries out of bridging equipment; these ferries were later improved and fitted with engines at Fécamp and Le Trait near Rouen, with help from the Luftwaffe. The 3rd Company was redeployed at the beginning of September in order to take over some of these ferries at Antwerp, where an Engineer Special Command (*Pioniersonderkommando*) under Major Böndel and Bridge Construction Battalion 655 (*Brückenbau Bataillon 655*) with the aid of the Siebel Special Command had also built ferries out of bridging equipment.

How the Luftwaffe came to be involved in these non-aviation activities is a curious bit of history. Luftwaffe Major F. W. Siebel had been on the staff in the First World War not only with the Commander-in-Chief of the Luftwaffe, Reichsmarschall Göring, but also with Udet, later to become Air Minister (*Generalluftzeugmeister*). Siebel had been put in charge of reviving a French aircraft factory at Albert in June 1940. In mid-July he received a visit from an officer from Engineer Battalion 47, who requested a number of old aircraft floats, explaining that his battalion was building rafts for an invasion of England.

This sparked Siebel's curiosity and he arranged, via Udet, to meet the head of the Merchant Shipping Division, Captain Montigny. He was not impressed with the Navy's amphibious capabilities, and decided to pursue his own ideas. Pressed for time, he had to make do with available materials. Siebel proposed using the Engineer Bridge (*Kriegsbrückengerät*) pontoons as floats and that the resulting craft would be propelled by the many antiquated water-cooled aircraft engines gathering dust in Luftwaffe depots. The first design, however, based on the B Bridge, was rejected as unseaworthy by both the Army and Navy.

However, a Siebel Special Command was established in August 1940 for the motorisation of unpowered barges. Along with the engineers this unit developed the far more seaworthy heavy pontoon bridge (*schwere Schiffsbrücke*) and Herbert ferries with combined air and water propulsion. A Captain Dr Koch was also involved in the design process and he later headed the Ferry Special Command (*Sonderkommando Fähre*) as the unit in Antwerp was known, which designed and built landing craft after 1940. The Engineer Special Commands under Böndel and Gantke were working not far away; these commands were renamed the Ferry Construction Command (*Fährenbaukommando I [sF]*) in spring 1941.

These commands generally worked on the technical side of the barges, though the one at Emden also trained the barge crews. The Sixteenth Army ran training courses in August under the direction of Colonel Dinter at Le Touquet.

When Operation Sealion was reduced in alert status in late autumn 1940, Colonel Zühlsdorf's training unit in Le Havre took over. Later this unit was transferred to Antwerp and Terschelling. Engineer Landing Boats 39 (*Pionierlandungs-boote 39*) in late September 1940, and an additional one in October created new opportunities.

Problems like landing unpowered barges and withdrawing from the beach were not forgotten. VII Corps tested one of these boats, and XIII Corps two. A new era in amphibious technology had dawned, but by that time Operation Sealion had been shelved for 1940.

Transports

Aside from the barges, the vast majority of vessels for troop transport were converted freighters and passenger ships taken up from the merchant fleet. In all, 174 ships were commandeered and converted. Most were German, but some had been confiscated from foreign countries during the war, especially from France and the Netherlands. The Navy's Maritime Transport Regulations (*Seetransportvorschrift*) of 1 March 1939 defined ships considered appropriate for sea transport of troops as being between 6,000 and 8,000 grt and capable of speeds of about 12 knots. They have to have deep through decks, large hatches, good fire precautions and loading equipment and at least one heavy cargo derrick at one of the larger hatches. Modern communications and navigation equipment were also necessary. Due to the discrepancy between these standards and the

Transport *Ro 25*, the former Dutch *Gordias* from 1939.

Transport *Ro 3* (*Aldebaran*) from 1920, also Dutch. In the bows are the spars for the protection system and a platform for the Army guns.

actual ships available, many of these requirements had to be scaled down. For instance a minimum speed of 8 knots had to be accepted in order to make use of a number of slower freighters. Most of the ships were faster, however. The most modern transports were the *A 3* (*Moltkefels*) and the *A 4* (*Neidenfels*) with speeds of 16 knots. Although some of the transports were in fact motorships, they were all referred to as 'steamers' in documents relating to the programme, since this term was more understandable to the layman than 'transport'. The ships also varied considerably in size. In Le Havre such large ships as the *H 20* (*Kerguelen*, 10,123 grt) and the *H 17* (*De la Salle*, 8,400 grt) were berthed alongside smaller ones such as the *H 11* (*Cap Guir*, 1,536 grt). Next to the *Ro 12* (*Damsterdyk*, 10,155 grt) in Rotterdam lay the tiny *Ro 17* (*Gasterland*, 317 grt) and the *Ro 16* (*Opsterland*) and *Ro 18* (*Haskerland*), each 374 grt. The vessels in Antwerp varied just as much, though the ships in Ostend tended to be more uniform, being between 2,000 and 4,000 grt in order to fit in the smaller harbour.

Most of the transports were freighters, but there were seven passenger ships: the *Ro 19* (*Batavier V*), *H 9* (*Flandre*), *H 15* (*Mar del Plata*), *H 17* (*De la Salle*), *H 20* (*Kerguelen*), *H 21* (*Ango*), and *H 22* (*Ville de Reims*).

Transport *Ro 19*, the former Dutch liner *Batavier V*.

The fast German *Neidenfels* from 1940 as transport *A 4*.

The German Navy was able to redeploy those German ships which had already been converted to troop transports for the Norwegian campaign, and which were still properly equipped. There were also several ships which had seen service in the Spanish Civil War as special transports (*Sonderdampfer*), but in all probability they had had their equipment removed.

A standard procedure was adopted for fitting out the transports. After thorough cleaning, modifications were made to the coal and cargo bulkheads. Next came the installations for troops and horses: gangways, hatches, horse stalls and quarters for troops, who had straw sacks. Lights, fresh water supply and waste disposal systems had to be enlarged or added. Since the cranes and derricks could not be strengthened, heavy loads were assigned only to ships with a lifting capacity of 25 tons. In order to use the aft holds for vehicles, the shaft tunnel was buried beneath a sand bedding and then covered with planks. Lifebelts and floats were added to supplement the existing rescue equipment. Rafts which could be easily dropped were installed in special slips. Signal and communications equipment also had to be added. Installation of bow protection and degaussing equipment

Transport *A 18* (*Urundi*) at the Schelde quay in Antwerp.

Transport *H 4* (*Ville de Metz*) in Le Havre.

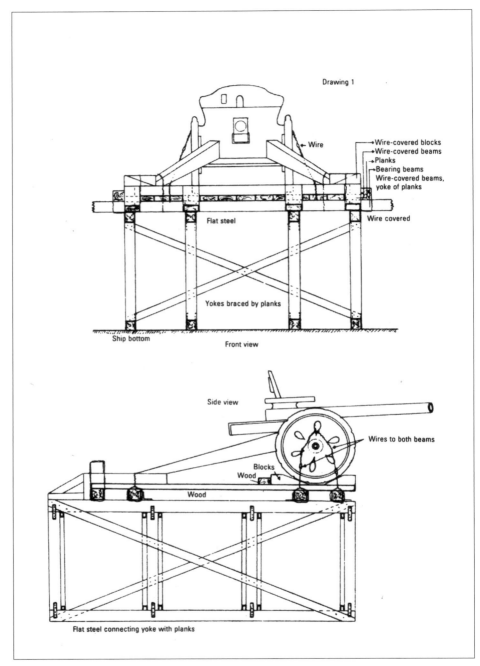

Gun mount for the Light Field Howitzer 18.

Transport *H 20 (Kerguelen)*.

against moored and magnetic mines posed organisational problems, since so much was needed. Due to an oversight, the degaussing coils were fitted externally and unprotected, and this often caused damage when the anchor was raised and while handling the barges.

The Navy installed only light anti-aircraft guns. For this purpose Navy Anti-Aircraft Detachment 200 (*Marine- Flak-Abteilung*) in Kiel-Holtenau was placed under the Commanding Admiral France on 3 September 1940. The Army considered heavy armament necessary, if only for morale, and had the engineers install Army guns on temporary mounts, since the Navy was not able to do so. Time did not allow the deployment of uniform types of guns, and various solutions were adopted depending on the type of ship, and in this respect the engineers proved to be very innovative. Various 7.5 cm guns (former *Feldkanonen 16*, French and Belgian Schneider guns or Polish M97) were mounted on wooden platforms fore and aft or alongside the superstructures where they would not interfere with loading, since the entire deck area was reserved for tall, heavy vehicles. The 17th Infantry Division developed a rotating platform for two guns, and since they were to be mounted permanently, they were allocated their own Army crews. Tests carried out on the steamer *R 1* resulted in six near misses at a range of 600–1,000 m with forty rounds fired and this result was considered good. Guns of this type and mounting are known to have been installed on the *O 5, O 8, O 15, R 1, Ro 3, Ro 6*,

Logistics ship *A 3 N* (*Capitaine le Bastard*).

Unloading exercise from *A 28* (*Mendoza*) in October 1940.
(*Historical collection, Naval School, Mürwik*)

Logistics ship *R 3 N* (*Thistlebrae*), originally a British vessel.

Ro 7, Ro 8, Ro 9, R 11, R 14, Ro 19, R 20, R 21, R 24, Ro 25, Ro 33, Ro 36, Ro 41 and *R 49*, but not until October and November 1940.

The civilian crews remained on board the German ships while foreign ships which were commandeered were manned by crews taken from the German merchant marine. In addition, there were to be fifteen men to operate the winches; these were dockers from German harbours. A representative from the KMD supervised fitting out and sailed as a supercargo on each ship.

Replenishment ships were a subgroup of the transports. They were under the direction of the Chief Quartermaster, England, and were to be used exclusively for the transport of supplies. These ships included the *A 1 N (PLM 23), A 2 N (PLM 26), A 3 N (Capitaine le Bastard), R 1 N (Maasburg), R 2 N (Dora Fritzen)* and the *R 3 N (Thistlebrae,* later *Altkirch).*

Passenger Liners

On several occasions during the war, the use of the large passenger liners already available in Germany was envisaged for a landing operation because of their high speed and apparently large cargo capacity. The *Bremen*'s successful dash to Germany made this particularly attractive. This was first mooted in June 1940 when, hard-pressed by Allied landings, the Dietl Group in Narvik was to be reinforced by landing additional mountain troops in the still-open Lyngenfjord east of Tromsö. On the Führer's orders, Norddeutscher Lloyd's two fastest

Barge alongside the *A 26* in a loading exercise. (*Historical collection Naval School, Mürwik*)

Unloading horses from a transport into a barge. (*Bundesarchiv*)

Troops disembarking from a transport into barges during an exercise on 24 October 1940 in Le Havre. (*Historical collection, Naval School, Mürwik*)

passenger ships, the *Bremen* and *Europa*, each of about 50,000 grt and with cruising speeds of 26.5 knots, were allocated to Operation Naumburg. After unloading 3,000 men, as well as light and medium tanks, they were to attempt to reach Soviet waters, possibly Murmansk. However, after it became known that the Allied troops had withdrawn from Narvik following the invasion of France, this risky plan was abandoned on 10 June 1940.

These liners were again in the limelight only one month later when Hitler was contemplating a landing operation in Iceland in order to encircle Great Britain after the successful Western campaign. Codenamed Ikarus, this operation involved not only the *Bremen* and *Europa*, but also the Norddeutscher Lloyd ships *Gneisenau* and *Potsdam* at 18,160 grt and 17,528 grt respectively and with cruising speeds of about 20 knots. In addition to these, the freighters *Moltkefels* and *Neidenfels* belonging to DDG Hansa were to be used. These last two were 7,838 grt and could cruise at 15 knots. However, the Navy opposed Operation Ikarus, using the argument that it would be unable to secure resupply lines, and the plan never materialised.

The four ships *Bremen*, *Europa*, *Gneisenau* and *Potsdam* were to be employed in the diversionary operation codenamed Autumn Journey (*Herbstreise*) (see

The passenger liner *Bremen* as a transport. Note the 8.8 cm gun in the bow. Landing pontoons can be seen below the bridge and along the sides.

page 275), and detailed plans were made to equip and deploy these ships. Three 8.8 cm Flak L/45 and several 2 cm anti-aircraft guns were installed on both the *Bremen* and *Europa* on 3 September 1940; some of these had come from the old battleship *Schleswig-Holstein*. The *Gneisenau* and *Potsdam* were probably also similarly equipped. Some 5,000 troops, 80 vehicles of up to 20 tons, and 37 of up to 10 tons were to be carried by both the *Bremen* and the *Europa*. The *Gneisenau*'s planned capacity was 1,506 troops, 244 horses and approximately 60 average-sized vehicles. For Operation Ikarus four landing pontoons (see below) were planned for each ship; for Sealion the *Europa* and *Bremen* were to have a minimum of eight and they were to carry four of these pontoons in their davits and land them by towing them ashore with powered lifeboats. The other ships were to unload them with their cranes and manoeuvre them with special motor launches.

The KMD Hamburg wanted to embark a field battalion on the *Potsdam* in Hamburg harbour as part of a decoy operation as late as 4 January 1941. After cruising down the Elbe the troops were to be disembarked under cover of night at Cuxhaven and the ships redeployed to a different harbour. But Naval Group North opposed this proposal on the grounds that Sealion itself had been downgraded to a deception operation pending the campaign against Russia.

Their large size and vulnerability and their relatively small cargo capacity militated against these ships, and it is not surprising that they were never deployed; they could not have been less suited to amphibious operations.

Landing Pontoons

Unpowered landing pontoons for unloading liners and transports were mentioned in the planning for Operation Ikarus. These were to carry horses and motor vehicles and have a capacity of 25 tons. Each was divided into seven watertight compartments and, with a draught of only 0.85 m fully loaded, were able to unload directly onto the beach via a flap bridge. Contrary to the reports of the Merchant Shipping Division (see page 22), these pontoons were not ordered at the beginning of the war, but on 12 June 1940 after a draft was produced by the KMD in Hamburg for Operation Ikarus. Thirty-eight were completed. They were used successfully in June 1941, as discussed above. Some of the pontoons were deployed with the Army Training Unit (*Armeeübungsverband*) in Antwerp and these were also tested with outboard motors. Others were taken aboard the liners, where they were supposed to be used in the diversionary operation Autumn Journey. This was the Navy's modest contribution to the development of amphibious vehicles before the planning began for Operation Sealion.

Vehicle and Railway Ferries

Ferries were considered early on in the planning for Sealion, principally because they were specially designed to transport motor vehicles on their spacious cargo decks. The proposal of Major General Dr Todt, Reich Minister for Armaments and Munitions, during the initial meeting on the technical aspects of Sealion on 1 July 1940, that ferries should be used to transport up to forty tanks each met with approval and the Navy pursued this proposal. The Army had called for a landing at Lyme Bay and in looking for a practical coastline it was found that there was a very steeply shelving pebble beach between Portland and Bridport. In peacetime passenger steamers beached there and unloaded using gangplanks, mooring at right angles to the beach after casting a stern anchor. In their response of 26 July the Navy advocated the use of ferries and freighters of 4,000 grt in these areas. The ferries were to unload cargoes of up to 20 tons using wide ramps, while freighters were to land troops and light equipment over the bow; heavy equipment was to be moved using barges. As noted earlier, the idea of landing at Lyme Bay was subsequently abandoned; nor was it possible to use ferries in a similar manner in other landing areas because the beaches shelved less steeply and so ferries were dropped – at least temporarily – from the planning.

Submersible and amphibious tanks (see page 92) were thought necessary to support the first wave of troops, since it would not be possible to offload heavy vehicles from the barges immediately. Launching submersible tanks (*Unterwasserpanzer*) from auxiliary sailing coasters proved to be impractical, so a small railway ferry, the *Rügen*, which was employed between Stralsund and Altefähr on the island of Rügen, was found and was fitted with a ramp at the Naval Dockyard at Wilhelmshaven. It departed for trials at Hornum on the island of Sylt on 7 August; these were reported successful on 19 August, and the *Rügen* returned to Wilhelmshaven on 25 August for the remaining modifications. Three ferries which had been captured in the Netherlands were also refitted in the same way. These were the *Moerdijk*, *Willemdorp* and *Dordrecht*. Modifications included the building of an unloading ramp, the overhauling of the engines, improvement of quarters and installation of degaussing equipment. On 4 September the Military Department for Naval Construction reported that the *Rügen* at Wilhelmshaven and the Dutch ships at Antwerp were fully operational.

Ferries with ramps were also regarded as the solution for transporting amphibious tanks (*Schwimmpanzer*) and the railway ferry *Pommern* was brought from Swinemünde to Wilhelmshaven to undergo modifications. The first tests were scheduled for 23 August and continued into early September at Emden. Despite this, there were no plans to modify additional ferries like the *Pommern*.

The car ferry *Pommern.*

An amphibious *Schwimmpanzer II* aboard the *Pommern.*

The railway ferry *Moerdijk* during the withdrawal of the German Fifteenth Army across the Schelde in September 1944.

Parallel to the trials with the ferries, special barges were being developed to unload the amphibious and submersible tanks (see page 89). During the final stages of planning for Sealion only barges were chosen to carry the special-purpose combat vehicles. It appears that the use of larger ships for landing the first wave of troops was considered too dangerous since they would have presented too good a target. The use of ferries was rejected from the outset for the diversionary Operation Shark (*Haifisch*) in 1941.

Auxiliary Sailing Coasters

Once the Army and the Navy had agreed on the basis plan of the assault, an agreement was reached to land lightly equipped Army units in Brighton Bay using small boats. It was thought that this solution would reduce the risk of losses for an operation much of which would be carried out in close proximity to the British naval base at Portsmouth.

Reinforcements and the supply of these assault troops would be achieved either directly through unloading in Brighton Bay, or overland from Sector D to the east, depending on the strategic situation. The nucleus of this fleet was 200 motor fishing vessels (usually referred to as 'motorboats' in documentation) and 100 auxiliary sailing coasters. These craft were approximately 100–200 grt and equipped with 80–300 hp engines. Also included were vessels like the *Georgi*, a

Motor coaster *Gerfried* with assault boats and launching gear.

Motor coaster *Helma* with assault boats and launching gear.

steam yacht built in 1902 which the Navy had captured. The German ships were further augmented by vessels captured in occupied countries, among them the British ship *Innisulva* from London, whose engine proved unsatisfactory, however. Minimum speed was set at 7 knots, but since only a few ships were capable of appreciably higher speeds, this figure was probably too optimistic, especially in view of the standard of the engines on the coasters. They were poorly equipped, lacking even radios, and were crewed by civilians. The commander of Transport Fleet E, Captain Scheurlen, had certified that the captains were 'ready and willing' and had trained their crews hard, but he could not ignore the fact that they were made up almost entirely of 15–17-year-old boys.

Since most of the coasters did not have a flat bottom, they would not be able to run aground on the beaches and the seventy-five infantrymen with light equipment on board each one were to be landed by assault boats, rafts and fishing trawlers. Two ramps which could be lowered were fitted on every coaster for launching the assault boats (see page 47) but most of these ramps proved to be too short for the average 2.5 m freeboard of the ships, and so during the autumn lifting equipment, so-called 'assault boat launching cages', was fitted.

Wooden mounts were also installed on the motor coasters for 10.5 cm, 7.5 cm and 3.7 cm Army guns. Since the ships were not intended for any return voyage, it is probable that these guns were meant to provide support for the troops which had landed.

Landing Equipment for the First Wave:
Assault Boats and Rubber Dinghies

The *Leichtes Pioniersturmboot 39* (Light Engineer Assault Boat) was considered early on during the planning for Operation Sealion as suitable for carrying advance commandos. It had proved so successful in earlier campaigns that it was thought to be suitable for deployment in coastal waters.

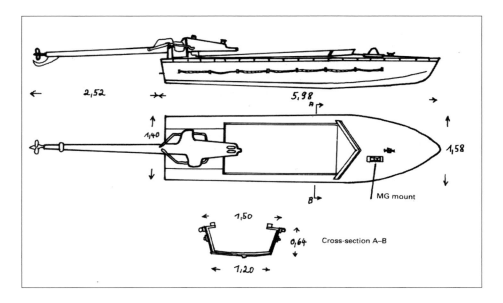

Decked light *Pioniersturmboot 39* engineer assault boat.

Assault boat ramp on a motor coaster. (*Bundesarchiv*)

The assault boat slides down the ramp into the water. (*Bundesarchiv*)

The German Army had adopted this design from the Hungarian Honved Engineers in 1936. The hulls were produced by the Engelbrecht company in Berlin-Eberswalde and the engines by Frankfurter Maschinenfabrik (FMA).

The hull was of simple wooden construction of light plywood boards on a wooden frame and was 5.98 m long and 1.58 m wide. It weighed 492 kg and using the Otto 30 hp outboard engine it could reach speeds of 25 km/h. The propeller could be quickly raised, allowing the boats to ride over obstacles and it also made manoeuvring relatively simple. They could be run onto the beach at full speed. Wooden covers attached with simple bolts were intended to prevent any swamping at sea, and 1,300 of these covers were ordered after they had been proved successful in tests at Sylt and Emden. Each assault boat had a two-man crew and could carry six men and their equipment, and a pedestal-mounted machine gun was fitted in the bow.

A requirement for 1,500 assault boats was established after these craft were successfully tested and, by October, 490 had been delivered to the Sixteenth Army. It appears that only about 800 of these boats were ever available.

Tests by the Assault Boat Trials Staff under Major Gantke in Emden showed that a slide was the most effective means of launching these boats. Two types were developed. The first was a wooden version designed for vessels with a low freeboard such as tugs; vessels with higher sides such as trawlers and minesweepers were

An assault boat returns to the ramp.

Assault boat launching gear on a coaster with high freeboard.

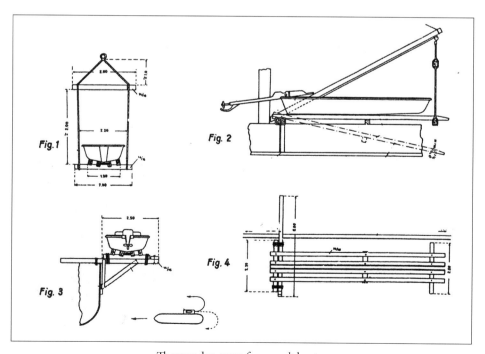

The wooden ramp for assault boats.

Assault boat clearing an obstacle.

The so-called 'assault boat spider' made up of two assault boats and a rubber dinghy.

to be fitted with more rigid steel slides. It was calculated that 4.7 m of slide was needed for every metre of freeboard. The supporting block was fitted permanently, while the slide was to be mounted shortly before the beginning of the operation in order to avoid it being damaged during the crossing. The assault boats were to be launched bow-first while the transport ship was travelling at half speed ahead, and the procedure proved quite effective even in rough seas.

Manoeuvring the boats back onto the ramp again required rather more skill on the part of the helmsman and ship's crew, since the slide had to be hoisted into the horizontal position at the right moment in order to prevent the boat from sliding back into the water. A high degree of skill in this manoeuvre was eventually achieved by the assault boat commandos, especially on the s.S. ferries.

Rubber dinghies were also used. These included the *Grosser Floßsack 34* (large dinghy) which measured 5.50 m by 1.85 m and weighed 150 kg, and the *Kleiner Floßsack 34*, measuring 3.00 m by 1.15 m and weighing 55 kg. It was easy to launch these light dinghies over the side and the crews then used rope ladders to get into them. Manoeuvring them by rowing while under fire was thought to be nearly impossible and so outboard engines were fitted. It was planned that all these small craft would be launched at varying distances from the beaches: the assault boats 1,000 m from shore, the small dinghies 500 m and the large dinghies only 300 m from the beach.

Auxiliary minesweeper with troops and rubber dinghies. (*Bibliothek für Zeitgeschichte*)

Motor Fishing Vessels

The list of the vessels assembled for Operation Sealion included a great variety of craft which were described as 'motorboats' and which had a broad spectrum of tasks. What they had in common was that they had been requisitioned and equipped by the Motorboat Section of the Navy. The 1,600 vessels were divided into the following types:

- motor fishing vessels for transporting First Wave infantry
- boats of various sorts for pushing the unpowered barges ashore
- fast police or customs craft as group leaders assigned to a naval officer commanding a tow group.

Transport Fleet E, for instance, had at its disposal 100 coasters as well as 200 seagoing motor fishing vessels to transport First Wave infantry to the western sector.

Transport fishing trawler with troops and dinghy. (*Bundesarchiv*)

Few modifications were made to these boats, aside from the addition of imaginative camouflage paint schemes. On the Baltic fishing boats the wet fish wells were sealed. Wooden blocks and rings were fitted on deck for the machine guns, of which there might be any number between six and thirty, depending on the ship's size and deck layout. The proposed landing procedure – running the boats onto the beach where the troops would disembark – proved to be impractical because of their draught and so each fishing boat had to be allocated one or more dinghies and in certain cases one or two assault boats. The trawlers were between 25 and 40 grt on average and since, when loaded, their engines would often not be powerful enough to achieve the required minimum speed, the boats from Transport Fleets B, C and D were to be towed behind the minesweepers and patrol boats to cross the Channel. Some of the larger river vessels were also allocated to this group.

Pusher Boats

Since tugs had too great a draught, numerous small 'motorboats' were to be used for pushing unpowered barges ashore; these included inshore fishing craft, harbour service boats and inland waterway craft. Sports boats from the Wannsee in Berlin were even requisitioned as well as small launch tugs. But the problems associated with this varied flotilla of small craft were considerable. Many of them were hopelessly underpowered and would have difficulty keeping their tows on course; many lacked thrust-bearing blocks strong enough for towing; and many had already suffered engine breakdowns during the transfer to the Channel ports.

Furthermore, the relatively deep draught and slow speed of the fishing vessels meant that they themselves had to be towed across the Channel.

The head of the motorboat section, Commander Strempel, a former commodore of the German Motor Yacht Club, was well aware of their limitations and voiced his reservations but the Merchant Shipping Division was confident that they would be able to do their job. In the end it was decided to lash powered barges alongside the unpowered ones, eliminating the need for these 'assault boats' altogether.

Two fishing trawlers pushing a barge during a training run with the 6th Mountain Division, 23 October 1940 in Le Havre.

The motorboat *B 32 Mo* with Transport *H 46* (*Hanau*) in the background.

Group Leaders

Six tows were organised as a single tow group under the command of a naval officer and to keep this flotilla together he required a high-speed command boat with communications and navigation equipment. Customs and police boats proved equal to this task and about eighty boats having minimum speeds of 10 knots were requisitioned and sent to the various embarkation ports; Boulogne received thirty-two, while Calais and Dunkirk were each assigned eighteen. On 26 October 1940 Vice-Admiral von Fischel complained that Transport Fleet B still did not have enough leader craft; there were only three at Dunkirk which could be fitted with the required communications equipment.

No boats were officially assigned to the commanders of the tow formations and convoys though some commanders appear to have acquired boats for themselves by shortcircuiting the process. Vice-Admiral von Fischel himself managed to obtain the *Weser*, a fishery protection vessel, for his Tow Formation 1. Captain Lindenau, who had the enormous task of leading the 165 tows of Transport Fleet D, managed to acquire the tender *Hela*, while the commander of Transport Fleet C, Captain Kleikamp, planned to cross the Channel with the commanding general of VII Corps on a minesweeper of the escort fleet; the commander of Convoy 3, Captain Wesemann, likewise opted for the *M 1502*. Transport Fleet E's commander, Captain Scheurlen, complained that his group had no leader craft; nor did Convoy 2 whose commander requested the use of the fleet escort *F 6*.

A former customs cruiser became the command boat B 31S Mo.

The complement on these police and similar craft usually comprised one pilot, one or two mechanics and two to four crew. The crews which came with the vessels requisitioned from the harbour and river authorities were generally retained; others were manned by conscripts and naval personnel. The untrained crews did not always know how to handle the boats, but the KMD Boulogne praised their good discipline.

Tugs

Since most of the barges were unpowered and the motorised ones did not have powerful enough engines to make a crossing in an acceptable time-frame, tugs with at least 250 hp engines were assigned to tow the barges across the Channel. A tow was to consist of a tug, one unpowered and one powered barge. A total of 1,400 barges was assumed and it soon became apparent that not enough seagoing and large harbour tugs could be mustered from Germany and from occupied territories. Though inland steam-powered tugs had enough power and good seakeeping qualities, they were nevertheless unsuitable, as their steam engines were generally fitted with injection condensers which used river water to cool the exhaust steam; the mixture was then channelled back into the boiler. This cycle was not possible with seawater. Some large Rhine and Seine motor tugs, however, could be requisitioned.

Large trawlers were commandeered to make up the necessary numbers of towing vessels, although they lacked manoeuvrability in restricted waters. The

H 24 S was the 650 hp Navy tug *Föhn.*

H 1 S was the 500 hp tug *Spiekeroog.*

R 88 S, the former 400 hp river tug *Baden XIV*, temporarily aground during a landing exercise.

140 German trawlers were supplemented by a similar number of ocean-going and inland tugs from occupied countries, as well as by almost 100 German ocean-going tugs and 20 Rhine tugs. To increase the numbers, the transports were to tow two barges each; to avoid problems in Antwerp, they were lashed alongside until the open sea was reached.

The tugs and transports were fitted with auxiliary communications equipment, including hand Morse lamps, signal flags, flare pistols and course and rudder indicators. A telephone line was installed between the bridge and the stern on the transports. Since the majority of the tugs had only limited navigational equipment, 425 magnetic compasses had to be provided.

The trials report from Transport Fleet C commented that most of the smaller tugs were not able to sustain the required 6 knots and asked for them to be replaced. All tugs were to burn only the best coal to maximise engine performance.

Lightly armed Army shock troops were to travel on the tugs in order to strengthen the First Wave. They were to land simultaneously with the advance detachments. With this in mind, each tug was fitted with one slide and the steam trawlers with two. The tugs were able to carry between one and four assault boats and the trawlers three or four. Since they were in constant use towing barges to the Channel ports, the tugs could not be as heavily armed as the transports, but some had minimal protection for the wheelhouse.

Steam trawlers configured as tugs in Rotterdam in October 1940.
Note the gun pedestals and boat ramps.

Manning the tugs presented fewer difficulties than it did for the other landing craft, since the crews were generally retained. Many of the crews of the trawlers were also kept on.

Each formation, of 8–12 tugs each towing an unpowered and a powered barge, was 300–500 m long. The best procedure was to tow the unpowered barge using two lines of equal length while the powered barge came along astern of it on a single line, using its engine but keeping the tow line just taut. Signalling within the formation was done by whistle. Tow lines often snapped and so barges were to be equipped with a 30 m manila line which had more give. Later trials showed that the two barges could be towed lashed together as long as the sea was reasonably calm. This reduced the length of the towed formations by one-third, though the Army was concerned that the coupled barges would present easier targets.

Type A Barge

A whole fleet of barges was to unload troops and equipment and lighten the large transports off the coast. Before turning to the technical aspects, it seems pertinent to discuss several terms which could cause confusion.

Although both types might be called barges in English, in Germany a distinction is made between river craft capable of carrying freight (*Kähne* or *Prähme*) and coastal vessels (*Seeleichter*). Furthermore, lighters (*Leichter*) are generally smaller

Part of the landing fleet off Boulogne on 4 September 1940. Strings of tows deliver barges (*Kampinen*) to the embarkation ports. The tug *Eversand* (810 hp) heads the formation. (*Historical collection, Naval School, Mürwik*)

than inland vessels and serve to 'lighten' freighters anchored offshore which are too deeply loaded to enter harbour. In harbours, another form of lighter (*Schuten*) is used as a floating warehouse and for ship-to-ship transfers. Lighters (*Leichter* and *Schuten*) are generally unpowered, but by 1940 a number of *Prähme* were already motorised. Since lighters did not have the necessary load-carrying capacity and could not pass through much of the inland waterways system, it was decided to use river craft for Operation Sealion. The term *Prähm*, which is a Czech term, came to be used for this type of craft, although files on the operation often use the incorrect term *Leichter*.

Most of the 2,318 converted barges came from the Rhine and its reaches and canals. At the time of the Second World War there were more types of inland craft than there are today and these were designed to fit the various sizes of locks and the different depths of the particular waterways. Two types commonly used on the Rhine serve to illustrate the types of barges that were requisitioned.

The *péniche* was Flemish in origin and measured 38.5 m × 5.05 m × 2.3 m, with a cargo capacity of 360 tonnes. It was used on the canals of Flanders, the Alsace and the Saar River, and was the smallest standard type in German inland waters. All barges up to these dimensions were generally termed *péniche* or Type AI; for Operation Sealion 1,336 barges were of this type. All larger barges were embraced

A trawler with two barges in tow.

The Army Trials Unit at Le Havre manoeuvring a tow formation with shortened
double lines. (*Bibliothek für Zeitgeschichte*)

in a single category, *Kempenaar*, or Type A2. This type, which was designed for the Belgian canals, was 50.0 m x 6.60 m x 2.50 m and had a cargo capacity of 620 tonnes. They were known as *campinois* in French, from which the German name *Kampine* was derived. This was the name commonly used in 1940; 982 barges were of this type.

Of the 2,318 modified barges, approximately 860 came from Germany, 1,200 from the Netherlands and Belgium and 350 from the Seine region. Approximately 800 of the requisitioned barges were motorised. This figure should not be taken too strictly, however, since their crews' inexperience and the state of the engines meant that not all them were fully operational at any one time. For example, the Commanding Admiral France reckoned that about 30 per cent of those modified in his territory could not be relied upon.

The theoretical requirements for the landing barges were as follows:

1   To be able to cope with open water up to sea state 2;
2   To land on beaches with a slope of about 1 degree;
3   To transport 25-ton tanks;
4   To be able to use all the Dutch, Belgian, and north French canals.

For the first criterion it was calculated that the barges would need a freeboard of at least 2 m and would have to be in a good state of repair. As it turned out, the barges were more seaworthy than expected, shipping little water during exercises in winds of force 4 or 5 and coping well with the waves. Even at wind forces of 6 or 8 only two barges reported damage to the external bow doors during one exercise with the 17th Infantry Division.

The second requirement meant limiting loaded draught forward to 0.75 m, to allow easy landing of horses, vehicles and troops. Tanks could be carried only by reinforcing the barges and building an internal ramp. A minimum length of 35 m was set in order to accommodate several vehicles.

The fourth requirement could only be met by the *péniche*, which could be transferred to Ostend via the inland waterways; the *Kampinen* were too large for some canals and had to be towed to their embarkation harbours by sea from the western Schelde.

Given the tight deadline, the conversion programme required careful planning, to have all the components – many prefabricated – ready for installation as soon as possible after the barges reached their conversion yards.

The first step in the conversion process was to prepare the hold for tank transportation. The hold was generally completely open and to compensate for its lack of transverse strength, diagonal braces were installed at about every sixth frame. The struts used for this were attached to the deck beams and frames by knee plates. The trackway for the tanks was strengthened by three I-section

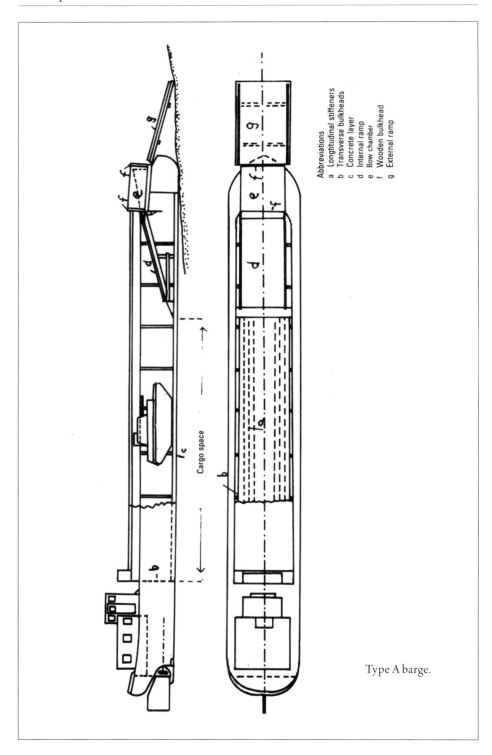

Type A barge.

Abbreviations
a   Longtitudinal stiffeners
b   Transverse bulkheads
c   Concrete layer
d   Internal ramp
e   Bow chamber
f   Wooden bulkhead
g   External ramp

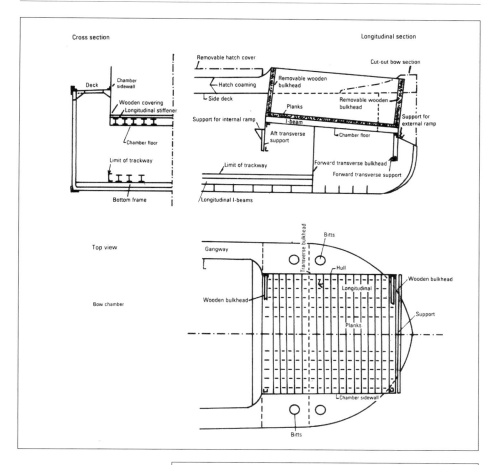

Cross section

Longitudinal section

Top view

Bow chamber

Above: Installation of the chamber in the bow.

Right: Transverse bracing in the body of the barge.

beams on each side running the length of the hold and welded to the transverse frame below. In order to spread the local stress from the weight of the tanks as much as possible, a layer of concrete was laid over the bottom; the

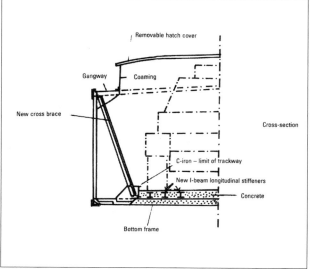

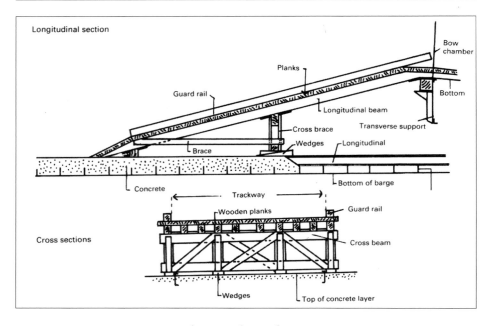

The internal ramp design.

increased draught had to be accepted. Three tanks could be carried in the *péniche* and four in the *Kampine.*

Rebuilding the bow was more difficult. An exit had to be constructed for tanks and other vehicles which was above the waterline of the loaded barge so as to provide sufficient freeboard. A watertight bulkhead was fitted in the bow for this purpose. In order to avoid too acute a track angle over this bulkhead, a nearly horizontal trackway equal to the length of the largest tank track tread was fitted and was supported fore and aft by strong transverse braces. Vehicles reached this trackway from the floor of the hold via a ramp. The bottom of it, under the trackway, was reinforced with strong longitudinal girders and there was a thick layer of wood on top. The whole trackway protruding from a cutout bow was inclined slightly forward to allow better run-off of water, while on passage the bow opening was sealed by two timber bulkheads forming a reasonably watertight chamber. The internal ramp leading up to it was made of wood for ease of production.

Aside from the two watertight transverse bulkheads in the bow and at the end of the hold in the stern, there was no protection against leaks. Only a few special barges for the advance forces had concrete-lined sidewalls. Later landing craft generally had double bottoms and sidewalls, which were greatly subdivided by bulkheads.

The external ramp leading from the trackway chamber to the shore proved to be the most problematical aspect of these early landing craft. At first the usual practice

Conversion of the barges began with cutting out the bow. Here, the bottom has not yet been reinforced. (*Bundesarchiv*)

Once the longitudinals had been laid, the spaces in between were filled with concrete. (*Bundesarchiv*)

Chamber and internal ramp installed in the bow. (*Bundesarchiv*)

Completed barges at the Schimag yard in Mannheim. The sharpness of the stems varies between
the barges and the hull of the barge to the right has bracket supports.

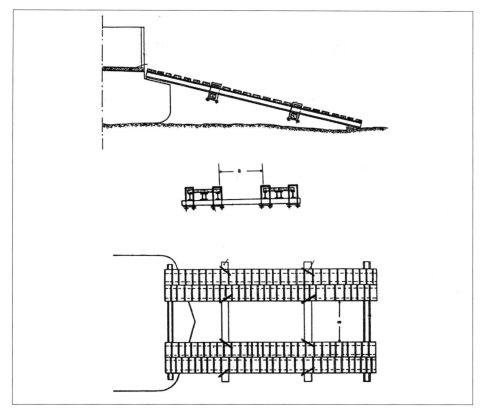

The external ramp design.

was followed of constructing the external ramp out of wooden beams laid across longitudinal members. Assembling this, however, proved to be too laborious and time-consuming. A solution was found in mass-produced track supports, which could be slotted into a U-shaped bracket on the bow. Four supports were used and they could either be laid flush together for unloading troops and horses or laid apart for tanks and other vehicles; for unloading larger combat vehicles they had to be braced by using two transverse beams. At sea the track supports lay on the internal ramp ready for use. Just before beaching, the wooden bulkheads of the trackway were removed and the track supports were pushed halfway forward of the bow. Once the barge grounded, some of the crew jumped into the water and helped draw out the track supports and rest the ends on a beam onshore, slotting the other end into the bracket on the bow. Ideally, this manoeuvre was supposed to take about four minutes and it required a team comprising the engineer NCO and four engineer troops, as well as sixteen infantrymen. In order to speed up the laying of the ramp, a frame was built to pick up the completed ramp and position it forward of the bow.

Above: The search for a practical external ramp:
building it from segments in 20 minutes during a test at Petkum with the barge *Rhemosa*.

Opposite, top: Motorised barge under tow. The wheelhouse has been given makeshift protection.
The sign *EM* was probably added after degaussing. (*Historical Collection, Naval School, Mürwik*)

Opposite, middle: Barge with gun platform and protected wheelhouse at Calais. Engineer jetty for
boarding at left. (*Bibliothek für Zeitgeschichte*)

Opposite, bottom: After an exercise, *H 61 P* is towed into Le Havre by a trawler, 21 October 1940.
In the background is *FB 20* (ex-*Alexis de Tocqueville*). (*Historical collection, Naval School, Mürwik*)

Landing exercise with the standard ramp. Track supports are being readied.
(*Bibliothek für Zeitgeschichte*)

The barge is secured by running lines onshore. (*Bibliothek für Zeitgeschichte*)

The complete ramp in use. (*Bibliothek für Zeitgeschichte*)

This was known as the *portalramp* (see page 72). During the crossing the frame was on deck and was set up shortly before beaching. Cables and winches were used to raise and lower the ramp. However, this system proved too complicated and vulnerable in operation and it was not possible to use the ramp if the vessel was listing. In the end, all the ramps which had been installed had to be removed.

The real shortcoming of all of these ramps was the fact that the barge had to be firmly aground in order to ensure sufficient stability for the ramp. This could generally only be achieved on a falling tide on gently shelving beaches. On a rising tide the barges shifted and pressed the track supports out of the brackets. Landing on a falling tide had its disadvantages because the barges went aground and were useless until refloated on the next tide. It was also a cause for concern that many of the barges would have been forced to wait half an hour or so between beaching and the tide dropping enough for lorries to be put ashore (unlike armoured vehicles they could not be driven into relatively deep water). This is where the limitations of these makeshift landing craft were most in evidence.

The barges were an important link in the transport chain, but their clumsiness and the dearth of transports meant that the Navy could provide the Army with only a very inadequate shipping capacity.

In the late autumn and early winter of 1940 efforts were redoubled to design a better ramp which could be used during any state of the tide. On 30 November, Lieutenant General Model, Chief of the General Staff of the Sixteenth Army,

Landing exercise on 24 October 1940 in Le Havre. In the background is the transport
H 25 (*Ange Schiaffino*). (*Historical collection, Naval School, Mürwik*)

Track supports being put into position. (*Historical collection, Naval School, Mürwik*)

A vehicle from a *Panzerjäger* anti-tank unit backing into a barge at Le Havre
in October 1940. (*Historical collection, Naval School, Mürwik*)

An armoured scout car is unloaded during a landing exercise of Engineer Training Battalion 1
(*Pi.Lehr.Btl.1*) on Memmertsand near Emden.

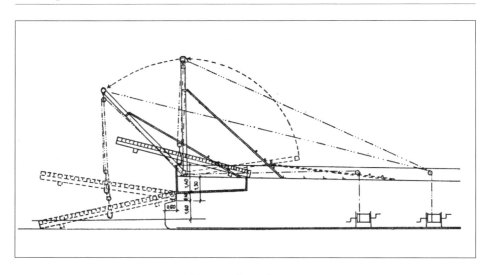

The *portalramp* design.

Test barge *Rhemosa*, later *R 34 Pmot*, with a *portalramp*.

Two types of ramp being tested in April 1941 at Ostend: in the foreground an improved *portalramp*, in the background a double folding ramp of Engineer Training Battalion 1 (*Pi.Lehr.Btl 1*). (*Bundesarchiv*)

A double folding ramp being opened. (*Bundesarchiv*)

Trials with a test ramp designed by Krupp at Le Havre in October 1941.

Extending the ramp using a block and tackle.

The ramp lowered.

even offered a prize of RM 3,000 for engineering improvements, particularly for better ramps. The bracket design for the track supports was rethought and skids for the lower end were introduced. Some improvement was noted, but only for light loads. Another approach to the problem was to use only two wider supports which were more easily moved using rollers. The track supports were laid using an outrigger and winch in the bow. The advantage of the outrigger was that it reduced the number of crew needed to handle the ramp to six or eight men and they did not need to enter the water; but the quick set-up time was offset by the ramp's weight limit of only 16 tons, which precluded transporting Panzer III and IV tanks. Engineer Training Battalion 1 developed folding ramps capable of carrying loads of 12 and 20 tons; when the barges were under way the ramps were folded upwards on the bow and could be quickly lowered when landing.

A more complicated solution was the Ramp System B (*Rampengerät* B), a closed 7 m ramp which was produced by Krupp Stahlbau. Two iron sections at the end of the inclined ramp ran on rollers in the hull, so that the ramp was held on a horizontal plane until it dropped into the supports on the bulkhead. The forward end could then be lowered with cables controlled via a hand winch. However, adopting this ramp design and converting the barges accordingly would have been very costly. The lack of test reports is frustrating for it would be interesting to know whether the powered barges, using this ramp, would have equalled the performance of 'real' landing craft.

For the rapid disembarkation of the shock troops, the Sixteenth Army built 100 light ramps each with a load carrying capacity of between 8 and 12 tons and similar to the production version of the track supports. These were earmarked for the First Wave barges.

Further modifications to the barges included the addition of bow and stern anchors, lifesaving equipment (a raft and two safety buoys), horse stalls and racks for bicycles. The rudder blades were decreased in size and the barges were degaussed to reduce the risk of magnetic mines.

*

The Army placed great emphasis on the installation of weapons and the Reinhardt Trials Staff developed a number of wooden platforms for this purpose. The engineers fitted a wooden platform amidships in many of the barges when they arrived at the embarkation harbours. Weapons could be old 7.5 cm guns, 10.5 cm howitzers, 3.7 cm and 4.7 cm PAK (*Panzerabwehrkanone*) anti-tank guns, as well as 2 cm and 3.7 cm AA guns. High-trajectory weapons such as the 8 cm and 10 cm mortars could also be used. A pedestal-mounted machine gun provided each barge with a limited degree of air defence. Although most of the guns could be shifted in their mounts to increase their arcs of fire, they were not particularly effective

Temporary gun mount for Army 3.7 cm flak guns.

Light field howitzer.

against surface targets but they would probably have been quite effective during the landings, especially in view of the fact that the Navy was unable to provide larger-calibre weapons for this purpose. The Sixteenth Army assigned 140 7.5 cm guns and 35 4.7 cm anti-tank guns to XIII and VII Corps. After the landing they were to reinforce divisional artillery. The 1st Mountain Division planned to arm 44 of the 76 barges assigned to it in the First Wave with a 7.5 cm FK 16 and 18 with a 4.7 cm PAK anti-tank gun.

German civilian crews were put aboard the 300 German and 150 Dutch barges when they were requisitioned and these crews were assigned to the local construction battalions of the engineers. Other crews, mostly dockers, rafters, harbour and river personnel, were trained to man the barges in two- or ten-day courses at Emden. To try to keep discipline tight, the barge captains were designated petty officers (*Bootsmaat*). They commanded three men and on the motorised barges four, the additional member being a mechanic. A non-commissioned officer and four men from the construction troops operated the outer ramp. The barge crews were a colourful crowd; Army construction troops wore grey uniforms, civilians and Army troops blue, as did the regular Navy crew. The chain of command was rather vague and the construction troops often refused to handle the lines, since their primary task was to operate the ramps. Discipline was lax due to a general lack of supervision, and constant air raids forced the crews

Light infantry gun.

to sleep in cellars and perform their tasks under threat of more raids during the day. It is no wonder that complaints were rife about poor performance and the recalcitrance of the barge crews.

*

For landing these barges a standard procedure was to be adopted. The tow approached the beach bow-on and just before the tugs grounded, at about the 4 m mark, they turned into the current to anchor. At the same time, the motorised barge aft cast off and beached under its own power. The towed pusher boats also cast off and tied up aft of the unpowered barge. Just before reaching the shore, that is when the draught of the pusher boat made it necessary, they dropped the forward line, turned and then dropped the aft lines. The barges dropped their stern anchor about 20 m from shore and then at 10 m their bow anchor so that they were positioned bow on to the shoreline. An additional four forward lines were taken ashore to keep them steady. The outside ramp could then be readied and unloading begin, though the water level had to drop before wheeled vehicles could be unloaded; in some tidal conditions this might take only fifteen minutes, but forty-five minutes was the norm.

Since pusher boats were generally unsatisfactory as manoeuvring units, a system was developed in late September and early October of towing the barges in pairs alongside each other, one unpowered and one motorised, the latter being responsible for beaching. Two unpowered barges were also to be towed by each transport but in this case the transport fleets' own tugs and pusher boats would have been responsible for landing the barges.

As soon as the barges had begun to float on the next tide, they were to be picked up by the tugs. They were to tie up lengthwise to the transports to be loaded and depending on the size of the ship, one or two barges could be loaded simultaneously on each side. Trials were run by the 17th Infantry Division in Ostend Harbour on 27–28 September on the steamer O 5 (*Wolfram*) with 28 officers, 136 NCOs and 693 men aboard. They were followed by 80 horses, 84 motorcycles, 25 automobiles, 30 trucks (including towing and bridge-building vehicles), 2 ambulances, 1 command vehicle, 1 light infantry gun, 7 PAK, 1 light tracked vehicle (*Karette*), 1 field vehicle (*Feldwagen*), 7 field kitchens, 284 bicycles, and 200 tons of supplies, amounting to 26 barge loads in all. It took 14 hours to unload the soldiers and equipment in calm harbour waters, and four barges were alongside all the time. Under operational conditions things would have been very different. In heavy seas, for instance, the loading could have taken place only on the lee side of the transport; night would have hindered work still further and it was uncertain whether there would have been sufficient barges. Thus it was estimated that it could take as long as 50 hours to unload a transport completely.

Under way (*above*) . . . and landing (*below*), the coupled barges *D 122 P* and *D 9 Pmot.* (*Bibliothek für Zeitgeschichte*)

Right: Stern of a Type AF barge.

Despite their deep draught, motorised barges capable of 6 knots or more were used in landings on the Russian Baltic islands in 1941. Many of these barges were retained as reserves in amphibious flotillas or were used for transport later in the war.

The Germans were not alone in adapting barges for amphibious operations during the Second World War; the Royal Navy had to compensate for the lack of specialised landing craft by converting over 2,000 barges, most of which were unpowered.

Special Barges

In addition to the Type A barges, four other types were developed and produced; these were the AF, AS, B and C.

Type AF

These were the barges which the Luftwaffe had fitted with two aircraft engines and airscrews as proposed by Major Siebel and Captain Koch (see page 26). The Navy was sceptical of this incursion into its sphere, but the Army High Command was convinced of its merit. In early September, the *Maria II* apparently ran successful trials in Walsum and the Luftwaffe began to fit unpowered barges at Rotterdam

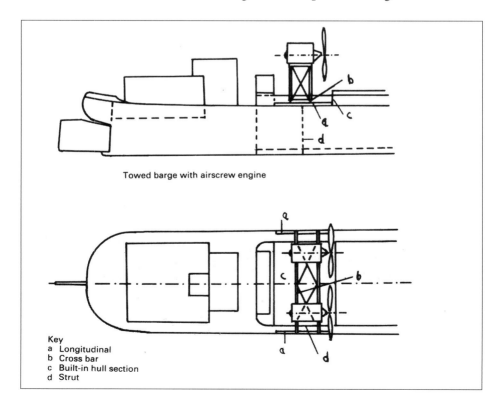

Towed barge with airscrew engine

Key
a Longitudinal
b Cross bar
c Built-in hull section
d Strut

Barges fitted with aircraft engines at Rotterdam Mervehaven.

Both engines of a Type AF barge operating. Note the cooling water pipes.

and Antwerp. By 1 October 128 *péniches* and *Kampinen* had been converted. An additional 22 were modified at Rotterdam by 7 October and a further 25 a few days later at Antwerp. Further conversions brought the total of Type AF barges to 201.

The *Prince Charles*, a Type AF barge, with one engine running.

The engines were BMW 6U aircraft engines that had been taken out of service or which had exceeded their service life, and large numbers of these were stored in Luftwaffe depots. Despite their combined 1,200 hp (2 x 600 hp), they were not efficient and were only capable of pushing the barges at 6 knots, giving them a range of just some 60 nautical miles without auxiliary fuel tanks.

In order to achieve a stable platform for the engines, a watertight iron deck was constructed immediately forward of the after end of the hatch between the two longitudinal coamings. This compartment rested on two U-shaped longitudinal girders on the side deck. Two U-shaped transverse girders were placed on the longitudinal girders and the deck to accommodate the framework for the engines. Diagonal braces supported the transverse girders; two vertical stanchions were placed in the cargo hold on each side. Cooling water for the engines was stored in tanks on deck. Unfortunately, no test reports exist on this type of barge, but it is probable that they were not particularly well suited to their task. They were unable to go astern and they had limited manoeuvrability; further the noise must have been deafening. They had two additional crew members in the form of Luftwaffe engine mechanics – a tri-service crew.

The Type AS barges did not differ externally from the normal ones.
Seen here is *C 102 PI* (*Uckermark*). (*Frädrich*)

The reinforced sides of this barge at Le Havre probably indicate that this is a Type AS.
The track supports can be seen on the inner ramp.

Type AS

An armoured infantry barge was necessary to protect the advance detachments during landing and for this purpose a powered Type A barge was armoured by reinforcing its sides with concrete, though this reduced load-carrying capacity to 40 tons. These barges were to carry up to ten assault boats which were to be launched via slides. Eighteen of these AS type were produced by mid-August, and on 30 September a further five were ordered. The validity of the concept was to be proved by the introduction of an armoured fast patrol craft by the Japanese amphibious forces and the production of lightly armoured British landing craft.

Type B

The Type A barges were unable to land armoured vehicles rapidly in support of the initial landing forces. A way around this was to make the tanks watertight, fit them with a snorkel, and allow them to land themselves once they had been unloaded, keeping the transports out of the range of enemy fire. In this way the transports were able to unload their armoured vehicles into 4 m of water, several hundred metres offshore, and this also cut landing and unloading time.

Trials with the coasters which were to be used as transports, as well as with ferries, proved to be disappointing and as a result, the Type B barge which had been developed as an alternative was incorporated into the fleet.

The *peniche Leine* using a test ramp from a bridgelaying tank. The ramp is kept afloat by an inflatable dinghy.

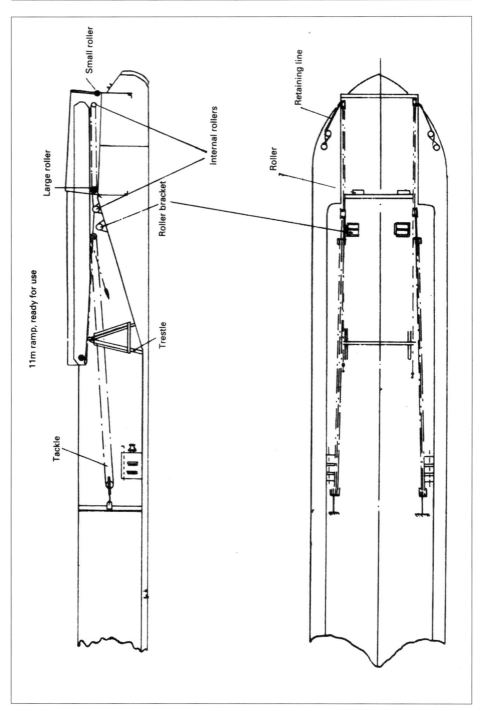

Type B barge, with ramp retracted.

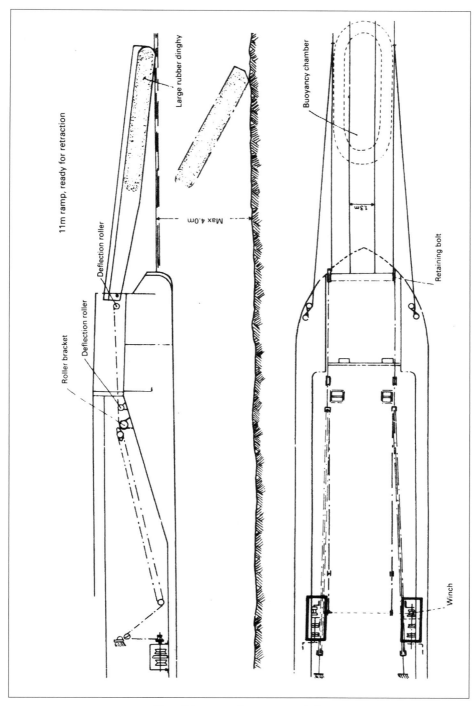

Type B barge, with ramp extended.

The *peniche Hans Herbert* with a newly-designed ramp which was later series-produced.

A Panzer III (U) submersible tank driving down the ramp of the *Hans Herbert*.

For unloading the submersible tanks the normal Type A barge was slightly modified by adding a long ramp. Since the tanks could only negotiate a ramp inclined to a maximum of 30 degrees, the ramp had to be 11 m long for a water depth of 4 m. The ramp had to be sturdy enough to bear the weight of the tanks, and so was itself fairly heavy. A quick solution was found in the assault bridge of the *Brückenlegepanzer IV* bridgelaying tank; this Krupp design, which was of the right length, was fitted to the *péniche Leine*. Its performance was disappointing, however, and an improved design was ordered. Further trials were conducted on 3 August 1940 using powered *péniches Leine, Wutag* and *Hans Herbert*, the last having been fitted with the new ramp.

Series production of the Type B barge had already begun at the Rheinwerft at Walsum and by 25 July twenty were near completion. Initially, sixty were planned for but this figure was subsequently increased to seventy to compensate for losses. On 30 September the Navy High Command (OKM) placed an order for an additional five as reserves. The requirement for barges of this type came too late and practically none of them were motorised, except for the trial *péniches*. However, since the tugs were able to tow the barges to the 4 m depth, where the tanks were able to enter the water, the lack of power was not that critical. Once released by the tug, the barge would lower its stern anchor and two bow anchors,

The tank has gained the beach and tows the buoy on the hose.
A radio aerial can be seen on the buoy.

while facing in the direction of the beach. During the crossing the ramps rested on rollers, roller brackets and a trestle in the hull over the internal ramp. To lower the ramp, two tackles were used, each of which was operated by five men. The ramp was drawn forward until it tipped over a small roller into the water. A float mounted at the front of the ramp between the longitudinal girders under the trackway held the ramp afloat while there was no load. The tank drove through the opening in the hull and onto the ramp, which slowly sank onto the seabed under the additional weight. Once the tank drove off the ramp it floated upwards again and the next tank could drive on. Once their special job was completed, the barges were to land troops, vehicles and conventional tanks directly on to the beach with their ramps.

The crew consisted of a non-commissioned officer and six men; in addition there was an engineer commando force of an NCO and fifteen men to operate the ramps. A non-commissioned officer and a radio operator from the armoured troops were assigned to controlling the submersible tanks via radio link.

Type C

Panzer II tanks were designed to complement the U-Panzer III and IV submersible tanks. The light weight of the Panzer II allowed it, with the addition of floats, to be driven on the surface of the water. These added floats, however, made the tanks too wide for the Type A barges, and they required an entirely new type of transport,

Stern ramp of Type C barge and wheel platform. (*Bundesarchiv*)

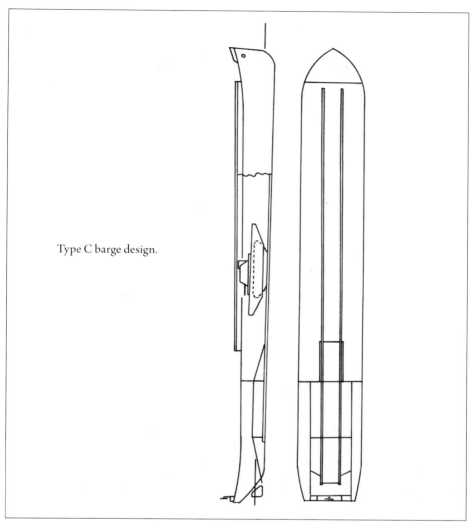

Type C barge design.

based on the *Kampinen*. Since a wide bow exit ramp, needed for the broad tanks, would have reduced the ship's seakeeping and handling, the ramp was installed in the stern, which had to be cut out to fit it. The permanently installed ramp was placed between the remaining aft parts of the ship (see above). As in the case of the other barge types, the trackway had to be raised to allow for a transverse bulkhead. The helm was designed as a bridge over the aft side compartments to which the rudders were attached. No modifications were necessary to the bow. Thus equipped, the Type C barge could transport four amphibious Panzer IIs. This type's design had been agreed upon by representatives from the OKM and the WaPrüf 5 on 10 August at the Rheinwerft Walsum. Testing was begun on 19 August at Duisburg but it is not known how many of these barges were actually produced. The first batch was to have consisted of twelve conversions, later

Type C barge seen from the stern at the conversion yard.

seventeen, with four of these in reserve. Final plans for Operation Sealion cited a total of fourteen of these craft.

A parallel programme aimed at transporting the amphibious tanks on the *Pommern* type ferries. This project seems to have been abandoned in favour of achieving uniform ship types and greater flexibility (see page 40).

Unloading the Type C barges was very simple and the fact that the tanks could operate independently eliminated the need for powered barges. The trackways of the Type C barges were widened in 1941 to allow easier off-loading of the amphibious tanks. The fact that no movable ramp was needed for unloading them eliminated the need for any specialised crew.

Submersible and Amphibious Tanks

At the end of the Western campaign, during the early deliberations for Sealion, it was thought that submersible and amphibious tanks might provide the necessary rapid concentration of firepower since no one in Germany knew at that time how such heavy tanks were to be disembarked on an open coast line. It seemed much simpler, at least in theory, to unload the tanks far outside the breakers but still in shallow coastal waters, and this was the tack taken.

The relatively heavy production version Panzer III battle tank and the Panzer IV infantry support vehicle seemed suitable candidates for submersible use due

A closed-down Panzer III being lowered into the water.

to their weight, while the lighter Panzer II could easily be made amphibious by adding floats. Since it took quite a long time to produce these floats, and because the lightly armoured Panzer II was not deemed to be very combat effective, attention was focused on the submersible tank.

Captain (Ing) Paul Zieb, who was Director of Equipment at the Naval Shipyard at Wilhelmshaven, has described the initial trials with a closed down tank fitted with a snorkel in his book *Logistical Problems of the Navy* (*Logistische Probleme der Marine*, Neckargemünd, 1961):

> At the end of June 1940 a tank was delivered with no forewarning. It had to be tested as quickly as possible for its amphibious capabilities and had been delivered without any directives or instructions regarding a test programme. The tank commander told us it was the first time any such trials had been run...
>
> In a brief meeting with the Director of the shipyard I was put in charge of testing; the site chosen was Schilling at the northern mouth of the Jade.
>
> Three floats of different sizes and designs for the top of the snorkel had been delivered with the tanks. On the float was a 1 m long tube which served as an extension of the snorkel as well as an antenna for the radio, via which the director of the tests could maintain constant contact with the tank crew during submerged travel.

Every safety precaution was taken during the trials. In order to maintain visual contact with the tank at all times, two 7 m depth gauges were mounted on the tank, painted red for port and green for starboard. Two shallow draught floating cranes were anchored nearby; on board both were doctors and medical personnel with resuscitation equipment in case water or exhaust gases penetrated the tanks. The crane ships were supported by two diving vessels, two tugs and two motorboats, kept at the ready. Radio transmitters were installed on both crane ships.

The first exercise was an emergency rescue operation. The tanks had been fitted with a divided strap for this purpose, so that the diver had only to fit the crane hook into the ring and the tank could be quickly lifted. It took only a few minutes to raise the tank from 5 m of water to the surface once the alarm was sounded; the doctors concluded that this allowed a reasonable length of time to resuscitate the crew.

The tank used its compass during the first underwater trial, but after it turned on its own axis several times the command was given via the radio link to halt, and a diver sent down to check how far the tracks had sunk. It turned out that there was no appreciable difference to travelling on wet beach sand. Thereafter the tank was guided by the test director, who made constant visual checks. After these trials the tank was able to navigate successfully even with its own compass and could keep on a prescribed course with changes of direction without any difficulties.

The water during these tests was no more than 7 m deep. Greater depths would have overtopped the floats and thus would have allowed water into the tank. The trials were conducted initially in dammed-up waters and then during strong flood and ebb currents. The tank remained firmly on the sandy bottom at every test depth in every position – against, with or diagonal to the current – as long as it was in motion. If it was stopped in the current for tactical reasons, for instance to allow another tank to close ranks, it quickly sank about 20 cm into the sand. The diver who was observing this reported via the telephone link that the tank was unlikely to be able to free itself under its own power and that the exhaust lay on the sand. A floating crane was ordered, but the tank managed to free itself without too much difficulty before the crane's arrival. The lesson learnt during these tests was that an immobile tank would soon become mired in strong currents.

All of the tests were conducted in warm, sunny weather. There was no time for trials in bad weather or for acoustic ranging tests. The maximum underwater duration of a tank during the trials was an hour. In general, the experiments showed that the tanks were able to travel underwater in sand up to a depth of 7 m; the tank commander did not feel it was necessary to test its performance in silt. A demonstration was given on 26 June to a high-ranking audience, including Dr Todt, the Armaments Minister.

Four armoured detachments were probably set up as early as July. These Divisions A, B, C and D were comprised of volunteers from Panzer Regiment 2. Crews were prepared in two-day courses in a Training Battalion at Westerland on the island of Sylt, under the supervision of the Reinhardt Trials Staff, before active service in mid-July.

While WaPrüf 5 was responsible for developing launch methods for the tanks, WaPrüf 6 was in charge of equipping the tanks. Making the submersible tanks watertight entailed sealing all openings such as sighting ports and hatches with tape and caulking, securing the main turret hatch from inside and completely closing the engine's air intakes. Rubber covers were fitted over the main gun's mantlet, the commander's cupola and the radio operator's machine gun. All coverings could be released by explosive cables. An inflated rubber hose formed a seal between the hull and the turret. Fresh air was brought in via a rubber hose 18 m long and of 20 cm diameter encased in a wire mesh; attached to the end were a buoy and the radio antenna. The tank's exhaust pipes were fitted with overpressure valves which had the disadvantage of reducing engine power during submerged travel, while the engine was converted to operate on seawater for cooling. Seepage could be extracted via a bilge pump. Thus equipped, a submersible tank could drive at a maximum depth of 15 m and could navigate on its own via a directional gyro, but co-ordinates for underwater travel were generally provided via radio link from the transport. On General Reinhardt's orders the tanks were painted to match the anticipated colour of the sea more closely.

Several accidents occurred during testing and there was at least one death due to exhaust gases being recycled back into the tank. On 20 July a submersible tank drove into a trench and became stuck. Rescue attempts with an amphibious tractor proved fruitless and so the crew flooded the tank and escaped using their life-saving apparatus. Two days later a tank stalled on a rock and had to be lifted out.

These incidents clearly reveal the real drawback of the submersible tank: it could not avoid underwater obstacles. In the end, the order was given that they should be unloaded from the ships at high tide so that those vehicles which became bogged down could be recovered when the tide fell.

During initial testing the tanks were lowered by crane ships directly or via ramps attached to them. This was different where steep ramps had to be used and these were very difficult for the tank crews to cope with. At first coasters were envisaged as transports. The first experimental ship, the coaster *Germania*, was finished by the end of July at the naval shipyard at Wilhelmshaven. The three tanks were to be carried on a wooden skid over the loading hatches and could be pulled forward to the 8.5 m long ramp on the side. At sea this ramp rested on a wooden support and was handled by a derrick. The *Germania* had to load 200 tons of ballast from its 300 tons capacity to enable it to cope with the heavy tanks and had actually to ground on the beach, since it would have capsized with the weight of the tanks on the side ramp. Since this manoeuvre proved impractical, the conversion of fifty motor coasters was abandoned and the *Friesland*, *Roland* and *Gretchen*, with their different types of folding ramps, were converted into fire-support ships, (see page 109). The Type B barge proved to be best suited to operating the tanks.

*

The first trials version of the *Schwimmpanzer II* was tested in early August on Sylt. Aluminium boxes filled with plastic bags for protection against small arms fire were fitted to the sides. The propeller shaft also ran through these boxes, driven by a rod from the tank's tracks. The drawbacks of these floats were their extreme vulnerability, the large number required, and the expense of production, which required 1,000 skilled workers.

The tank travelled at 5.7 km/h in the water. A rubber hose provided a seal between hull and turret but the 2 cm gun and coaxial MG remained operational. WaPrüf 6 tested this tank design extensively in the Tegeler See in Berlin before

Schwimmpanzer II amphibious tank. Note the floats on the sides. (*Bibliothek für Zeitgeschichte*)

the go ahead was given for production. By 29 August the landing force had 160 Panzer III (U) submersible tanks with 3.7 cm guns; 8 Panzer III (U) with 5 cm guns; 42 Panzer IV (Schwimm) with 7.5 cm guns, and 52 Panzer II (Schwimm) amphibious tanks with 2 cm guns.

The combat power of these tanks equalled that of an armoured division. The four battalions comprised of these tanks were to advance to the embarkation harbours immediately before the operation, initially from Putlos, and then from Eutin, Bremen and Hamburg also. During the actual operation each tank was to carry a substantial fuel and ammunition supply which would give it a combat radius of 200 km. The organisation of detachment C is shown on page 255.

Production of submersible tanks was to continue until April 1941, but in all probability no further conversions were carried out. The bulk of the units were allocated to the 18th Panzer Division in November, and some of them saw action when crossing the Bug River during the invasion of the Soviet Union.

An innovative project which would have converted the submersible tanks into 'real' submarines by adding floats with flotation and trim tanks never reached beyond the design stage. Naturally, specially designed amphibious tanks are admirably suited for reaching the beach. Normal tanks which can be made more or less amphibious or submersible will always be needed for a first wave, however. When these German tanks are compared with the Allied Sherman DD tanks, which proved to be not as amphibious as first estimated during the Normandy landing, they do not come off so badly. Even today, the draught of Russian LSTs forces them to unload amphibious tanks in several metres of water.

Rafts and Ferries

In July 1940 the engineers of Engineer Battalion 47 from VII Corps received an order from General of Engineers Jacob to design 'seagoing ferries from any available auxiliary and bridging equipment' in their capacity as an Army High Command trials battalion, an unusual task for this unit, whose quarters were at Munich. According to Colonel (retd) Dennerlein, former company commander of Engineer Battalion 47:

> Anything and everything which would float was commandeered. Amphibious aircraft floats were obtained from the Potez aircraft factory at Albert and Caudebec-en-Caux and sturdy aircraft fuel tanks came from the Breguet and Schneider aircraft factories at Le Havre and Paris.
>
> Combing Rouen produced numerous wine barrels and a French Army engineers depot yielded watertight kapok-filled floats covered in sailcloth which had belonged to French infantry assault bridges. Petrol drums also came in handy.

Once everything was collected the rafts were built. The thorniest problem was finding the correct size beams, since there were no suitable trees in the nearby forests. The largest beams had to be shipped from Germany.

To construct the rafts, the floats were placed in rows, with a framework of longitudinal and transverse beams secured with wire. The outboard engines powering the assault bridges proved a failure, since they cut out every time a wave washed over them. The decision was thus taken to tow the rafts using small seagoing tugs. The battalion began testing this technique at Bray-sur-Somme and then redeployed to Carteret on the west coast of the Cotentin peninsula. Off this coast was the island of Jersey, which the Germans had occupied during the campaign in France. The approximately 20 km between the coast and the island were to serve as a 'test track'. In mid-August the first convoy with the makeshift ferries sailed for Jersey in good weather and in reasonably calm seas. Aside from the fact that some of the men became seasick and several of the wine barrels came adrift from their wire bindings, there were no untoward events. However, during the long sea crossing the kapok sacks absorbed so much water that some rafts were barely able to limp back

The beach at Carteret with the rafts designed by PiBtl 47. In the foreground is a dinghy raft; behind it a ferry made of petrol tanks. In the row behind to the left is a B ferry; next to it a ferry made of wine barrels. Behind this row is an additional B ferry; in the distant background to the left a Herbert ferry.

A raft made of petrol tanks with a light field howitzer on board.

Wine barrel raft with splashplates.

to Carteret. These rafts had reached their limits, but the rafts made of petrol tanks appeared to be suitable for transport of troops or as a platform for light guns in calm seas.

The Pontoon Bridge B was tested at the same time. The normal 16-ton B Ferry consisted of four half pontoons arranged in tandem pairs. The resulting two floats were attached via the two sections of the bridge, which served as the cargo area [see below]. Two of these rafts, alongside one another and attached via the locking bars which were part of the bridge fitting, formed a raft with twice the width and greater stability. The principal drawback of the B ferries was the use of open floats, which were quickly swamped in any sort of a seaway. One solution was to cover them with sailcloth. This enabled them to survive reasonably calm waters, but in rougher seas the water found its way in. Empty tanks were then installed inside to help buoyancy. Petrol tanks from the French aircraft factory were a real boon but there were not enough tanks to fill all the pontoons and other canisters and empty barrels were more difficult to tie down so ripping the sailcloth as soon as they started to float. Fitting splashboards on the forward surfaces did not improve matters. Accordingly this type of craft proved to be unsuccessful in heavy seas.

Other engineer units tested makeshift rafts in the late autumn and winter of 1940. Engineer Battalion 296 of the 35th Infantry Division constructed a raft

A B ferry with outboard engine.

B ferry with Siebel superstructure for troop transportation.

out of three B pontoons placed side by side. An additional ten B ferries in Bruges were fitted with two 75 hp Ford engines each. Even rafts made out of tree trunks were built during training courses run by Colonel Winter in Le Touquet, but they proved worthless. The engineer training unit Pionierlehrbataillon 1 and the Navy formed a test group for trials of heavy transports such as barges and ferries in Emden. On 29 July they tested a raft 22 m long and 12 m wide built by the engineers. It was towed by two tugs to the River Ems, but it could only manage 2.5 knots.

Another ferry, constructed from two barges 8 m apart, also proved unsatisfactory. On 17 August 1940 the Emden Test Group also ran trials with a B Ferry which had a Siebel superstructure; this vessel had already been demonstrated on 3 August on the Rangsdorfer lake near Berlin to the Commander-in-Chief of the Army, Field Marshal von Brauchitsch, and Halder and had been developed by Major Siebel using four half pontoons of the Engineer Pontoon Bridge B lashed together to form two floats. These were held together by beams and not by the bridge sections as in the case of the engineers' raft. A 40 cm high splashboard was mounted to protect the pontoons from spray. An airscrew was fitted in the stern of the pontoons while the crews sat in the pontoons with tanks and equipment on the platform in between. The Luftwaffe supplied enough parts for 150 of these ferries to St Omer but neither the Army nor the Navy were enthusiastic, and the project was cancelled on 5 September 1940 on the grounds of their susceptibility to foundering.

A search for better-designed floats resulted in the discovery of some closed pontoons from British assault bridges which had been abandoned on the Continent. There were very few of these, but they did serve as a reminder to the German Army that it had also had two types of closed pontoon in service in 1939, the Herbert bridge and the heavy pontoon bridge (*schwere Schiffsbrücke*). The Herbert bridge was named after its designer, an Austrian colonel in the engineers. An earlier version of this assault vehicle had seen service in the First World War in the Austrian Army and had been acquired by the Wehrmacht when the Germans annexed Austria and Czechoslovakia.

The heavy pontoon bridge had been developed in 1938 to carry the increasingly heavy tanks then entering service. At the beginning of the war there were four

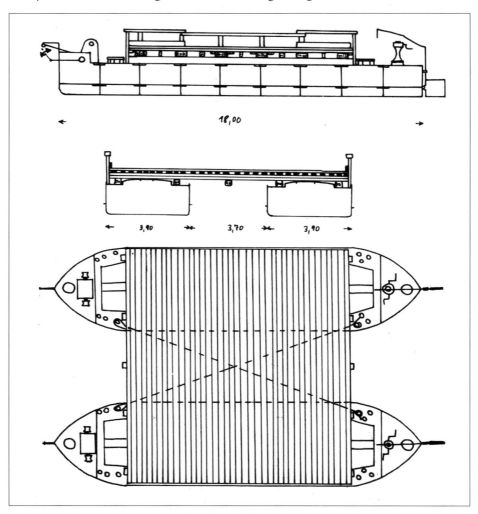

Herbert ferry without engines.

A Herbert ferry with two aircraft and three lorry engines fitting out.

units with Herbert bridges totalling some 64 pontoons, and 24 units with heavy pontoon bridges consisting of 384 pontoons. Both types had nine sections: two pointed end pontoons and seven middle units.

Once Field Marshal von Brauchitsch and General of Engineers Jacob became convinced of the uselessness of the makeshift rafts at Carteret, materials for building the Herbert ferries were sent to Pionierlehrbataillon 47 on 19 August. The Herbert ferries had two pontoons arranged to form a catamaran. The end pontoons were pointed and between these were fixed the square pontoons; a platform was placed over them. The superstructure had to be made of wooden beams cut in Germany in record time and shipped to Carteret. The Herbert ferries and their equipment were ready by 10 September and five days later they sailed from Carteret to Fécamp via Cherbourg.

At the same time, the Engineer Special Command under Major Böndel was building ferries at Antwerp from Herbert and heavy pontoon bridge units and Siebel's Luftwaffe Special Command fitted these craft with airscrew propulsion (see page 26). Two 750 hp BMW engines were fitted on two mounts on the aft part of the platform over the pontoons. The airscrews produced a tremendous amount of suction and this resulted in several fatalities before protective grids were fitted. Three 75 hp Ford V8 truck engines were placed between them which drove the propellers via cardan shafts. The aircraft engines were to be used only during the actual landing, since they were noisy and thirsty, and the truck engines for cruising. These rafts were able to carry a load of 40 tons under normal conditions

A Herbert ferry sailing.

and could travel at up to 17 knots. The crew of the Herbert ferry comprised three sailors, two aircraft-engine mechanics from the Luftwaffe, three engineer vehicle mechanics and four deck crew.

Eight Herbert ferries were completed at Antwerp during September and the six Herbert ferries of Engineer Battalion 47 were similarly fitted with engines. According to a report dated 23 September, an additional eight Herbert ferries from this battalion had been produced in a yard at Le Trait, on the Seine not far from Rouen. These craft had 20 per cent less cargo-carrying capacity than the other ferries and were only to be used as reserves. It seems improbable that any other Herbert rafts were produced after these twenty-two.

The Navy expressed grave doubts about the seaworthiness of the Herbert ferries right from the outset. A naval architect, Drießen, had already criticised the Herberts and heavy pontoon bridges because they had no rigid longitudinal fixtures which meant that weapons could not be fired from them. On 28 September the Naval Design Bureau produced an especially critical report on the Herbert ferries, which stated that their pontoons, which were lighter than those of the heavy pontoon bridge, as well as the wooden superstructure could not be made seaworthy. The arrangement of the shafts for the propellers was also considered to be unstable. Nevertheless, the Naval Operations Office (*Seekriegsleitung*) dismissed these concerns and reconfirmed the place of these ferries in the planning. Naval prejudice against Army amphibious developments must be suspected.

Large-scale production of the Herbert ferries was out of the question due to the limited number of pontoons available, but the heavy pontoon bridge was deemed to be the better solution anyway. First trials were run by the Emden Test Group. The original vehicle platform design joining the two pontoons for seagoing use was not satisfactory, so at the request of Major Siebel, Krupp-Rheinhausen built a wood-covered steel platform in co-operation with WaPrüf5. In this the pontoons were only 5.5 m apart instead of 6 m as in the case of the bridge. In later versions of the heavy pontoon bridge, this gap and the dimensions of the platform and thus the cargo area, were increased.

The siting of the propulsion system proved problematical. The only systems readily available in sufficient numbers were diesel truck engines and aircraft engines. The engineers found that each end pontoon was large enough to carry two commercial 75 hp Ford V8 or Opel Blitz truck engines side by side, thus making a total of four waterscrew engines. Communications between the wheelhouse and the engine operators in the stern was via a bell operated by an engine-room telegraph. If the engine operators did not react at exactly the same time and to the same degree the ferry would begin to turn since it was almost as broad as it was long and this movement could barely be counteracted by the rudder.

Other teething troubles included engine failure due to cooling difficulties; this was solved by linking the three aircraft engines with the waterscrew engines as an alternative to the Siebel concept. The BMW 6U 750 hp aircraft engines were located aft on the vehicle platform.

The Herbert ferry *Loch Ness* at Dieppe.

Heavy bridge pontoon ferry cruising with only underwater propulsion during trials.
On deck are two 8.8 cm flak guns.

The Special Command of the Merchant Shipping Division tested the Luftwaffe's heavy bridge pontoon ferry propelled only by the aircraft engines on 31 August in the Ems estuary. The three engines produced a cruise speed of 14 km/h and a good 15 km/h at full throttle. The engine throttles in the wheelhouse allowed the engines to be run at different speeds which helped manoeuvrability. The aircraft engines were extremely noisy, though, and voice communication was out of the question. It was finally decided that they would be used only as a back-up to the truck engines shortly before the landing, or in an emergency.

Test cruises with the heavy bridge pontoon ferry powered by four Opel Blitz engines were conducted on 4 September, and on the next day with the Ford V8 engines, both again in the Ems estuary. Cruising speed was thought to be 13 km/h, though it was hoped to boost this by using better propellers.

Both the Herbert and the heavy bridge ferries were considered good platforms for heavy and light anti-aircraft guns because of their large cargo areas. The Luftwaffe's anti-aircraft guns, especially the 8.8 cm, had been combat-proven in land warfare. Motorised flak units armed with an 8.8 cm and two 2 cm guns were formed for deployment against air, ground and – during the crossing – surface targets. The 8.8 cm guns acquitted themselves well during trials, and so the decision was taken to use the ferries for flank defence of the towed formations

Ferry *D* 5 with a combined propulsion system at Dunkirk.

and then to help unload the transports once their flak guns had been landed. In blissful confidence, the Army termed these types of ferries 'destroyer substitutes'.

The heavy pontoon bridges were able to carry an entire flak combat unit including three towing vehicles. The two 2 cm guns were mounted on a raised platform forward of the wheelhouse. However, Flakkorps I, which was assigned to the Ninth Army, decided to use the 8.8 cm gun only on the heavy pontoon and Herbert ferries, and to transport the combat towing vehicle as well as the remainder of the troops in barges. Flakkorps II assigned to the Sixteenth Army elected to transport an entire flak combat unit on its ferries and the heavy pontoon bridge was able to carry a standard load of 50 tons, though later engineer versions could manage up to 100 tons.

Series production of the heavy-bridge pontoon ferry was begun in September 1940 by the Bandel Special Command of the engineers in Antwerp. The Siebel Special Command of the Luftwaffe mounted additional aircraft engines on the ferries. Twenty-five of these ferries were completed and delivered to Flakkorps I and II by the end of September. Those rafts which were completed by the beginning of Operation Sealion were to be kept in reserve.

The heavy pontoon ferry required three sailors, three Luftwaffe aircraft-engine mechanics, four engineer mechanics, and four deck crew who were also from the engineers.

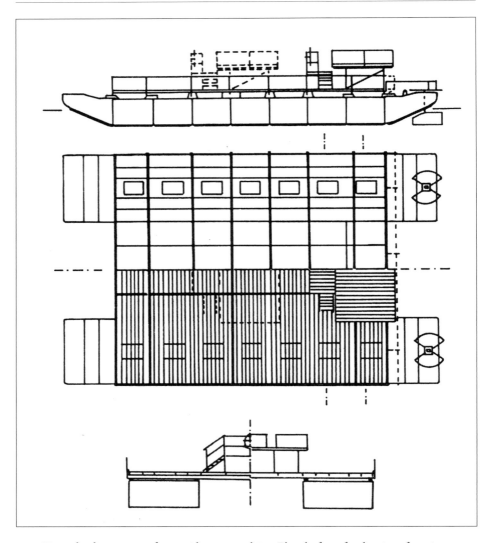

Heavy bridge pontoon ferry, without propulsion. The platform for the aircraft engines
is outlined.

Despite earlier problems with the heavy pontoon ferries, they ultimately
proved themselves handy for a variety of amphibious tasks. They were the only
'real' landing craft in the Sealion fleet. The heavy pontoon ferries of Flakkorps II
for the eastern landing sector were self-propelled, though Flakkorps II took a
more cautious approach to the western sector due to the longer crossing and
rougher seas and opted for towing assistance. The heavy pontoon ferry could be
transported by railway and, with its simple design, good seakeeping qualities,
general stability and ability to mount guns on its roomy cargo area, was an ideal

amphibious craft for short or long distances. This raft, unlike the other types, could easily carry bulky vehicles on its platform and that it could not be deployed from the transports was not regarded as a serious drawback in Germany.

These ferries were first produced in Antwerp as a joint Army–Luftwaffe project, but the Luftwaffe later decided to build them itself after the autumn of 1941, instructing its Special Ferry Command accordingly. This unit also produced other landing craft. BMW and other aircraft engines were used for propulsion. These engines drove waterscrews via a reversing gearbox and were installed in enlarged end pontoons divided in two lengthwise, four engines to each ferry. Some of these ferries with mixed crews were assigned to the Army, while the Luftwaffe used others for its own purposes in the Mediterranean, turning them over to the Navy in 1943. The Army had found the aircraft engines prone to catching fire and too thirsty. The Engineer Ferry Construction Command I, also stationed at Antwerp, produced a series of ferry types propelled by vehicle engines. These were also installed in larger end pontoons divided in two lengthwise. The Luftwaffe had inaccurately called the heavy pontoon bridge 'Siebel ferries' despite the fact that the engineers had had an equal share in their development. Nevertheless, the name stuck.

Auxiliary Gunboats

The topic of fire support for a seaborne assault was brought up at a meeting with the Chief of Staff of Naval Operations, Admiral Schniewind, on 17 August. Although the Luftwaffe would bear the brunt of suppressing enemy defences, ships of the invasion fleet would have to engage point targets. To this end, single 15 cm guns were to be installed on twenty barges to cover the landing zones against enemy naval forces once a bridgehead had been established. However, it proved impossible to procure barges that were stable enough, and they were also difficult to integrate into the landing fleet due to the shortage of tugs. The more sensible approach was to use the fifty coasters already designated for the transport of the submersible tanks. These were able to operate without tugs and were large enough to carry guns up to 15 cm. Initial planning called for twenty heavy fire-support ships each capable of carrying two medium guns, and twenty-seven light fire-support ships each with three small-calibre guns.

However, only five coasters were converted into heavy fire-support vessels. The conversion of these craft at Wilhelmshaven entailed the fitting of a 15 cm gun on the *Helene*, *August*, *Ost* and *West*, and two 10.5 cm guns on the *Robert Müller 6*. Two 2 cm Oerlikons provided air defence. The 120 tons of sand ballast needed to compensate for the gun on deck was usually stored in outboard compartments where it protected crew quarters and munitions stores. Both the gun mounts and the ship's waterline were lightly armoured and concrete blocks or sandbags

The heavy auxiliary gunboat *West.*

Light auxiliary gunboat *Fortuna* (*II*) with a 3.7 cm flak gun on deck and a 7.5 cm gun on a bow mount.

protected the wheelhouse; degaussing systems as well as bow protection gear were fitted.

The heavy auxiliary gunboats proved satisfactory, and they later acquitted themselves well against Soviet destroyers in the Baltic. The light auxiliary gunboats, however, of which twenty-seven were converted at the Naval Yard at Wilhelmshaven in autumn 1940, were much more makeshift. In this case the forward derrick was replaced by a mount for a captured 7.5 cm field gun. The crew were squeezed into temporary quarters in the hold along with 40–60 tons of sand for ballast. The 7.5 cm gun and 350 rounds of ammunition were intended to engage coastal targets after landing as well as naval targets, though the latter only at a pinch. Two Luftwaffe 3.7 cm anti-aircraft and two machine guns were fitted on the hatches for air defence and against fast attack craft. Once the landings had been accomplished, the Luftwaffe anti-aircraft guns and their mounts stored in the hold were to be landed.

After a training period – transfer to the embarkation ports was not scheduled until two days before the operation – the fire-support vessels were taken out of service in November. The former light gun vessels were mostly assigned to harbour-defence flotillas, while those with medium artillery, some of which had been rearmed, were taken back into service with the Baltic Trials Unit, and were used for the assault on the Soviet Baltic islands. They performed so well during that operation that twenty additional motor coasters were subsequently converted into heavy and light auxiliary gunboats.

Later both the US Navy and the Royal Navy produced dedicated landing support ships which provided fire support for assault forces.

On the Beach

The difficulties that the landing forces would face on the beaches and narrow coastal strips did not go unappreciated. Barriers and minefields laid by the British Army on the most vulnerable beaches would be encountered. The Germans also assumed that the British would mine the sandbanks and at first decided that the best approach in this case would be to detonate them with depth charges at high tide. However, the Naval Operations Office rejected this proposal on 14 August, reasoning that depth charges had only a limited effect in shallow waters and that it was difficult to install launchers in small craft. The engineers were thus assigned the unenviable task of removing these mines and other barriers.

The steep cliffs along part of the southern English coast were to be scaled with rocket-assisted lines similar to the equipment which was later used by the Allies in Normandy in 1944. The Germans settled on commercial pulleys to hoist their equipment up the cliffs.

Broken-down vehicles had to be towed off the barges, and others might become bogged down in the dunes or mud. The engineers and artillery corps troops

Land-Wasser-Schlepper amphibious tractor. (*Bundesarchiv*)

assigned to the armies formed tow groups of tracked vehicles which would be landed with the first echelon; these were reinforced by an additional 101 vehicles from the Sixteenth Army on 1 September consisting of 70 captured light tracked *Cheniletten* and some old German armoured vehicles.

The amphibious tractor (*Land-Wasser-Schlepper* – LWS) was also called into play. In autumn 1940, Tank Detachment 100 had three prototypes of this unarmed, fully-tracked vehicle which had twin screws and two rudders. WaPrüf5 had been developing this vehicle for the engineers since 1935 and the first prototype was completed during the preparations for Operation Sealion. The Reinhardt Trials Staff on Sylt demonstrated it on 2 August to General Halder, who was critical of its large silhouette on land, but it proved its value pulling unpowered barges ashore and towing vehicles over the beach. When combined with the Kässbohrer amphibious trailers which could carry loads between 10 and 20 tons, it could be used as a landing boat which could carry any load directly ashore. Tank Detachment 100 found this combination amply suited for use during the six hours of the falling tide when the barges were grounded. The department proposed mass production of enough LWS to give each transport two to four tractors and trailers. Captain Kleikamp responded to this proposal on 28 October, by pointing out the difficulties involved in mass-producing the LWS, and the fact that the trailer had only one-third the capacity of the barge, which would lengthen the time to unload the transports. It made more sense to build genuine landing craft, as was eventually done by the Army, Navy and Air Force.

The LWS was well designed for towing and pushing other vehicles but the Germans never produced amphibious troop transport vehicles such as the American DUKW or LVT in any numbers.

The problem of unloading the barges on a rising tide still remained, and the Sixteenth Army tested a prefabricated landing stage in the winter of 1940/41. This mobile *Landebrücke 674* (landing bridge) for loads up to 16 tons was to be carried on the pontoons of the First Wave and assembled in about four hours on shore. It ran on a steel trackway which could be set up during low tide, allowing the barges to tie up to a ramp which could be raised or lowered depending on the water depth. The barges were then unloaded via a folding bridge.

The barges would be channelled toward the ramp through two rows of pilings arranged like a funnel which would take about twelve hours to construct. VII Corps planned to transport four of these ramps.

Sixteenth Army came up with another solution to the problem of unloading troops and light equipment from the barges, and in September started work on fixed landing bridges which would take about eight days to build and would be used for unloading until English harbours became available. Several wooden versions were tested which were capable of withstanding quite rough conditions for several weeks. The Army provided 600 m long temporary bridges capable of carrying a 16-ton load; each First Wave division was to transport an 80 m run of this bridge, 120 m of an 8-ton bridge, 340 m of the trackway for bridges of inflatable boats and 400 m for trestle bridges. The amount of timber necessary

Mobile Landing Bridge 674 ('landing wedge') with moored barge. (*Bundesarchiv*)

Landing bridge elevated. (*Bundesarchiv*)

for this was divided among the individual armies. VII Corps had to transport 379 tons of baulks of timber, and 64 loads of planks; some was used as temporary gun mounts for the barges and the remainder was to be shipped in four barges.

The corps troops would have towed their timber in two rafts. XII Corps had the idea of carrying its 224 tons of baulks and 76 loads of planks in the unused area of the propeller tunnels of the barges. V Corps of the Second Wave decided to carry its seven floating bridges on the transports.

The Ferry Special Command (*Sonderkommando Fähre*) developed a landing bridge made from gas pipes similar to present-day steel tube scaffolding, but tests conducted near Misroy in 1941 showed that it could not carry the required loads. Captain Lehmann, commander of the KMD Ostend, took this thinking one stage further, calling for the construction of artificial harbours in the landing area.

Medium-sized steamers were to be sunk and used as breakwaters. As innovative as this idea was, it could never have been carried out due principally to the lack of ships. Since Sealion was at first officially only postponed, both the Army and the Navy continued to develop components for artificial harbours. The Navy held a competition for the development of a 65 m long heavy landing bridge which was to serve as a jetty for the transports. Krupp Stahlbau's proposal consisted of 32 m long platforms, the corners of which rested on four piers on the seabed. Winches raised and lowered the platform to adjust to the tide. Several platforms placed in a

Krupp landing bridge: On the left-hand platform are the mounts for pile-driving the anchors. (*Bundesarchiv*)

Krupp landing bridge, the left segment is being moved into position.
(*Bundesarchiv*)

Dortmunder Union's design for a landing bridge. The left pier support is just being lowered.

The 'German Jetty' on Alderney made of Krupp (*left*) and Dortmunder Union (*right*) landing bridges, shortly before its demolition in 1978–9. (*K. Tough*)

row formed the bridge, which could be linked to the shore in shallow water via an auxiliary bridge or a jetty if available. The bridge was to be transported by three auxiliary coasters connected side by side by transverse girders. On arrival the piers could be lowered onto the seabed, the platform lifted and the ships floated free. The piers were fixed to the seabed using iron piles inside them. The jetty head was to be protected by dolphins. Two of these designed by a Professor Agatz of MAN were produced in September 1941 for testing; they were floated up to the pier and then sunk by flooding and sand ballast and rods hammered into them gave them stability. Two experimental landing bridges were completed and erected on 15 and 31 July off Zeebrugge. The auxiliary coasters *Welle, Holsatia, Wittekind, Otto, Lucie Eckmann* and *Immanuel* were used to manoeuvre the bridges into place.

A competing design by Dortmunder Union was tested off Zeebrugge at the same time. It consisted of three lattice piers suspended between two coasters and connected by a lifting gantry. After being lowered on to the seabed the piers were winched into the vertical position and secured by eight rammed-in piles. One of the piers was used as a scaffold for the actual construction of the steel lattice-type bridge, which could be made of individual elements or prefabricated bridge segments. The bridges were transported and erected by the coasters *Rheinland, Jan, Franz, Heinrich, Antonius* and *Dorothea Weber*. The time needed for their construction was twenty-eight days so it is no wonder that the Krupp design which could be erected in one day was chosen.

The order for eight complete six-part Krupp-Stahlbau landing bridges was reduced to six in autumn 1941 and finally cancelled. In mid-1942 both test bridges were shipped to Alderney in the Channel Islands, and installed there for unloading materials with which to defend the island; they came to be known as the 'German jetty' (though their original purpose was never known to the island's inhabitants) and were not torn down until 1978–9 when they were due for major repairs. A further Krupp platform which was used by the French Navy as a torpedo testing base after the war still is preserved today at Querqueville near Cherbourg.

Seeschlange ('Sea Snake') floating bridge tested in Le Havre.

The Army developed a floating bridge nicknamed the *Seeschlange* (Sea Snake) which was designed as modules that could be joined to one another. It was easily transported by rail and was easy to tow. It was tested by the Army Training Unit at Le Havre in autumn 1941 and was later intended to be used during an assault on Malta in 1942. It was also used in the Mediterranean as a temporary jetty for transports which were secured to buoys; their cargo was then unloaded onto the bridge or loaded from it using their heavy duty booms. The *Seeschlange* was last used during the withdrawal from East Prussia and Pomerania. Though these German developments were insignificant compared to the two artificial harbours which the Allies used in the Normandy invasion in 1944, they at least demonstrate the independent yet parallel developments which were then going on.

Countering Burning Oil Barrages

The Naval Operations Office noted on 10 August 1940 that the British might use burning oil as a coastal defence and this immediately spurred the Germans on to developing countermeasures. Tests at the Chemisch-Physikalischen Versuchsanstalt on 18 August at Wilhelmshaven using 100 tons of a petrol–oil mixture demonstrated the obvious dangers, at least in calm conditions, for the oil burned for almost 20 minutes and produced a great deal of smoke and heat.

One early solution involved the use of depth charges, but it was soon discovered that water jets were quite sufficient to counter oil-slick fires. Pumping and fire-fighting vessels were deemed necessary to protect the First Wave and in addition 150, and then 200 and finally 800 small fire-fighting pumps from the *Reichsluftschutzverband* (Reich Air Defence Organisation) were earmarked for installation on the individual craft of the First Wave. The Luftwaffe, however, refused to provide these since they were needed for air-raid defence, but nevertheless, forty-nine tugs requisitioned for Sealion had pumps and fire-fighting equipment and these were to be distributed as evenly as possible amongst the assault harbours, mainly for use by the advanced detachments. These ships were the *Herkules, Löwe, Stier, Bardenfleth, Wangerooge, Vulkan, Steinbock, Widder, Karl, Fairplay V, VI, VII, XV* and *XVII, Brunshausen, Steinwärder, Stade, Moorwärder, Ernst, Albert Forster, Danzig 2* (150 hp), *Neufahrwasser, Danzig* (350 hp), *Brösen, Richard Damme, MS II, Haff, Ostwacht, Roland, Hermann, Thor* (350 hp), *Titan, Seeteufel, Möwe, Vegesack, Eversand, Georgswärder, Baumwall, Oliva, Auguste, W. Th. Stratmann, Willy Charles, Emil, Elsfleth, Rechtenfleth, Hermes, Albatros, Spiekeroog* and *Seeadler.*

The Director of the Naval Technical Department (*Technisches Amt der Marine*) proposed yet another method of fighting burning oil slicks which involved tugs towing logs chained together and encircling the oil slick before towing it out to sea; this idea anticipated modern-day methods but was never fully implemented.

Whether the German precautions were necessary seems uncertain. In *Invasion 1940*, Peter Fleming says that one of the few successful trials of such a weapon took place on 24 August 1940 in calm seas off the north coast of the Isle of Wight using oil from ten railway tank wagons. The enormous amount of oil that was required to achieve an effective barrier, and which would have had to be stored in the landing areas because of its short burning time and ineffectiveness even with slight waves, made the value of this defence rather suspect; but burning oil slicks might have been conceived more as a useful psychological deterrent than anything else – otherwise the ineffective German intelligence network in Britain would not have caught wind of it!

Hospital Ships

In view of the obvious risks inherent in a landing operation, the Army High Command requested hospital ships at the beginning of August. The Army foresaw the need for a thousand beds, on twenty ships with fifty beds apiece. The idea behind using many small ships instead of a few large ones was that the Army planned not only to treat casualties but also to retrieve casualties and shipwrecked personnel quickly from the fighting zones and this requirement could only be met by small fast transports. Only surgical facilities were necessary.

Rescue ships would have to accommodate a number of personnel in addition to their normal crews; ships of about 800–1,000 grt were suitable for this purpose and were also big enough to remain comfortably at sea. The additional crew

The small hospital ship *Alexander von Humboldt*.

members were to consist of a chief surgeon, a naval officer, up to ten medical staff and orderlies, and a pair of signalmen.

KMD Bremen, Hamburg and Stettin requisitioned and converted fifteen vessels as hospital ships, which was five short of the number the Army had wanted, but they did at least make up the total number of beds required.

KMD Bremen fitted out five ships, KMD Hamburg seven and KMD Stettin three. Degaussing coils and bow protection gear were fitted in addition to the medical facilities. Since the ships did not reach their conversion yards until later in August the work had to be done quickly to meet the deadline for Sealion, first 15 and then 20 September. This gave the yards only ten days in which to modify the ships.

Ships which were converted included the *Flora* (1,272 grt, 148 beds), *Ceres* (1,078 grt, 104 beds) and *Alexander von Humboldt* (783 grt, 56 beds) completed at the Atlaswerke at Bremen; *Minos* (1,127 grt, 103 beds) and *Latona* (1,126 grt, 103 beds) at Vegesack. The Hamburg Howaldtswerke equipped the *Indalsälfven* (658 grt, 70 beds), *Königsberg* (999 grt, 70 beds) and *Pitea* (962 grt, 70 beds), and the Deutsche Werft converted the *Hermia* (997 grt, 61 beds) and the *Stubbenhuk* (934 grt, 63 beds). The *Birka* (1,000 grt, 120 beds) and *Portia* (968 grt, 61 beds) were fitted out by the African Lines yards. KMD Stettin sent the ships it had requisitioned to various yards: the *Leipzig* (795 grt, 50 beds) to the Lübecker Flenderswerke, the *Danzig* (797 grt, 52 beds) to the Lübecker Maschinenbaugesellschaft and the *Claus* (302 grt, 64 beds) to the Nobiskrug yard in Rendsburg.

The ships entered service between 3 and 9 September, when they sailed to Hamburg. Additional equipment and medical supplies were taken aboard later on. Training cruises in the Baltic in October brought the deficiencies of both the ships and their crews to the fore, most especially the qualifications of the medical personnel as most of the ships were without experienced operating-theatre staff. Communications and signals crew were also not up to scratch, and it became obvious that it was not always easy to transmit even reasonably simple radio messages quickly.

Most of the ships proved to be at least of use for limited transport duties, but only a few of them for rescue services, since their freeboard was too great and they did not have suitable ship's boats. Hospital ships already in naval service were also to be employed; according to a plan of 3 August, the *Wilhelm Gustloff* (25,484 grt, 500 beds) was to sail to Rotterdam, the *Berlin* (15,286 grt, approximately 400 beds) to the Schelde estuary, the small hospital ships *Oberhausen* (1,250 grt, 150 beds) *Rügen* (2,170 grt, 240 beds) and *Glückauf* (1,062 grt, approximately 100 beds) to Le Havre and the large hospital ship *Stuttgart* (13,387 grt, 485 beds) to Cherbourg. Once Cherbourg had been rejected as an embarkation harbour, the

Tugs as rescue ships in Rotterdam in 1940.

Chief Quartermaster of the Army requested on 25 October that the *Stuttgart* be transferred from Cherbourg to Boulogne or to the Schelde estuary. All these ships assembled in German harbours, where some conversion work continued, but in the end they never sailed to their embarkation ports. An interesting example is the *Meteor* (3,613 grt, 200 beds) which remained in Norway, where it was on call from mid-September for the diversionary operation Autumn Journey (*Herbstreise*) (see page 275). Little is known about a number of pilot vessels given hospital ship colouring but retaining the Dutch flag.

There is an interesting sidelight to the history of the fifteen small hospital ships. The Germans tried to register them with the International Red Cross in Geneva but the application was rejected by Britain, which declared itself 'unable to recognise these ships as hospital ships, since due to their small size they did not have the necessary facilities to transport and treat wounded'. In fact, the British had recognised the hospital ship *Portia* in the First World War, but were undoubtedly using every means possible to stop an invasion and were not prepared to accept the rescue of troops during any such attempt: indeed, during the Battle of Britain, German rescue seaplanes were repeatedly attacked in order to prevent the rescue of downed German pilots.

Naming the Transport Fleets

In order to make some sense of the thousands of makeshift transport vessels they were given identifying letters and numbers and these designations were painted in white on the bow. The first letter stood for the embarkation harbour: R or Ro for Rotterdam, A for Antwerp, O for Ostend, D for Dunkirk, C for Calais, B for Boulogne and H for Le Havre; and the numbers, which ran consecutively, identified the position of the vessel within the group, which in turn could be identified by a group of letters at the end of the code. The transports, which were larger, had no letters after the number. In the case of the smaller vessels, S stood for tugs, which also included fishing trawlers; KM for motor coasters and Mo for pusher boats, group leaders and fishing vessels; P for barges (*Prähme*) and PM or Pmot for a powered barge. The special barges were designated separately: the armoured Type AS barge with PI; the aircraft-engine-propelled barges with PF; Type B for submersible tanks with PU and Type C for the amphibious tanks with PS. In Ostend and Boulogne the special barges had their own numerical sequence, but at the other harbours the sequential numbering of the other barges was used.

The only exception to the sequential numbering of the units was the motorboat flotilla at Le Havre. Here, one flotilla was formed for each division which was to be transported: for example, the 60th Motorboat Flotilla for the 6th Mountain Division; the 80th Motorboat Flotilla for the 8th Infantry Division, and the 280th Motorboat Flotilla for the 28th Infantry Division. Each flotilla comprised four groups of eight coasters each and sixteen motor fishing vessels. In order to make this organisation obvious in the boat designation, the following system was devised. The first, or first two numbers stood for the flotilla, that is, a 6 for the 60th Flotilla, an 8 for the 80th Flotilla, and a 28 for the 280th. The subsequent number designated the group in the flotilla and the final number the boat in the group. The motor fishing vessel numbers were duplicated, since two of these were allocated to each coaster. An 'a' after the number indicated the boat sailing in the starboard file and a 'b' the one on the portside. An example of a designation would be H 611 aMo.

Most of the barges were given a temporary designation by the yard doing the modification until they reached their embarkation harbours. Those barges modified in Germany had a combination of numbers beginning with 14/. . . for the area under the Commander of Construction Corps 14 in Mainz and Mannheim, and 35/. . . for those produced by Construction Corps 35 in Duisburg. The following letters and numbers pertained to the Netherlands shipyard command:

GU   Gusto Yard, Schiedam
DR   Rotterdamsche Droogdok Mij
AD   Amsterdamsche Droogdok Mij

ND   Nederlandsche Dok Mij NV, Amsterdam
NS   Nederlandsche Scheepsbouw Mij, Amsterdam
V   Verschure & Cos Scheepswerf 6 Machinefabriek NV, Amsterdam
WF   Wilton-Fijenoord, Schiedam
GK   Cvd Giessen, Krimpen/ljssel
BC   Belliard Crighton & Co, Antwerp
EC   Engeneering & Co, Antwerp
PS   Machinefabriek aan Scheepswerf P Smit NV, Rotterdam

No yard designations are known for barges modified in France.

The Invasion Plan

IN HIS DIRECTIVE NO. 16 of 16 July 1940, Hitler established the organisation of Operation Sealion and its chain of command: 'The Commanders-in-Chief of the services are to deploy their forces under my command and in accordance with my general directives.' The Führer Headquarters and the headquarters of the Commanders-in-Chief were to be combined, and Hitler intended to transfer his base to Ziegenberg near Giessen for the duration of the operation. Army Headquarters was to be at Giessen and the Navy Headquarters at Wildungen; the Luftwaffe was to relocate its headquarters train to Ziegenberg.

In addition, Army Group A headquarters, which during the autumn of 1940 was at St Germain near Paris, was to move to a barracks near Amiens three days before the start of the operation; there was also to be a forward base at Boulogne. The Sixteenth Army transferred its headquarters from Tourcoing on the Belgian–French border to Guines near Calais and the Ninth Army was headquartered that summer at Limesy near Rouen. Each army's command staff was to be landed in England with the second echelon of the First Wave.

There were actually very few changes in the high command staffs for the operation; the only step taken was to establish a special staff in the Army High Command under the Chief Quartermaster for England, Kretschmer, who was to be responsible for supply after the landing, and who was given six ships for this purpose.

The Navy Prepares

The Navy had already had to make substantial changes in its command structure during the occupation of the western areas of the Continent, and Sealion brought further restructuring and the creation of entirely new positions. One of the new posts was that of Naval Commander West, filled by Vice-Admiral Lütjens, which was created on 3 August from Fleet Command in Trouville. He was responsible for the tactical command of warships and transports in Naval Group West before and during Sealion, as well as performing the duties of the Commander for Western Defence (BSW) until this post could be filled.

Admiral Otto Schniewind (*foreground*).

Another new position was that of Chief of Sea Transport, held by Captain Degenhardt in Paris, who oversaw the requisitioning and movement of ships in France. After the landing of the First Wave he was to function as the Special Commander of the Naval High Command in England. The requisitioning of ships in Germany was run by the Merchant Shipping Division, which set up a special staff for this purpose. The Main Naval Construction Office, K III M, directed the conversion of these vessels in Germany and designated shipyard officials supervised the work outside the country.

The Naval War Staff of the Naval High Command in Berlin and the Army General Staff were jointly responsible for the operational side of the invasion, the embarkation harbours and landing zones, as well as for the procurement and equipping of ships. Admiral Saalwächter, Commander-in-Chief of Naval Group West, was responsible for the planning and implementation of the naval side of the operation. Naval Group West was to operate jointly with Army Group A and Air Fleet Commands (*Luftflottenkommandos*) 2 and 3; his subordinate, Naval Commander West, was to liaise with Army Commands (AOK) 9 and 16.

The Commander for North Sea Defence (*Befehlshaber der Sicherung der Nordsee*, BSN) was responsible for shipping in German harbours as far north as the island of Texel. The commanders of Transport Fleets B, C, D and E were given operational command during the actual crossing and command of combined training with the army groups before the operation. They were also to oversee the composition of the tow formations and convoys and were to be given technical support by the naval bases (KMD) at the embarkation harbours. Commanders of the transport fleets were authorised to issue orders to these naval bases in regard to preparations for the invasion.

The KMDs in Germany were responsible for the requisitioning of German ships and for their transfer to the yards where they were to be converted. KMD Bremen set up a new office in Koblenz for this work from where it was easy to monitor inland shipping. Outside Germany, equipping, distributing and the loading of the ships at the embarkation harbours was performed by the various Naval Equipment Offices which reported to the Commanding Admiral France.

Harbour commandants and captains had to ensure the readiness of the ports and of the loading facilities as well as the supply and accommodation of troops.

The Commanding Admiral France, in Paris, was responsible for the overall co-ordination of preparations, delivery and completion of the ships. Engineer staff under his command carried out special tasks such as the maintenance of inland waterways, assisted by Fortress Construction HQ Units 22 and 9, a Director of Construction, a supervisor for the yard and a resupply group.

The Naval Commanders of the Netherlands (at the Hague), of the Channel Coast (at Wimille, near Boulogne) and of Northern France (at Trouville) were to ensure the safe passage of vessels through their command areas to the embarkation ports. The Harbour Commanders reported to them. The Chief Quartermasters of Belgium/Northern France and of Paris oversaw the operation and local security of the canals and inland waterways in Belgium and France.

When the invasion was postponed in September 1940, a special staff of the BSW at Trouville under Captain Brocksien assumed the duties of Naval Group Commander West in regard to Sealion effective from 27 October. Their staff report of 23 November indicated that the top command for this operation was inadequate because of the lack of an overall commander of the armed forces. Areas of responsibility in the Navy were vague, particularly at the embarkation ports, where transport fleet commanders under the Chief of Sea Transport would receive orders from the Commander-in-Chief of the KMD in regard to preparations, but who generally received all types of orders from the Merchant Shipping Division, the Commanding Admiral France and his naval commander as his superior. Thus the Naval Group Commander West and the transport fleet commanders were circumvented. There was a plethora of others entitled to issue orders: naval and harbour commandants, harbour captains, supply directors, harbour department chiefs, commanders of the patrol and minesweeping flotillas, and newly formed transport units.

It was suggested that a Wehrmacht staff be formed under the operational supreme commander of Sealion in order to put all of these commands under one roof. He would also deputise for the OKW and be authorised to command all three armed services. In addition, a top command at each embarkation harbour was proposed which would report directly to the Wehrmacht staff.

The Naval High Command was not long in rejecting a Wehrmacht staff from all three services; in its report of 22 December it argued that such a staff would undermine the authority of Group West in implementing the entire operation and that of the BSW for transport. The Navy pointed out that the contradictions and vague lines of command would require the intervention of the Naval War Staff and the Army General Staff. Perhaps bad experience in the past made the Naval High Command reluctant to co-operate with the other armed services, especially with the Luftwaffe, but the main reason was their negative attitude to the whole operation.

Preparing the Transports

The Navy faced far more daunting problems with Sealion than did the Army or the Luftwaffe. After all, the invasion fleet had to be produced virtually out of thin air, a fact emphasised in a paper submitted by the OKM at the Führer Conference on 26 July:

1.   Requisitioning the majority of inland barges and the tugs required to tow them to the conversion yards, and transporting them to their embarkation ports will bring inland shipping to a virtual halt. It is not possible to assess the exact effect upon the defence industry, food industry, retail trade and transport, but it is considered that the implications will be very serious. The Reich Economics Ministry and the Reich Transport Ministry support this view.

2.   Material required
     a)   30,000 tons iron and steel. This will require rolling mills to work on this project exclusively for ten days, thus postponing work for other contracts accordingly.
     b)   40,000 cubic metres of lumber must be available which will have serious effects on the building sector and the armaments industry.
     c)   concrete: 75,000 cubic metres must be provided; negative impact on entire construction industry.

3.   Shipyards
     a)   Inland yards: full capacity of all inland shipyards on the Rhine and in the Netherlands/Belgium needed for at least four weeks; all repair work and new construction will have to be postponed for that time.
     b)   Coastal yards: a substantial portion of their capacity will be needed for the preparation of ocean-going ships (coasters, transports, freighters, etc.); this

will have priority over submarine construction. Moreover, several hundred auxiliary ships and transports with degaussing systems are to be fitted out. This work will require the use of the workshops in all German dockyards for approximately four weeks, and will take priority over the submarine programme. This will mean, for example, that work on the *Tirpitz* will also have to be postponed for four weeks.

4.   The German cable industry [*Drahtseilverband*] will be heavily taxed with completion of the approximate 1,000 sets of towing equipment, taking precedence over other production such as of mining cables, submarine nets, etc. for about three weeks. Furthermore, many workers from harbour construction projects are required, so that these must be postponed for four weeks.

5.   Movement of materials between the manufacturers and the processing plants (dockyards, etc.) will require a great deal of transport, most of which is supervised by the Todt organisation. Its other work will necessarily suffer.

In order to perform this work, which will have serious implications for the armaments industry, trade, transport and private industry in the Reich, the Netherlands and Belgium and which will lead to the postponement of top priority projects for the Navy and the other armed forces, authority must be granted at the highest level for Operation Sealion to take precedence over other top priority programmes.

Hitler and Jodl agreed to this demand at the conference and the Navy, determined to complete all the preparations by the end of August, started work immediately.

Looking at it realistically, the Navy decided it could requisition and convert 2,000 barges in this time frame. KMD Koblenz was to provide 860 barges and the rest were to be found by the KMD at Rotterdam in the Netherlands and Belgium. On 15 August the Merchant Shipping Division reported it had procured 825 barges in Germany and the KMD at Rotterdam had found 898. Of these, 432 in Germany and 858 in Holland and Belgium were already in shipyards. The situation was not as good as these figures suggest, however, and the Merchant Shipping Division was forced to concede on 10 August that deliveries of the barges to the German yards for conversion was not proceeding according to plan. On 8 August only 331 of the planned 436 had reached German yards. The daily delivery rate was planned at 44, but in the last few days before the deadline it had been only 29, 22 and 19 per day. The Division concluded that the delays would mean that the goal would not be achieved in the next 20 days.

The outlook in Holland and Belgium, where deliveries were on schedule, was better. Since the Commanding Admiral France was reported to have found

Barge conversion by Fortress Construction Battalion 82 at the coal quay
at Ivry near Paris. (*Bundesarchiv*)

additional barges, the Naval Commander-in-Chief sent him an order on 9 August
to commandeer 200 (later 300) barges in France via the Chief of Sea Transport
and convert them, obviously in order to circumvent a potential bottleneck before
it was too late.

All the modification work for them was to be done in France, with the exception
of the beaching ramps which were produced in Germany. This heavy workload
caused no end of aggravation. On 26 August, Admiral Schuster, the Commanding
Admiral France, was alarmed to discover that only between 150 and 175 of the
projected 244 barges would be finished by the end of August. In a report he cited
the inadequate delivery rate of the barges and the difficulty in procuring materials
as the principal reasons. Trees had to be felled and cut up; and since there was not
enough sheet steel, small pieces had to be welded together. Deliveries of material
to the French yards were much slower than anticipated and the barges themselves
had many deficiencies. Admiral Schuster reported that many, for instance, did not
have hatch covers.

On 21 August Fortress Construction Battalions 82 and 88 (*Festungsbau-
bataillone*) were assigned to the barge programme to help fill the gaps in qualified
personnel. Companies of construction troops were assigned to the following
French yards:

2 Kp. Brückenbaubataillon 84: Chantiers Franco-Belges, Villeneuve-la-Gorenne;

1 Kp. Baubataillon 99: Ateliers & Chantiers de la Haute-Seine, Villeneuve-
le-Roi;

2 Kp. Baubataillon 99: Atelier & Chantiers de Choisy-le-Roi;

3 Kp. Festungsbaubataillon 88: Worms & Cie, Le Trait;

4 Kp Festungsbaubataillon 88: Arbeitsgemeinschaft Rouen, Ile Lacroix

2 Kp. Festungsbaubataillon 88: Ateliers de France, Caen Blainville

3, 4, 6 Kp. Festungsbaubataillon 77: Arbeitsgemeinschaft Le Havre;

1, 3, 4, 5 Kp. Festungsbaubataillon 82: Chambre de Commerce, Ivry.

The supervisor of shipyards under the Commanding Admiral France described the progress of the work in a report on 30 August 1940:

Five examination units from the administrative area examined and requisitioned the normal barges described as part of the overall ship capacity by the AOK. This examination proved to be very time-consuming, since the search encompassed the area from Le Havre up the Seine to 150 km above Paris. The barges were widely scattered and were hidden, to some extent, in the Seine tributaries. At the beginning the daily intake was 15, which rose to 50 barges. In about 14 days 450 barges were seized [by the Army]. These barges had to be unloaded by the Transport Chief with the assistance of the Wehrmacht Transport Directorate [*Wehrmachtverkehrsdirektion*] and distributed to the various shipyards. The daily target was 30–49 barges. Conversion work was increased by about six days due to the lack of facilities at the yards, the dearth of qualified personnel, especially welders, and tools. The Navy was still coping with the shortage of materials, particularly wood, cement and iron. The first barges were not completed until 24 August.

Overcoming the difficulties cost time and effort, especially since the French authorities were not very co-operative. Increased work by engineers at the yards stepped up the pace so that the original conversion quota could almost be achieved by the deadline. After that, production reached 20–25 barges a day. Continuing effort will result in conversion of up to 300 barges by 10 September. There are enough materials allocated and reserved for this purpose. Some double shift work is being done. (RM45/298/37309)

The supervisor of yards concluded in his report of 27 September 1940:

The 200 barges cited in the Navy's telex of 21 August as a target for conversion were ready for delivery on 13 September. The reserve of an additional 100 barges which were to be finished by no particular deadline were ready by 21 September. In Top Secret letter 1772 of 21 September, OKM (Skl) issued an order to cease conversion of barges. Thus only those which had already been delivered for conversion were to be completed. On 27 or 28 August a total of 347 were reported as ready for delivery or already delivered.

Completion dates would have been 13 days earlier if supply of the barges, which was not the responsibility of the supervisor of yards, had been on time.

The main reasons for the successful conversion of 300 barges in about five weeks – that is, from the time the work was ordered on 9 August until completion – are as follows:

1.   Using the Army to locate and bring the barges to the shipyards, to transport the materials and to help in modification. The Wehrmacht Forestry Administration assisted in locating suitable stands of timber, since there was insufficient wood in Paris. Construction battalions helped in felling trees, supervising lumber production and its transport from distant forests . . .

2.   The shortage of welders and welding equipment was solved by searching through Army suppliers and French companies via the German commissars and through advertising in newspapers.

3.   The work of building hulls was assigned to many companies outside the shipyards and enabled hull construction, concreting and production of ramps to be done at the same time.

4.   The Economics Office [*Wirtschaftsabteilung*] Section IV/Iron of the Belgian and Northern French Military Administration helped procure the necessary materials.

[*Signed*] *Rhein*

Barge conversion in Germany was better organised and proceeded at a faster pace. Raeder was able to report favourably on the rapid pace of work at the Führer Conference on 31 July at the Berghof:

Iron: Production of supports, plates, hulls and transverse frames has started; completion expected 12 August.

Wood: Enough available. Production started of internal ramps; 200 daily starting 1 August, completion expected 8 August.

Concrete: Delivery of raw materials expected 12 August.

Canvas: Allocated by the Reichsbahn [railway]. Delivery to German conversion yards anticipated by 10 August.

Life jackets: 213,000 completed by 15 August. Subsequent delivery to assembly points of the barges and vehicles. Completion and distribution by end of August.

Exit ramps: Supplied by the Army; promise of timely delivery to assembly points of barges.

A branch of KMD Bremen was opened in Koblenz on 23 July 1940 at the Waterway Directorate to distribute the appropriated barges to the conversion yards and then to the mounting ports. The first head of the directorate was Commander Bade, who had overseen the establishment of the Rhine Flotilla in 1917. He was quickly succeeded by Captain Lutter on 4 August, who was immediately embroiled in a conflict between the Merchant Shipping Division (OKM A VI), which wanted the Waterways Departments to confiscate as many barges as possible, and the OKM Design Bureau (*Konstruktionsamt*) represented by Councillor Sohrweide, which insisted on using only ships that were absolutely safe for Sealion. The conversion yards, which were under the direction of the Design Bureau, had rejected 140 of the 245 barges that had been delivered to them, which put them short of their target. After discussions and consultation with Captain Kiederlen and Construction Councillor Driesen from the Design Bureau in which it was agreed to reduce the length to depth ratio of the barges (12–15:1 for ocean-going barges as opposed to 25–35:1 for inland ones), thereby improving their seakeeping qualities. However, there were still insufficient barges with a ratio of 19.5:1 or less, and the figure was only lowered to 22:1 for craft in good condition.

KMD Koblenz had to deal with a mass of details. The barge crews were an early problem: while the pilots could be conscripted, their families had no other place to live and had to be rehoused by the social services. KMD Koblenz also had to ensure air defence of the yards and assembly areas by the Luftwaffe after an air raid on Mainz on 22/23 August – albeit a relatively unsuccessful one.

Three conversion centres were set up at inland yards and steel works at Mannheim, Mainz-Gustavsburg and Duisburg-Ruhrort, each under a director. Materials could thus be centrally ordered and distributed systematically. Duisburg was given a target of 400 barges to modify, Mainz 300 and Mannheim 160. In order to achieve this goal, Dutch, Belgian and two Swiss ships in Germany were commandeered, as well as ships in the territory of the director of shipyards in the Netherlands.

Defended assembly areas were set up at Hitdorf, Neuss, Düsseldorf, Krefeld, Brohl, Oberwinter, Gotorf, Köln-Mühlheim and Köln-Niehl, at which convoys were formed to the embarkation ports. The barges were first sent to degaussing facilities in Duisburg and Cologne to reduce the risk of magnetic mines.

Seven thousand civilians worked at the shipyards in Germany cutting out the bows and installing side struts and floor supports in the hulls. Engineer troops worked at specially allocated and equipped harbours, pouring in the concrete floors and installing the internal ramps supplied by the timber yards. This work was performed by Lieutenant-Colonel Baeck commanding Bautruppen 35 (Construction Corps 35), assisted by Baubataillone 55, 62 and 108 in Duisburg and Major Bartmann commanding Bautruppen 14, assisted by Baubataillone 51 and 52 in Mainz and 219 in Mannheim.

In the Netherlands and Belgium the teams responsible were the commander of Bautruppen 26, to which reported Baubataillone 1, 3 and 107 in Amsterdam and the commander of Bautruppen 8 which supervised the supporting work by Baubataillone 131, 134, 144, 208 and 222 at Rotterdam and 96 at Amsterdam.

After the conversion work was finished most of these units were assigned to man the barges. Most of the modification work was under the direction of the shipyard supervisor for Netherlands and Belgium who was supported by the engineer staff of Colonel Hellwig and the construction troops assigned to him and it is interesting to note that the vast majority of the barges (1,140) were converted in his area; this is all the more remarkable since most of the raw materials came from those countries, as had been the case in France.

A report by the shipyard supervisor notes the obstacles the teams encountered in their work, which was done in about three weeks from signing of contracts. Three districts were responsible for the conversion work and one for repairs and these, along with the shipyards, are listed below (the figures in parentheses indicate the number of barges which were converted):

Amsterdam
> Amsterdamsche Droogdok Mij, Amsterdam (25)
> Nederlandsche Dok Mij, NV Amsterdam (117)
> Nederlandsche Scheepsbouw Mij, Amsterdam (177)
> Verschuren & Co's Scheepswerf & Machinefabriek NV Amsterdam (71)

Rotterdam
> Wilton-Fijenoord, Schiedam (170)
> Rotterdamsche Droogdok Mij, Rotterdam (170)
> Werf Gusto, Schiedam (130)
> C. van den Giessen & Zn, Krimpen ad Ijssel (50)
> Machinefabriek aan Scheepswerf P. Smit, NV, Rotterdam (129)

Antwerp
> Mercantile, Antwerp
> Belliard Crighton & Co, Antwerp (50)
> Engineering & Co, Antwerp (50)

Ostend (repair work only)
   A. Seghers, Ostend (Phare) (130)
   Belliard Crighton & Co, Ostend
   L. Hermanns, Bruges
   Repair yard, Zeebruge

The yards around Amsterdam, Rotterdam and Antwerp were primarily involved with the actual conversion work, while the Ostend yards mainly repaired the ships from Holland and Germany that were to be sent on to the southern embarkation ports.

One constant problem was the shortage of materials from Germany, which meant that the construction supervisors continually had to redirect deliveries in order to keep shipyards supplied. Rerouting was costly and transport scarce; deliveries did not keep pace with the production schedules set by the individual yards. As a result supervisors were often compelled to have parts which were either missing or not yet delivered manufactured on site, an expensive but nevertheless essential solution.

The supply of sufficient numbers of barges also proved difficult. In the early stages they were easily located, but by the end of the modification work the Rotterdam Naval Base was scratching around to find them and this caused further delay.

At the same time the conversion yards were carrying out other work such as fitting out twenty-six transports and smaller vessels.

The German troops who had advanced across Europe in May 1940 had found a large number of steamers in Dutch, Belgian and French harbours; there were 130 alone in the Gironde estuary, for example, and some of these vessels lent themselves easily to conversion into transports. One of the ships commandeered was the French passenger steamer *De la Salle*, which had failed to elude advancing German forces on the Gironde estuary because of a leaky hull; it became *H 17* of the Sealion fleet. Nevertheless, most of the transports came from Germany. On 31 August 111 of these had been appropriated and converted. In the Netherlands and Belgium twenty-six had been captured which were scheduled for completion by 3 September. France yielded thirty-one ships which were available two days later.

The massive conversion programme kept almost all large German yards working hard and all other projects were shelved to meet the end of August deadline, including the completion of the *Tirpitz* and fitting out the auxiliary cruiser *Kormoran*.

Of the twenty-six ships seized in Belgium and the Netherlands, two were converted in Amsterdam, six in Antwerp and eighteen in Rotterdam. Equipment for conversion was supplied by German companies and some Dutch ones; loading equipment, for example, was produced by various Dutch yards and workshops.

Captain Degenhardt, the *Seetransportchef*, reported on 9 August that the following ships were being worked on:

BORDEAUX: Chantiers et Ateliers de la Gironde: Steamers *Cournouaille*, *Penthièvre*, *Sainte Maxime*, *Ville de Metz*, *Nicole Schiaffino*, *PLM 23*, *PLM 26*, *Dunkerquois*, *Madali*, *Ile d'Aix*, *Flandre*.

BORDEAUX PAUILLAC: Société des Chantiers et Ateliers de Rhin & Trompeloup-Pauillac: Steamers *Espagne*, *Cap Guir*.

ST NAZAIRE: Steamers *Jean et Jacques*, *Cambronne*, *Saint Firmin*, *De la Salle*, *Ronwyn*, *Château Palmer*, *Yang Tse*, *Kerguelen*, *Ango*. Motor vessels *Mar del Plata*, *Moero*.

NANTES: Chantiers de la Loire: Steamers *Capitaine le Bastard*, *Ville de Reims*, *Grandlieu*.

NANTES: Dubigeon: Steamers *Elima*, *Marcel Schiaffino*, *Ange Schiaffino*.

NANTES: Bretagne: Steamers *Grängesberg*, *San Mateo*.

LA ROCHELLE: Demas et Vieljeux, la Pallice: Steamer *Hélène*.

(*Elima* and *Hélène* are not in the later list of transports).

The Troop Transport Depot at Frauendorf which was working on the transports produced a report, quoted here in part, which attests to the massive problems in preparing for an operation on the scale of Sealion:

KMD Stettin received an order at the beginning of the year to prepare for Operation Sealion. The Navy depot at Frauendorf was to convert 38 ships. This order was unexpected and only three weeks were allowed for completion of the work. The number of personnel had to be increased since most of the original staff had been reassigned to Aalborg. A request to the Bureau of Labour for more workers could not be met since they had only skilled personnel who were to be assigned to defence contractors for the Wehrmacht. We were given only 75 Poles who had been assigned to transport duties. Some of the staff at the Naval Shipyard Training Depot volunteered to put in overtime for us after their normal workday.

Conversion work was further hampered by the fact that there was insufficient room at the Frauendorf Naval Depot to berth all the ships. Only one ship could tie up directly in front of the warehouses and five or six ships at a breakwater or piles some distance away. The other ships had to be distributed around the harbour at Stettin and fitted out there. Tugs and barges had to ply back and forth constantly with materials.

The Naval Depot's stores had been fairly well depleted by the operation in Norway in spring 1940. Immediate provision of the following was necessary for Operation Sealion: 50,000 lifejackets, 2,000 rafts (iron), 200 rafts (wooden frames with barrels), 4,000 paddles, 10,000 vehicle chocks, 100 boathooks, 100 assault ladders, 150 horse boxes, 4,000 horse stalls, 200 wash stands, 100 cranes for loading motor vehicles, 50 cargo nets, 10 gangways, 350 hatchways, 200 hatches, 100 WC cabins, 100 lifebelts, 1,000 fenders, etc.

Equipping a large number of ships posed considerable problems for the Depot, but this was alleviated by diverting raw materials directly from the producers; 130 tons of sheet metal for rafts could be produced and delivered in three days and bar iron for vehicle lifting gear from the Bismarckhöhe rolling mill in Silesia in seven days.

Though deliveries of sufficient raw materials to the Stettin shipyard were achieved we were unable to produce the relatively large amount of equipment ordered in that short time, due to the shortage of skilled personnel. Several companies were thus formed into co-operatives:

1. Carpenters to produce 200 large wooden rafts made of eight drums.
2. Plumbers and the company Stoewer-Stettin to produce 2,000 iron rafts.
4. Painters to paint the rafts.
4. Blacksmiths to produce loading equipment.
5. Ropemakers to produce various tackles and splicework.
6. Sailmakers to produced 50,000 life jackets, assault ladders, horse stalls and fittings.

The carpenters, painters and ropemakers worked at the naval depot, at temporary facilities which had been provided for them; the ropemakers, who had come from Pomerania and who had been conscripted, were housed at the naval depot.

Our lorries were sent directly from Berlin with the paint in order to keep the work going, requiring a large-scale transport operation. Since there were not enough lorries at Frauendorf to keep pace with the daily work, eight additional trucks had to be hired from private companies or from the air defence (Flak) forces. In addition to the supply of the new material and its onward transport for distribution to the various ships, 1,000 tons of straw for the straw sacks had to be obtained, as well as wood for internal construction, for horse stalls, etc, from a distance of up to 300 km both day and night. Moreover, six to eight railway wagons had to be unloaded daily and the cargo dispatched.

The other ship types to be used for the operation, such as the tugs, coasters and motorboats, did not need any significant modifications. Nevertheless the sheer numbers of these craft made equipping and fitting out a major task. One of the more problematical tasks was mustering enough tugs for the 1,000 or so barges of the First Wave. The Merchant Shipping Division recorded on 15 August that the Navy had already requisitioned fifty-nine tugs; thirty-five more could come from the Navy itself and about a hundred from private owners in Germany. It was estimated that about eighty vessels could be obtained in Holland and Belgium; in contrast, none had been procured from France by this date.

These shortfalls meant requisitioning the few remaining fishing trawlers still in civilian hands as makeshift tugs. On 15 August ninety of these were assembled at Wesermünde and a further forty-seven at Cuxhaven. The KMD at Rotterdam was able to obtain sixty-five tugs in their area and received an additional twenty Rhine motor tugs from KMD Koblenz. Finally, quite a few tugs were found in France – most of these being inland waterway craft – to make up the 426 required.

The list of the vessels which arrived at the embarkation ports (see table on page 142) creates a misleading impression in regard to the tugs, since many were still involved in delivering barges and were not recorded as having arrived at their destination.

It was relatively easy to requisition sufficient numbers of motorboats, though many were not up to the task; indeed, 30 per cent of them were assumed from the outset to be unsuitable. It was calculated that 1,062 boats were needed, and the Motorboat Section of the Navy, with its headquarters at Neustadt/Holstein and branches at Emden and Rotterdam, had seized some 1,600 boats by the beginning of September, a remarkable job for this relatively small organisation. The Motorboat Section, under Commander Strempel was also responsible for the equipping, manning and operational readiness of a number of boats.

The acquisition of a hundred auxiliary sailing coasters by the German KMDs seems insignificant in comparison and apart from fitting the assault boat slides very little fitting-out was necessary. Manning did not pose any particular difficulties since the original crews were retained and the only delay occurred in their delivery to the embarkation ports due to a spell of bad weather.

A complaint in the War Diary of the Commander for Northern Defence (BSN) for 25 August 1940 sheds some light on the difficulties faced during these preparations. During an inspection of the slides for the assault boats on the escorts by representatives of the BSN, the Merchant Shipping Division and the unit's engineer, four former whalers for the 15th Patrol Flotilla drew adverse attention. The engineers had installed the slides against the protest of the commander.

Since whalers are inclined to heel with even a slight change in the rudder angle, this design was doomed to failure at sea. No maritime authority which could have prevented this was present and construction continued. Finally, the slides had to be ripped out. It was decided to launch the assault boats from the whalers directly over the side through a gap in the bulwarks, which was easily done because the ships had only 30 cm of freeboard amidships.

*

The landing fleet began to move from the assembly points to the embarkation ports in late August and thirty-four training barges had already reached Ostend by 29 August. There were two different routes. The transports, coasters, fishing trawlers, *Kampinen* and special barges as well as the large motor boats and tugs took the 'red' and 'pink' routes out of the German Bight along the West Frisian islands to the river estuaries in the Netherlands and the Channel harbours. The escorts of Group West were hard put to clear the routes of mines and protect landing craft cruising in convoy from attack from the air or sea. Smaller vessels travelled via inland waterways.

For instance, the barges rebuilt at the Rhine shipyards in Germany and Holland were towed down the river and reached the West Schelde through the inland waterways of the Netherlands and the South Beveland Canal (see Map 1 pages 196–7). The *péniches*, small tugs, and motorboats (including motor fishing vessels) took an inland route on the Flemish canals from Terneuzen via Ghent and Bruges to Ostend, Dunkirk and Calais. The commander of the Motorboat Section was able to report the departure of the following convoys from Emden on 30 August:

> Convoy 506 on 30 August. Departed Emden via inland route. 37 large motor fishing vessels. Destination Le Havre.
>
> Convoy 504 departed Emden on 30 August. One group leader boat (*Hannibal*), 12 motorboats, 23 motor fishing vessels.
>
> Convoy 505: two command boats (*Hurtig, SW 3 Lindau*), one motorboat. Destination Boulogne. 504 and 505 together.

By 12 September 223 *péniches*, 38 motorboats and 541 trawlers were underway on inland waterways, while 516 barges, 7 AS barges, 30 B- and 3 C-type barges, 143 tugs and 21 group leader boats were at sea en route for the embarkation harbours.

In order to speed up the transfer, the order was given to sail from dawn to dusk on the inland routes, though as inconspicuously as possible. No flags were to be flown and the crews were to wear civilian clothes.

Engineer troops under the Commanding Admiral France maintained the necessary inland routes through Belgium, north-east France and along the Seine, and an idea of the problems that they faced is well illustrated by an incident on the Seine.

A weir had been destroyed on the Seine. The water engineering authority responsible had it repaired by a French company. Work was delayed and the level of the Seine continued to drop. Tugs were unable to navigate the Seine and the departure of the barges was delayed. The problem was solved only by employing German engineer troops.

Nor did everything run smoothly at the embarkation ports.

A flotilla of motorboats arrived around noon at Calais. It had to take provisions on board and the crews had to report to the various authorities. The boats were thus forced to lock in and out no fewer than five times, causing two days' delay.

Despite all these difficulties, the Sealion fleet was beginning to take shape at the embarkation ports by September and the table that follows shows the number of vessels that had arrived by specific days in August and September.

The table on pages 143–4 shows that the number of vessels in the individual harbours did not necessarily increase; a possible explanation could be that in harbours all vessels were counted as having 'arrived', even if some were shipped west later on.

This list was compiled from daily reports to the Shipping Division from the KMDs. A few points are not clear in this list: for example, how many motorboats actually arrived at Ostend, as only boat numbers up to 013 Mo are known. In addition, 200 reserve barges were noted in both the Antwerp and Rotterdam lists, and fifty for Ostend, Dunkirk and Calais. Twenty-five barges were planned as a reserve out of the 200 for Le Havre. The barges for Nieuport and Gravelines were intended initially as reserves to replace losses. Later, troops were assigned to Gravelines to help with loading, since Calais appeared to be full (see page 236).

Group leader boats were included in the lists of motorboats. Only Calais and Boulogne noted, at the beginning of October, the arrival of fourteen leader boats each. In Boulogne this figure had increased to twenty-five by early November.

Reports on transport issued by the Motorboat Section in early September indicated that thirteen leader boats had sailed for Boulogne, twenty to Calais and one to Dunkirk. On the other hand, sixty-one leader boats as well as 344 motorboats were stopped in their tracks in late September by Hitler's order to halt the preparations.

Some harbours reported the motorboats and trawlers separately, though both types of vessels, with the exception of the motorboats at Le Havre, had to act as pusher tugs.

Bad weather delayed the arrival of the forty-eight auxiliary sailing coasters until late September. They were distributed equally to Fécamp, Trouville and Le Havre to protect them from air raids. Thirty-one coasters were held up at

Vlissingen, sixteen at Borkum and five at transit harbours when the order to halt the assembling was received on 19 September.

Many tugs in the assembly area were never listed, since they were being used to deliver the barges. On 24 September, for example, there were 227 tugs under way and 45 at transit harbours. If the tugs that had arrived in the meantime were counted, there would have been a total of 402, just about the required number. Indeed, it would seem that, if there had been no order to halt, 87 per cent of the transports, 94 per cent of the barges, almost all of the tugs and approximately half of the motorboats and auxiliary sailing coasters would have been ready by 24 September, the earliest possible start of Operation Sealion. These figures do not include reserves. Apart from the requirement for more pusher boats (as mentioned on page 51), the figures support the Navy's later assertion that as far as transport was concerned, the operation could have been mounted in autumn 1940. Ronald Wheatley covers this aspect in greater depth in his book *Operation Sealion*.

Tightly packed barges ready for operations. The tanker *Rekum* (ex-*War Shikari*) is in the foreground.

Modified Craft in Readiness at Assembly Areas

	19 Aug	20 Aug	21 Aug	22 Aug	23 Aug	24 Aug	26 Aug	27 Aug	28 Aug	29 Aug	30 Aug	31 Aug
Rotterdam												
Barges A1	4 (2)	10 (4)	15 (5)	19 (7)	28 (10)	31 (11)	34 (11)	55 (12)	65 (18)	72 (20)	115 (27)	78 (22)
Barges A2	29 (3)	83 (6)	111 (8)	122 (8)	139 (8)	151 (15)	183 (11)	227 (13)	301 (24)	343 (25)	489 (37)	295 (15)
Barges B	0	0	0	0	0	0	0	0	0	0	0	0
Koblenz												
Barges A1	0	0	0	0	22 (8)	4 (2)	12 (6)	16 (6)	19 (12)	74 (7)	22 (8)	22 (0)
Barges A2	0	0	0	0	81 (43)	51 (35)	75 (61)	90 (65)	69 (69)	85 (33)	74 (44)	84 (16)
Barges B	0	0	0	0	0	0	0	0	13 (1)	22 (2)	36 (1)	47 (1)
Barges AS1	0	0	0	0	0	0	0	0	0	0	0	1 (1)
Barges AS2	0	0	0	0	0	0	0	0	0	0	1 (1)	4 (4)
Emden												
Tugs	0	0	0	0	0	0	29	29	42	54	66	101
Wesermünde												
Fishing trawlers	0	0	0	0	0	0	24	24	82	82	22	22
Cuxhaven												
Fishing trawlers	0	0	0	0	0	0	30	30	24	49	9	9
Transports	0	0	0	0	0	0	0	.	.	.	.	111
Emden												
Motorboats	.	.	.	.	.	153 (21)	197 (23)	224 (23)	224 (23)	184 (27)	255 (29)	255 (29)
Coasters	0	0	0	0	0	0	0	0	0	0	0	35

(figures in parentheses indicate the number of self-propelled barges and leader boats)

Modified Craft in Readiness at Assembly Areas

	2 Sept	3 Sept	4 Sept	5 Sept
Rotterdam				
Barges A1	30 (6)	24 (8)	83 (16)	87 (18)
Barges A2	158 (6)	151 (4)	305 (17)	314 (18)
Koblenz				
Barges A1	14 (1)	6 (1)	15 (1)	15 (1)
Barges A2	83 (6)	52 (0)	111 (22)	108 (20)
Barges AS1	2 (2)	4 (4)	4 (4)	4 (4)
Barges AS2	6 (6)	8 (8)	4 (4)	4 (4)
Barges B	12 (2)	18 (5)	13 (0)	1 (0)
Barges C	2 (0)	2 (0)	2 (0)	2 (0)
Emden				
Tugs	32	43	46	–
Wesermünde				
Fishing trawlers	3	4	–	–
Transports	136	136	136	–
Emden				
Motorboats	153 (23)	106 (19)	106 (19)	–
Elsfleth				
Coasters	50	50	54	–
France				
Barges A	57 (48)	–	–	–

Music poured from loudspeakers at Dunkirk throughout September. The commander of the naval base there, Captain Bartels, had had them installed in a vehicle to greet the incoming vessels and to keep up the spirits of the workers. Everyone waited for the order to sail.

Craft Arrived at Embarkation Ports

	12 Sept	14 Sept	16 Sept	17 Sept	19 Sept	24 Sept	28 Sept	2 Oct	7 Oct	7 Oct	8 Nov	Target
Rotterdam												
Transports	–	–	–	–	–	49	49	49	46	46	43	49
Barges	–	–	–	–	–	308	308	300	300	298	297	370
Antwerp												
Transports	–	–	–	–	–	48	48	48	48	48	45	50
Barges	–	–	–	–	–	300	300	300	300	300	294	370
Ostend												
Transports	0	13	15	15	15	15	15	15	15	15	14	15
Barges	196	89	65	75	76	76	76	76	76	76	118	155
Tugs	98	0	0	0	4	0	0	0	0	0	5	25
Motor boats	0	0	0	0	0	0	0	0	0	0	0	) 50
Motor fishing vessels	0	0	0	0	0	0	0	0	0	0	0	
Nieuport												
Barges	25	25	24	24	24	24	24	24	22	24	24	24
Tugs	0	0	0	3	3	0	0	0	1	1	1	12
Pusher boats	0	0	0	0	0	0	0	0	0	0	0	24
Dunkirk												
Barges	127	128	132	136	136	163	163	201	228	228	192	200
Tugs	0	0	0	3	3	0	0	27	33	33	25	75
Motor boats	0	14	20	15	15							
Motor fishing vessels	0	0	3	0	7)	22	22	22	22	57	25	150

Craft Arrived at Embarkation Ports

	12 Sept	14 Sept	16 Sept	17 Sept	19 Sept	24 Sept	28 Sept	2 Oct	5 Oct	7 Oct	8 Nov	Target
Gravelines												
Barges	2	2	40	40	40	40	40	39	39	39	42	40
Tugs	0	0	7	7	7	7	7	0	0	0	4	20
Pusher boats	0	0	0	0	0	0	0	0	0	0	0	40
Calais												
Barges	138	157	163	202	204	214	217	218	223	223	207	250
Tugs	98	20	24	23	23	31	46	50	54	54	54	100
Motorboote	0	54	121	38	38	158	161	152	152	166	204	200
Motor fishing vessels	0	0		92	92							
Boulogne												
Barges	88	111	146	236	236	245	252	252	260	260	267	330
Tugs	6	15	19	49	49	68	68	68	45	47	51	165
Motorboats	132	100	100	151	151	296	294	294	264	278	285	330
Motor fishing vessels	57	119	119	125	125							
Le Havre												
Transporter	10	34	47	47	47	47	47	47	47	47	41	50
Barges	46	52	78	130	169	179	200	222	224	224	224	200
Tugs	18	20	20	24	24	24	24	25	25	25	25	25
Motor fishing vessels	0	0	0	100	100	106	156	156	158	161	39	200
Coasters	0	0	0	0	0	0	48	48	48	48	48	100

Assembly of the transport fleet at Le Havre.

Logistics

The scale of the German amphibious assault made it essential to consider the problem of resupply at an early stage. The directors of logistics from Kiel and Wilhelmshaven, Rear-Admiral Niemand and Captain Zieb, were briefed for the first time on 21 July 1940 by Admiral Saalwächter about the basic operational objectives of Sealion.

It became readily apparent after inspection of the Channel harbours in the following two days that they disagreed greatly on how long it would take to meet the logistical requirements, basically because of their differing definition of auxiliary equipment, such as the lack of condensers to produce distillate for the destroyers and in the completely inadequate tanks for storing heating and fuel oils. These problems were further compounded by the fact that there was no reliable information about the number and type of Sealion vessels and their berths. It was not known until August that there were about 4,000 ships to be supplied, in addition to the approximately 320 Navy ships.

Supplying the various lubricants for several thousand different types of ships was problematical, since their fuels were unknown. Samples had to be taken from over 100 vessels and analysed in the laboratory at Wilhelmshaven. All of these ships, including the barges, were to be equipped with as many containers for drinking water as possible, since it was assumed that the wells in the landing zones would be contaminated. Supplying thousands of these containers would not be easy.

Captain Zieb believed that the logistical requirements for Sealion could be met in the eight-week time frame, as long as three officers and thirty-eight staff were transferred immediately to Paris, while work continued at the Wilhelmshaven supply depot. This arrangement was to ensure the smooth shipment of supplies to Paris. He was given this assignment on 26 July by the Naval Operations Office and on 28 July moved to Paris with his staff.

There were many unforeseen complications. Fuels were delivered to the warships or Sealion vessels and thus to the naval depots which were just being set up, partly by the Navy's own or chartered ships or in railway freight trucks or tanker wagons. The naval depots used the existing storage tanks at the embarkation ports, but there were few of them. Bombed-out tanks had proved adequate for storing heating fuel with its specific gravity greater than 1. The destroyed tops of the tanks fooled British photo reconnaissance and the Germans hoped that they would be ignored in future. Large linseed oil tanks were also requisitioned for storing fuel but were hard to clean because of the oil coating. The Todt Organisation quickly built a number of small bunkers of about 200–300 cubic metres. Many French inland craft called *péniches*, with a capacity of between 300 and 500 cubic metres, were seized for heating and fuel oil. Using these craft for storage had the advantage of bringing the fuel directly alongside the Navy ships and making them less vulnerable to attack.

All of the ports had to contend with the almost insurmountable problems of supplying distillate to the Navy ships fitted with high pressure superheated boiler systems. Group West estimated that at least 200 cubic metres of distillate would be needed at each of the five ports for the destroyers. Even a tiny amount of impurities ruined the distillate for the destroyers and at that time it could be produced only in special evaporators at Kiel and Wilhelmshaven. In peacetime the distillate was supplied by purpose-built ships, but these could not be removed from their home ports. Since the evaporators could not be delivered to the embarkation ports in time, confiscated French railroad tanker wagons and inland craft, lined with enamel for transporting wine, were used. These could hold 200 cubic metres and thus met the requirements of Group West. Some of the wine-carrying *péniches* were directed from Bordeaux via Brest into the Channel ports. One of the *péniches* broke up and sank in high seas off Cape Ushant, though the crew were saved.

The military commander in Paris commandeered several thousand wine casks for the large drinking water supply. After cleaning they were filled only enough to float onto the beach if the ship were sunk ... All logistics were set up only after consultation with the KMDs and the military commander in

Paris. The chiefs of the naval depots had the most arduous tasks for Sealion and the staff were often pushed to the limit. There were naval depots in fourteen harbours and these often had branches as well. Since the telephone lines between Paris and the ports were usually jammed during the day, the directors were ordered to stand by at night for communications, which enabled the directors to obtain essential information in the first six weeks and take decisions accordingly.

Since the operation was not a long-range one, it was possible to reload the ships at their initial departure points. Admiral Raeder discussed supply at the Führer Conference of 25 July; an excerpt from his notes is quoted here:

> Supply: Anticipated daily requirements for transport fleet and escorts calculated; necessary supplies will be provided at the harbours. Transport difficult, since transport by sea not yet possible due to air raids and unclear status regarding mines; overland transport still disrupted, assistance requested from Army (300 railway tanker wagons have been promised).

The Navy posted one engineer officer at each of the most important harbours of the occupied territories along the Channel coast. At each port they were supported by two sergeant-majors, a supervisor, six non-commissioned officers and thirty-two crews for setting up and maintaining a naval arsenal. At that time, the occupied harbours were Ostend, Dunkirk, Calais, Boulogne, Le Treport, Dieppe, Fécamp, Le Havre, Trouville, Caen and Cherbourg, followed by Rotterdam, Antwerp, Nieuport and Gravelines. The decision was taken not to use the smaller harbours at St Valerie sur Somme, St Valerie en Caux or Honfleur.

The Naval Logistics Department produced a report on 'Preparations for Support of Operation Sealion' on 25 July, emphasising the following measures:

> Rapid completion of work on all auxiliary vessels, tankers and tugs. Report required on which supply ships (for heating oil, fuel oil, lubricants, water [drinking, cooking, distilled], petrol, coal), tugs and rescue craft are immediately available. Generally, 500- to 1,000-ton ships are suitable as tankers. All those ships not specially designed for transporting lubricants are to be loaded with barrels of special oils.
>
> One diving support vessel and one heavy salvage tug are to be stationed immediately off Cherbourg, Boulogne and Ostend to keep open the channels.

Lecture notes for Raeder dated 30 July indicated the readiness of support services:

> 1. Machine spares: On 28 July the first machine spares were shipped from Wilhelmshaven to Ostend, Boulogne and Cherbourg. Additional

rail transport being arranged. Transport means available. Shipment by sea presently not feasible.

2. Routes: Railways partially in service.

3. Transport: Requirement for 170 railway tanker wagons, fulfilled 40 per cent. Twenty-eight road tanker vehicles at 20 tons each available. Status unclear regarding tanker ship capacity and other vehicles.

The Merchant Shipping Division ordered the KMDs to commandeer: twelve colliers totalling 17,183 grt, equalling 24,000 tons load capacity; twenty-seven tankers (45,348 grt in total); 3,012 cubic metres capacity in six motor tanker lighters, 5,928 cubic metres in six tanker lighters; one tanker barge of 364 tons; five water carriers totalling 315 tons. Other vessels which had not been commandeered, but were nonetheless available to the naval supply depots, included seven motor tankers amounting to 2,190 grt; twenty-two tanker lighters totalling 11,051 grt; thirteen motor tanker lighters (3,503 grt); and seven water carriers (868 tons). The Military Commander in Belgium and France provided fourteen motor tanker lighters totalling over 2,685 grt to the Navy. All these vessels were delivered on schedule and the *Marine kommandoamt* was able to report on 20 September 'Thirty-three tankers are ready for maritime transport duties: all orders for supplies have been met in all the ports and even exceeded at Cherbourg, Le Havre, Antwerp and Rotterdam.'

Clearing the Ports

Harbours in the north of France had been heavily damaged by the retreating British Expeditionary Force. Dunkirk, focus of the action in May 1940, had suffered such destruction that at first the Germans had not even considered it as a suitable embarkation port for Sealion. Belgian and Dutch harbours had escaped more lightly. The only major damage was to the locks at Zeebrugge where the gates had been blown up and ships sunk in the harbour. Determined efforts made resumption of traffic possible by November 1940, but this was far too late for Sealion and only the pier there could be used. Ostend, Nieuport and Gravelines were largely intact.

At Dunkirk the Harbour Construction Office, soon after it was established, produced a map with the locations of 177 wrecks. Of course, many of these sunken vessels were small craft such as tugs, trawlers and barges, but they also included some steamers ranging from 3,000 to 5,000 grt as well as a tanker of 18,500 grt. The wrecks of four medium-sized steamers partially blocked the harbour entrance. Two wrecks lay in the middle of the channel, one behind the other. Two others rested on the east side in front of and next to these ships. These

Salvage work in Dunkirk harbour entrance. (*F. Hansen*)

were raised leaving a channel clear on either side of the remaining wrecks and was
kept so by sea marks.

Ministerialdirektor Eckhardt described the progress of the Dunkirk harbour
reconstruction in an article 'Construction of Naval Ports in War' (*Nauticus* 1944)
in which he stated:

> Clearing mines was only one of the tasks to be done in making the harbour
> usable again. Three locks fed into the harbour, one of which had been built
> by German companies after the First World War as part of reparations.
> Destruction of the bearings of the lock gates through damage to the gates
> themselves, the rams or the rotating supports rendered them completely
> useless. The gates no longer closed, allowing the tide to flow in and out of the
> harbour and docks. The gates themselves had to be repaired. Various repair
> troops were formed to work in the harbour, particularly on the locks, working
> on the electrical equipment, conduits, mechanical maintenance and ironwork.

Divers with underwater welding and cutting equipment also worked to repair damage. A total of 7,000 men was required; using them to the best advantage ensured that the harbour was in service after only a few months.

Organisations involved in rebuilding work included van Wiemen, a salvage company; Bugsier AG with its salvage vessel *Berger I*; the Todt Organisation; Teno (*Technische Nothilfe* – Technical Emergency Service); and the 1st and 3rd Companies of Engineer Battalion 208. Their work permitted the Trystram and Guillain locks to be brought into service, so meeting the requirement for there to be at least two locks at each embarkation port.

Calais had escaped lightly. By 16 September the small 14 m-wide lock and the small chamber of the larger 21 m-wide lock had been repaired and it was anticipated that the western outer portion of the large lock would be temporarily repaired by 23 September.

Boulogne had likewise suffered only minor damage and on 16 September the harbour and locks were declared operable. Pile-driving work had already commenced for a slip to accommodate eight barges.

Considerable salvage work had to be done in Dieppe and Caen. Originally they had not been cast as departure ports because of their location and small size,

Loading bridge. (*Bundesarchiv*)

but by late autumn they were being used as alternative harbours to disperse the assembled fleet more widely.

Le Havre had been severely damaged but was still usable. The thirty-five wrecks were only raised if they were a nuisance or the hulks were of value.

Once the various harbours had been assessed for their use as embarkation ports, Dr Gerdes from the Naval Construction Office (*Marineoberbaurat*) and Professor of Harbour Design Dr Agatz, produced a preliminary plan for accommodating the landing fleet based on the Navy's fleet disposition. Areas for loading troops onto the barges had already been fixed and they were to embark shortly before the fleet sailed, vehicles and equipment having been loaded several days in advance using the barges' own beaching ramps. Troops were to come on board the barges via iron loading bridges produced by Dortmunder Union, Klonne, Jucho, and Dortmunder Union Brückenbau (Werk Orange division). Boulogne and Calais were to receive six bridges each, Dunkirk and Ostend seven apiece, and Nieuport two. (The position of these bridges is shown on the harbour plans on pages 216 ff.) About half of the bridges were for tidal harbours and the other half for non-tidal basins. Dunkirk had an average tidal range of about 6 m and it was thought that the bridges in the tidal harbours could be used for three hours before and three hours after high water.

Personnel

If procuring enough suitable landing craft was a herculean task, it was equally hard to recruit the personnel to man them. Right from the outset, the Navy knew it would not be able to provide enough personnel from within its own ranks. The Operations Branch of the Wehrmacht Command stated on 18 July that,

> Further to Führer Directive No. 16, the Führer has ordered that the transports are also to be manned by conscripts in order to reduce the pressure on the commercial sector. ObdH and ObdL are to assign all suitable personnel to the Navy, except those specialists who are already needed for the same operation [Sealion].

The Navy estimated on 6 August that it would need the following personnel:

> For 1,000 barges one coxswain each.
> For 1,000 barges four crew members each totalling 4,000 sailors.
> Reserves for barges already in service totalling 2,000 crew members and 500 mechanics.
> Each motorised craft generally has one coxswain, one or two engine mechanics and two to four sailors.

One hundred motorboats will be manned by the Motorboat Section at Neustadt and three hundred by the VGAD (K) [*Verstärkter Grenzaufsichtsdienst (Küste)*] which provided reinforcements for the Coastal Border Patrol. Additional requirements for 800 coxswains, 2,400 sailors and 800 mechanics. As a reserve, 800 sailors and 400 mechanics.

The steamers are to be manned by merchant fleet crews as well as supplementary crews of fifteen men consisting of dockers, boat crews, etc. from German harbours.

Tugs: It is assumed that there will be full crews on tugs. Reserve: 100 pilots, 200 mechanics (steam), 200 mechanics (motor), 400 boilermen, 1,110 deck crew.

Total requirement for 14,700 men.

Met by:

3,500 Navy personnel, Career structure I, seaman branch (good sailors, former merchant marine personnel, crew on small vessels, towed barges, Naval boat crews, etc.)

500 active Navy personnel, Career structure II, mechanics with experience of engines and small craft.

Approximately 7,000 Army personnel (knowledgeable in inland navigation, fishermen, raft crew, etc.).

5,209 Navy reservists not yet serving.

Approximately 6,000 Naval Reserve conscripts who had not been called up including coastal and inshore fishermen.

200–300 corporals as coxswains. 300 Navy NCOs.

If necessary, Navy and technical NCOs and crew from Career structure I and II from ship crews and schools.

750 coastguard personnel (Navy) Career structure I and II.

A final reserve force of 4,000 who have not yet served, from inland navigation dockers, river and harbour workers, rafters etc. who are in supervisory posts with the other armed forces.

According to the directive of 6 August, the following Naval Reservists I were to be called up:

8,844 uncalled-up Naval Reservists I (all in strategic industries protected by exemption agreements).

4,169 additional Naval Reservists I born in the years from 1901 to 1919.

4,000 personnel from inland navigation, fresh-water fishing industry and river barges.

Total: 17,013 men

The difficulties in assembling such a force were awesome. Aside from the fact that of all the personnel only those from Engineer Battalion 2 had had any experience with amphibious technology at all, so many men were needed that they had to be seconded from other jobs such as fishing and timber rafting. Improvisation of materials and equipment was matched by that of personnel. Not only did landing craft have to be conjured up from every available source, but they were to be manned largely by inexperienced crews and only the most sketchy training could be given in the few weeks available.

It is a sign of the Navy's dedication to the mission that it assigned serving personnel to Sealion. The old pre-dreadnought *Schlesien*, used as a training vessel, had to be laid up in Gotenhafen and the crew of its sister-ship *Schleswig-Holstein* reduced to such a degree that it could only be used as a target ship. The large training crews of the light cruiser *Emden* and that of the cadet training ship *Tannenberg* were reduced to combat levels and the ships themselves assigned to duties as fleet cruiser and minelayer respectively for Sealion.

Crews from ships undergoing lengthy repairs were also used: the 'pocket battleship' *Lützow* (ex-*Deutschland*) for instance, was out of service until early 1941 after being severely damaged by torpedoes, but a proposal by Group West to use the crews of the battleships *Scharnhorst* and *Gneisenau*, the destroyer *Hermann Schoemann* and *Sperrbrecher 4* for Sealion was rejected and the Naval High Command pressed for early completion of repair work on the battleships regardless of whether they would be finished in time for Sealion or not (see page 287).

Conscription of those in the first and third categories drew mainly on naval dockyards and the armaments industry of the Navy, since these men were generally, and in the case of the first group, exclusively, skilled workers and engineers.

Naval flak gunners were to operate the few anti-aircraft guns on board the transports and those units which had been formed by 15 April 1940 were renamed the *Marinebordflakabteilung 200*.

The net for recruiting the best-trained personnel for the largest German amphibious operation to date was soon spread wider. In Rotterdam 470 German amateur sailors were conscripted and indeed, any membership of a sailing club was a ticket to becoming a sailor in Sealion. The Chief of Sea Transport, Captain Degenhardt, who reported to the Commanding Admiral France, was a strong supporter of the landing operation and the mobilisation of every conceivable group. In Austria radio announcements were followed up by recruiting drives for crew, and an attempt was made to attract men from the *Donaudampfschiffahrtsgesellschaft* (Danube Steamship Company) on the Hungarian side of the river, as well as to recruit ethnic Germans from Hungary.

When Captain Degenhardt extended his recruiting efforts to school-aged youths, the *Allgemeine Marineamt* (AMA – General Naval Office) which was responsible for personnel lodged a protest: 'Renewed effort or continuation of recruiting by the Chief of Maritime Transport must cease. School pupils will no longer be sent and those who have already been will be returned to their homes.'

The *Marinestammabteilung* at Munsterlager had provided 18,811 men for Sealion by 2 September, including 1,656 barge skippers; 2,786 helmsmen; 717 motor mechanics for the barges; 913 engine operators for the motor vessels; 1,159 engine-room crew for the steamers; 2,027 boilermen; 449 tug skippers and 9,104 deckhands.

Training of these crews was scanty other than exercises in the embarkation ports. Barge crews had two-day training courses at Emden and additional ten-day courses at Rotterdam. Conscripted civilian crews were given five weeks of military training. The landing fleet which was to make the assault on England was anything but a well-honed force.

It is interesting to recount the experiences of a former field artilleryman who had taken part in the Western campaign and found himself seconded to Sealion:

> Because I had been in the Naval Hitler Youth I was put into a blue uniform at Munsterlager and ordered aboard a Rhine barge as a deckhand. This barge had been rebuilt at the Rheinwerft at Walsum for landing operations and fitted with two airscrews at the yard in Rotterdam. These boats were manned by three men from the Navy, some of whom had previously been in the Army; five engineers operated the landing equipment (these were mostly from the Construction Battalions) and there were two aircraft engine mechanics. A platform was installed amidships for a 2 cm Luftwaffe flak gun. These guns were to be fitted just before sailing. I estimate that there were 200 to 300 barges in the harbour at Rotterdam after completion [of modifications]. Nothing much happened except a few trial runs of the barges. Logistical support was provided by the Army construction battalions.
>
> Otherwise we were pretty much left alone. Since there were many men who had never been in the military, such as dockyard workers and former members of the merchant marine who had simply been put into uniform, this lack of training led to real problems. We were taken off the craft in late autumn and put into organisations known as Naval Harbour Units and housed mostly in schools. Army and Luftwaffe troops were also on board but were later reassigned to these units. Almost every large port on the Dutch, Belgian and French coast had Naval Harbour Units. Later they were renamed Fleet Base Units [*Flotillenstammabteilung* – FSTA] and formed a third arm with the Baltic and North Sea Commands. Naval amphibious forces, most of which were

equipped with the *Marinefährprahm* landing craft, had been systematically trained and equipped from 1941 onwards. I was a boatswain first class from 1942 to 1943 and later commanded one of these craft in northern Norway, ending up in the 23rd Amphibious Flotilla.

This account points the way to later developments during planning for Sealion.

Army Planning

Army preparations for the landing were quite modest compared to the massive scale of the Navy's, but it too was embarking on a new type of operation, and was confronted with an entirely new element: the sea.

The first step was to restructure the First Wave infantry divisions, tailoring them to their particular mission. Since the combat forces could not count on the logistical support during an amphibious operation that they would have on land, each division was subdivided into two echelons. The first echelon contained two reinforced regiments, the bulk of the combat troops, which were organised for brief autonomous operations. They were to mount the assault. One battalion from each first-echelon regiment was specially organised and equipped; they were the advance detachments which would capture the beachheads ahead of the first echelon. The second echelon, with twice as many troops, comprised the third regiment and the divisional logistical support elements.

All the divisions assigned to the landing, particularly those of the First Wave, had to be reinforced and better equipped than the back-up support troops. Most

Artillery training with a 3.7 cm PAK on a wobbly platform to simulate ship movement.

A self-propelled 4.7 cm PAK during landing training.

of the German infantry divisions of that time were not fully motorised and were mostly foot soldiers in the truest sense of the word. Some signals units had horses and some artillery units used them to pull their guns and ammunition wagons. The deficiencies were alleviated somewhat by using captured vehicles, at least in the first echelons. British light tanks, commandeered during the Western offensive, were well suited for the first echelon. One company in each infantry and engineer battalion in the First Wave had bicycles for greater mobility. All existing mounted units were re-equipped with bicycles, because horses were difficult to transport.

Reassignment and distribution of weapons ensured that the First Wave divisions had the most modern equipment; everything possible was done to make the divisions of the First Wave an effective striking force. Each first echelon anti-tank company had a towed French or Czech 4.7 cm PAK gun, the German 3.7 cm gun having proved inadequate. Two batteries in every infantry division with the light field howitzer (*leichte Feldhaubitze*) were reequipped with the *Gebirgskanone 15* mountain gun, giving them more mobile artillery. First-echelon infantry battalions were also furnished with six heavy towed mortars. All First and Second Wave Armies were allocated one artillery regiment staff, a 10 cm gun detachment (motorised), a heavy field howitzer detachment (motorised) and a reconnaissance detachment. Each of the nine First Wave divisions had a company equipped with 2 cm flak, some self-propelled, which were advanced for their time. There was one flak battalion for each Army. These self-propelled Army guns were to provide air defence for the infantry. The anti-tank forces of each division were reinforced by a company of 4.7 cm self-propelled PAK anti-tank guns based on the Panzer I chassis, also a relatively modern weapon system.

A completely new weapon, the rocket launcher, was deployed with Nebelwerfer-regiment 51. Previously classified secret, it was assigned to the Sixteenth Army for Sealion. The regiment consisted of nine batteries with a total of seventy-two sextuple 15 cm launchers. These were capable of laying down a heavy bombardment over large areas in seconds. Both the Allies and the Germans developed weapons of this type during the war. Initially, on the German side, it was to be assigned to one battery in every division; by September, however, the decision was taken to concentrate the weapon, and the regiment was then to be transported in the second and third sortie.

Another new weapon which did not see action until the end of the Western Campaign was the *Flammpanzer* flamethrowing tank of Tank Detachment (Fl) 100. Essentially these were Panzer IIs with two flamethrowers instead of the main gun, which could attack pockets of resistance and bunkers under cover of conventional tanks. In the autumn of 1940 this unit comprised three companies, each with three platoons. Each platoon was led by a gun-armed Panzer III and had four flamethrowing tanks. The companies had twenty support vehicles

An assault gun being unloaded.

for refuelling, since the *Flammpanzer* were emptied after only fifteen minutes. Although the commander of the unit, Captain von Zezschnitz, favoured a massed attack which would have allowed sufficient cover by the conventional tanks, the Sixteenth Army chose to assign twenty *Flammpanzer* to the shock troops to spearhead a landing. These vehicles were divided equally between the XIII and VI Corps. The bulk of the unit was to be transported along with the remainder of the first echelon of the VII Corps from Ostend and join the troops which had already landed at Appledore. From then on they would be deployed with the Sixteenth Army.

Captain von Zezschnitz was an energetic supporter of the landing operation. He created a 'landing column' from captured vehicles and a fourth Panzer company, which were used during exercises. He had his own ideas about his company's role during the invasion of England, proposing that his vehicles be placed transversely on board the barges alongside the pier, and that the hatch covers could double-up as ramps. This proposal was not very practical, since loading and unloading from the side would be likely to capsize the barges. But his enthusiasm sometimes proved fruitful and he was probably responsible for the fact that the first three *Land-Wasser-Schlepper* amphibious tugs were tested by Tank Detachment (Fl) 100.

Assault guns were another relatively recent innovation. These were 7.5 cm forward-firing guns in a heavily armoured frontal casemate on a Panzer III chassis. They were designed to provide infantry support for brief engagements of point targets and were very effective.

During the preparations for Sealion there were only eight assault batteries each with six assault guns. This shortage meant, for instance, that the 35th Infantry Division was not assigned an assault battery. Depending on the division, these guns were to be used either in the advance detachment or at the front of the first echelon, where they certainly would have adequately supported the first troops to land on the beaches.

The four units equipped with submersible and amphibious tanks have already been described (see page 92).

Other reinforcements for the First Wave divisions included a bicycle reconnaissance battalion and a mixed signals company. An additional engineer regiment staff unit and a further engineer battalion provided amphibious capability. Each army had a towed ammunition supply company for resupply of the First Wave divisions.

The above account of equipment and its disposition merely gives a general impression of their assignments; in practice there were many reorganisations, sometimes due to the reduction of First Wave divisions after the decision on a narrower front was taken, sometimes due to the availability of new units such as the assault batteries. The strength of the landing divisions and army corps is described under the individual landing fleets.

Allocation of additional units caused considerable confusion. Frequent exercises were held to reveal any new problems and to solve them by liaising with other units. Colonel Dinter set up training courses for the Sixteenth Army at Le Touquet in order to familiarise his troops with the Reinhardt Test Staff's technical specifications. These exercises stressed the landing of the advance detachments in assault boats, rubber dinghies and motor fishing vessels, on-board firing of weapons and the laying of temporary roadways in the dunes, all without the aid of the training barges which had not yet been delivered. Courses were held from 5 to 18 August for 42 officers and 300 men; from 23 to 26 August for 36 officers and 168 men; and from 30 August to 9 September for 36 officers and 168 men.

When the first landing craft arrived at the embarkation ports the divisions began embarkation training and held landing exercises with the Navy. The advance detachment of the 34th Infantry Division held exercises on 27–28 September and those of the 26th Infantry Division on 10 October, which included an attack by a British bomber. Bad weather cancelled training of all three advance detachments of Transport Fleet D and one tow group. Transport Fleet E was able to train with the 6th Mountain Division, the 8th and the 28th Infantry Divisions on 26 October.

Night unloading operations were critical and were meticulously described in training reports. It was hoped that the Navy's tight schedule for the crossing could be mitigated somewhat by night loading of returning transports in home ports and offloading of the transports into barges off the beaches and in captured harbours. Loading the barges and beaching them at night was not difficult, but taking heavy equipment aboard the transports had to be done under lights, making the ships sitting ducks for enemy naval and air forces. The BSW opposed night training by Group West and the Army, fearing even more devastation to the Channel ports by British bombers. Though it was admitted that night training was too risky, loading at night under actual operational conditions was countenanced. Thus only a few of these exercises were held, one of which was in December at Rotterdam when steamers were offloaded under subdued lighting into barges tied up alongside; it was a success, a heavy lorry being unloaded in 15 minutes. Night-time loading was judged to take from 25 to 50 per cent longer than during the day, and in the case of the Army resupply items, 100 per cent longer. In the spring of 1941 lights were installed on various quays, including at Ostend and Zeebrugge.

Finally, an idea of the strength of a reorganised infantry division can be gained from the following list:

First echelon: two reinforced regiments
    6,762 men
    341 horses
    300 cars
    80 heavy machine-guns
    292 light machine-guns
    54 light mortars
    72 heavy mortars
    14 light infantry guns
    27 anti-tank guns
    12 air-defence machine guns
    8 rocket launchers
    8 mountain guns
    93 jeeps
    34 lorries
    135 motorcycles
    46 motorcyles with sidecars
    1,908 bicycles
    49 tanks
    9 light tanks (*Karetten*)

Second echelon: One division less two reinforced regiments
    12,376 men
    4,427 horses
    933 vehicles
    105 cars
    36 heavy machine guns
    204 light machine guns
    6 heavy infantry guns
    9 light infantry guns
    48 anti-tank guns
    28 light field howitzers
    12 heavy howitzers
    356 jeeps
    760 lorries
    605 motorcycles
    271 motorcycles with sidecars
    164 bicycles

The Luftwaffe Prepares

The Luftwaffe was exhausted after the Western Campaign and attacking Britain at that time was inconceivable. On the other hand, the Germans had gained an important strategic foothold, the occupation of France putting southern England within range of German fighters escorting the bombers on their daylight attacks.

Given this situation, the Luftwaffe Command had three options in prosecuting the war against Britain. The first was to attack British ships, harbours and economic centres with naval support. The second option was to launch an all-out air attack, neutralising the Royal Air Force and then systematically destroying British economic and communications centres in order to bring the country to its knees. The third alternative was to plan and support an amphibious assault.

The first option promised the greatest success and was also advocated by the Navy. The one snag was that the plan did not fit in with Hitler's strategy in the summer of 1940. Conquering Britain, the Führer thought, would gain little, and he cast about for other ways to overawe the British government in order to allow him to attack in the east, his real objective.

There is a regrettable dearth of German documents on the strategy of the Battle of Britain in autumn 1940, though some conclusions can be drawn from its course.

His work for the Nazi Party from the earliest days allowed Göring a more sympathetic hearing with the Führer than either Raeder or Brauchitsch, the other commanders-in-chief. Göring was probably well aware of Hitler's reluctance to undertake a landing operation and 'destroy the British Empire' and tailored his air offensive accordingly, making air superiority the prime objective. Afterwards, Britain was to be economically weakened and cowed. There is no direct link in German documents between this goal and Operation Sealion. Walter Ansel has correctly noted, though with slight exaggeration, that the only link between the two was the desire to strike fear into Britain.

There were also differing opinions within the Luftwaffe. An expert in the Luftwaffe Home Defence Office (*Abteilung Landesverteidigung*), Major Freiherr von Falkenstein, prepared a short report on the role of the Luftwaffe in a landing in England as early as 25 June. He touched on air superiority, naval air support, the role of the 7th Airborne Division as well as of the 22nd Infantry Division as an airborne force. Luftwaffe Chief of Staff Major-General Jeschonnek did not bother to respond to this report, as he believed that Hitler was not considering an amphibious landing at the time. The Falkenstein proposal was certainly the result of deliberations in the *Abteilung Landesverteidigung* by section head Colonel Warlimont and the naval liaison officer, Captain Wolf-Junge.

On 8 August the Luftwaffe inventory included 949 bomber aircraft, 336 dive bombers (*Sturzkampfflugzeuge*, also known as Stukas), 869 fighters, and 268 heavy fighters. Almost all of these, with the exception of a heavy fighter wing (*Zerstörergeschwader*) and a few fighter and bomber units, had been deployed to the Channel coast and to Norway. Air Fleets (*Luftflotten*) 2 and 3 controlled most of the bomber, dive-bomber and fighter units. Air Fleet 5 had parts of Bomber Wings (*Kampfgeschwader*) 26 and 30 and a heavy fighter wing. Bomber Wings 26 and 30 were specially trained for naval operations and had wreaked havoc on important British targets during the Norway Campaign, forcing the Allies to evacuate their amphibious troops. During the summer of 1940 their target continued to be the British fleet despite the lack of orders to this effect. The Luftwaffe also attacked targets on British soil at this time, though with little success, eventually being rested in Holland to prepare for a greater role in the air offensive against Britain.

On 1 August the following Luftwaffe forces were ranged against Britain:

Field Marshal Kesselring during an inspection of Luftwaffe ferries off Ostend.

Luftflotte 2 (Field Marshal Kesselring)

I. Fliegerkorps

KG 1 [Bomber Wing 1] comprising:
  Stab [Staff]
  I. II. III. *Gruppen*

KG 77 comprising:
  Stab
  I. II. III. *Gruppen*
  5 (F)/122 [Long-range flight]
  4 (F)/32

KG 76 comprising:
  I. II. III. *Gruppen*
  Lehrstaffel [Training flight]
  Korpstransportstaffel [Corps transport
    flight]

II. Fliegerkorps (*Colonel-General Loerzer*)

KG 2 comprising:
  Stab
  I., II., III. *Gruppen*

KG 3 comprising:
  Stab
  I., II., III. *Gruppen*

KG 53 comprising:
  Stab
  I., II., III. *Gruppen*

AufklGr (H) 30 [Reconnaissance group
    (Army co-operation)]
4 (H)/31 [Army co-operation unit]
5 (H)/32
II/StG 1 [Dive bombers]
IV(St)/LG 1 [Dive-bomber training]
ZGr 210 [Heavy-fighter Group]

9. Fliegerdivision (*Lieutenant-General Coeler*)

KG 4 comprising:
  Stab
  I., II., III. *Gruppen*

KG 406 comprising:
  Stab
  I. *Gruppe*

KGr 126
KGr 100 (to 16/8/40)
KüFlGr 106 [Coastal reconnaissance
    group]
3 (F)/122

Jagdfliegerführer 2 (Jafü 2) (*Major-General Osterkamp*)

JG 3 [Jagdgeschwader 3] comprising:
Stab
I., II., III. *Gruppen*
JG 26 comprising:
Stab
I., II., III. *Gruppen*
JG 51 comprising:
Stab
I., II., III. *Gruppen*

JG 52 comprising:
Stab
I. II. III. *Gruppen*
JG 26 comprising:
Stab
I. *Gruppe*
ZG 26

Nachtjagddivision (*Major-General Kammhuber*)

Stab NJDiv.
NJG 1
Flakscheinwerferbrigade [Searchlight unit]

LnAbt (H) (mot) 2 [Army co-operation signals unit]
Flugmeldeabt Kenzler [Communications]

Luftflotte 3 (Field Marshal Sperrle)

VIII Fliegerkorps (assigned to LflKdo2 from 29. 8. 40)

StG 1 [Stukageschwader 1] comprising:
Stab
I., II., III. *Gruppen*

StG 2 comprising:
Stab
I., II., III. *Gruppen*

StG 77 comprising:
Stab
I., II., III. *Gruppen*

II/LG 2 (in Böblingen)
V(Z)/LG1
AufklGr(H) 21
2 (F)/11
2 (F)/123
Transportstaffel

V. Fliegerkorps (*General Ritter von Griem*)

KG 51 comprising:
Stab
I., II., III. *Gruppen*

KG 54 comprising:
Stab
I., II., III. *Gruppen*

KG 55 comprising:
Stab
I., II., III. *Gruppen*

Erprobungsgr 210 [Trials group]
4 (F)/14
4 (F)/121

IV. Fliegerkorps (*Lieutenant-General Pflugbeil*)

LG 1 [*Lehrgeschwader 1*] comprising:
   Stab
   I., II., III. *Gruppen*

KG 27 comprising:
   Stab
   I., II., III. *Gruppen*

I., II./StG 1
StG 3 with *Stab* KGr 806
KGr 100 (from 17. 8. 40)
KüFlGr 606
AufklGr (H) 31 comprising:
   2/12, 4/22, 2/31
AufklGr (H) 41 comprising:
   2/13, 1/41, 2/41, 3 (F)/31 (assigned to
    StG 3 from 8. 7. to 12. 8. 40)

Jagdfliegerführer 3 (Jafü 3) (*Colonel Junck*)

JG 2 comprising:
   Stab
   I., II., III. *Gruppen*

JG 53 comprising:
   Stab
   I., II., III. *Gruppen*

JG 27 comprising:
   Stab
   I., II., III. *Gruppen*

JG 52 comprising:
   Stab
   I., II., III. *Gruppen*

Stab ZG 2

Luftflotte 5 (Colonel-General Stumpff)

X. Fliegerkorps (Lieutenant-General Geisler)

KG 26 comprising:
   Stab
   I., II., III. *Gruppen*

JG 77 comprising:
   Stab
   I., II. *Gruppen*

KG 30 comprising:
   Stab
   I., II., III. *Gruppen*

I./ZG 76

KüFlGr 506
AufklGr 22 comprising
   Aufkl Staffel OdbL [Reconnaissance
    flight C-in-C]
   1 (F)/120
   1 (F)/121

It should be noted that the 9th Fliegerdivision was also trained for maritime operations and had successfully mined British harbours and Channel routes.

The list of the Luftwaffe units includes several naval aviation units which had been withdrawn from tactical operations by the Navy. Only Coastal Aviation Groups 406 and 906 remained under naval command.

Flakkorps I and II of the Luftwaffe's anti-aircraft artillery had supported the push westward and were left in place to defend important installations. Flakkorps I was assigned to Luftflotte 3 and was to operate in conjunction with the Ninth Army, while Flakkorps II was placed under the command of Luftflotte 2, operating with the Sixteenth Army. These Flakkorps were tasked with air defence during loading and unloading of the landing craft: the support of advancing Army troops, as well as protecting the more vulnerable elements of the convoy against air and surface attacks.

The Flakkorps were organised as:

Generalkommando Flakkorps I
　　1st Flak Brigade
　　　　Flakregiment 102
　　　　Flakregiment 103
　　2nd Flak Brigade
　　　　Flakregiment 101
　　　　Flakregiment 104

Generalkommando Flakkorps II
　　　　Flakregiment 6 (Ostend)
　　　　Flakregiment 201 (Calais)
　　　　Flakregiment 202 (Dunkirk)
　　　　Flakregiment 136 (Boulogne)

Well aware of the need for adequate protection of beaches and troops during the landing, the Luftwaffe had requested the transport of fifty-two flak batteries along with the First Wave of troops as early as July. The Luftwaffe had to make do with only 30 per cent of this strength; the rest were to cross with the Second Wave forces.

'Provisional Directive 16 of the Army High Command (AOK) on Operation Sealion' of 9 September foresaw the mission of Flakkorps II as essentially:

> ...the suppression of enemy armour and fixed installations, besides providing air defence. Thus early deployment of these flak units is necessary and they should be set up as quickly as possible to ensure this.

Flakkorps II will provide air defence during loading and unloading of the landing craft and will also support the Sixteenth Army's offensive. The weaker elements shall protect the fleet during the crossing.

Its nine heavy and four light detachments will protect the massed troops and ships as well as loading operations at Ostend, Dunkirk and Calais. Two mixed detachments, each equipped with three 8.8 cm Flak batteries and two 2 cm Flak batteries will be assigned to each First Wave army corps (distributed among the two echelons). These Flakkorps will provide air defence during the crossing, the unloading and the assault on the British coastline, then attack British aircraft, naval forces and tanks during the advance.

Together with other units in subsequent waves, it will provide air defence of harbours.

Those units which will co-operate are Flakregiment 201 and VII Corps; Flakregiment 202 with XIII Corps; and Flakregiment 6 with the V and XLI Corps. Regimental commanders are to liaise with the army corps and make recommendations on the use of their forces for air defence.

Later lists mention only one mixed flak regiment for each Army, the lack of transport capacity having apparently been acknowledged. Shortly before the beginning of the operation each armoured and motorised division was to be assigned a light flak regiment. The disposition of the Luftwaffe units is shown in the table on page 170.

Relief of those elements of Flakkorps I and II which had sailed from Ostend, Dunkirk, Calais, Boulogne, Etaples and Dieppe, as well as from the fall-back harbours of Zeebrugge, Nieuport and Gravelines, was to be prepared by the *Luftgaukommando* of Belgium and Northern France. This command was also responsible for the defence of Antwerp harbour and strategically important locks terminating in harbours. *Luftgaukommando* Holland was tasked with the air defence of Rotterdam harbour.

The Luftwaffe had been involved in the development of the Herbert ferry and the heavy bridge pontoon ferry (*schwere Schiffsfähre*) (see pages 101–2) and it was thus not surprising that anti-aircraft guns were to be transported on them. These were to be free-standing on platforms, ready to fire on British ships or aircraft and provide cover during the landing. In late July and early August flak combat units were established which were equipped with an 8.8 cm and two 2 cm guns which were to follow the advance detachments during their attacks on British emplacements. These units and Army troops trained hard at Fécamp and Dieppe as well as at the Luftwaffe ground forces school at La Courtine.

An excerpt from a report on command and control of these Flak units details their composition:

1. *Organisation*
a) Personnel
   1 Officer (unit commander)
   4 NCOs (three gunners and one specialist)
   22 crewmen
   1 Luftwaffe medical corpsman and possibly 2 NCOs
   20 Army crewmen as auxiliaries
b) Equipment
   1 8.8 cm flak gun
   2 2 cm flak
   1 towing vehicle
   2 Kfz 81 trucks for the 2 cm flak
   2 motorcycles
   Ammunition:
   8.8 cm: 200 rounds common, 200 time fused, 100 armour piercing
   2 cm: 9,000 rounds common, 200 time fused, 100 armour piercing
   Large number of infantry
   Individual flak units to be reinforced by Officer Reconnaissance of Ln
Rgt 101.

2. *Missions*
The Flak unit operates autonomously under a commander. This unit will be
deployed as part of the advance detachments or the First Wave. It will provide:
   a) air and surface defence for advance detachments and First Wave troops
       during crossing.
   b) air defence for advance detachments and First Wave troops during
       landing and suppressing coastal defences.
   c) ground defence to enable the establishment, expansion and holding of a
       bridgehead; and air and surface defence as a secondary role.

3. *Implementation*
   a) Missions can only be accomplished in close co-operation with the local
       army commanders ...
   b) Maritime and ground targets are to be engaged while under way in
       accordance with Paragraph ... L.Dv. 400/ ... Air defence is only on an
       ad hoc basis due to the lack of fire control. Targets are thus to be engaged
       only at short ranges (up to approximately 1,000 metres). The gun sight
       is to be used to aim the gun diagonally across the target's trajectory, the
       time fuse having been set for the estimated range.
   c) The Flak units will provide the main artillery firepower for the landing
       forces. They will be able to do this only by using the maximum amount

of ammunition and opening full fire at short range in a timely manner. Proper placement of guns is thus essential for sustained fire.

d) Army support will be given during landing of the Flak troops, unloading ammunition, siting the guns and repositioning them as the operation unfolds.

The Flak units are to operate autonomously. Nevertheless, they are to make every effort to liaise with each other in achieving and holding a bridgehead, co-ordinating fire and supporting the shock troops.

e) The Flak troops should be fully aware that the success of the mission depends on them. All ground gained should be defended with every possible means.

A number of long- and short-range reconnaissance units were assigned to the Army on 30 August, and short-range reconnaissance specially for armoured units. A Luftwaffe commander (*Koluft*) was assigned to co-ordinate the army groups and armies. The table overleaf lists those units under the command of Army Group A as at 14 September:

Organisation and Allocation after 30 August 1940

Army Group Command and /or Army High Command	Army Corps and Panzer Division	Long-range flight	Army co-operation flight	Panzer units	Flak and/or light flak later allocated
Koluft A		4 (F)/11			
Koluft 16		3 (F)/10			
	VII		1 (H)/10		I/26
	XIII		4 (H) /12		II/14
	V		1 (H)/32		
	XLI			3 (H)/12	
	8 Pz			3 (H)/41	lei 94
	10 Pz			2 (H)/14	lei 71
	29 mot				lei 76
	IV		3 (H)/21		
	XLII		2 (H)/32		
	XXIII		2 (H)/14		
Koluft 9	VIII		2 (H)/10		I/36
	X		1 (H)/31		I/29
	XXXVIII		3 (H)/32		I/3
	XV			9 (H)/LG2	
	7 Pz			1 (H)/11	lei 86
	4 Pz			1 (H)/14	lei 77
	20 mot				lei 93
	XXIV		2 (H)/23		

Koluft = Commander Air Force   lei = leichte/light

Artillery Reconnaissance Squadron 3 (F)/10 and 3 (F)/11 are only deployed in support of the Artillery Air Defence [for the heavy coastal batteries at Pas de Calais] and are to be used by the Army High Command for reconnaissance only with the permission of the Army Group Command.

Artillery Reconnaissance Squadron 2 (H)/14 is assigned only for operational purposes and is to be trained with other branches as well. Their tactical deployment is under the control of the Army High Command.

Luftwaffe preparations were particularly concerned with airborne troops. All paratroops were part of the 7th Airborne Division, which did not reach divisional strength until the summer of 1940 when it comprised four parachute regiments and a glider regiment. It was inferior to an infantry division in terms of firepower and manpower. Infantry divisions were about 19,000 men strong, while the 7th Airborne Division had only about 10,000, of whom 7,000 were paratroopers.

After the campaign in Poland the 22nd Infantry Division was converted to an air-mobile role, that is, its troops and equipment could be landed at airbases using transport aircraft. These forces never reached the strength of an entire division.

The 22nd Infantry Division was placed under Luftwaffe command in the winter of 1940/41, forming the XI Fliegerkorps along with the 7th Airborne Division. Sealion plans for the latter underwent many permutations and are reasonably well documented, but relatively little is known about plans for the 22nd Infantry Division. Possibly, it was to be used as a contingency force for the Sixteenth Army, since it was first assigned to the Army High Command and then to the Sixteenth Army. The dearth of documentation is probably due to the fact that the Luftwaffe had only seven Transport *Gruppen* which were not even capable of transporting the 7th Airborne Division as a whole. The 22nd Infantry Division would then have been landed much later.

One of the Luftwaffe's interesting innovations was the heavy-lift glider, developed during the winter of 1940/41, but not used until the following spring. This was designed to transport a Panzer IV or an 8.8 cm flak gun with its towing vehicle, or 200 infantry troops and their kit. Messerschmitt and Junkers had been invited to tender designs by 1 November 1940; Junkers' was to be of wooden construction and Messerschmitt's of steel tubing and sailcloth. Junkers were in unfamiliar territory with wood and the project flopped, but Messerschmitt produced the Me 321. This aircraft saw a lot of service, initially in the occupation of the island of Ösel in 1941. Its chief disadvantage – that it had to be towed by one or more aircraft – was later overcome by fitting it with engines.

Transport

Vice-Admiral Lütjens, Naval Commander West, issued Operational Order No. 1 on 14 September. 'Transport for Operation Sealion' is quoted here, along with other pertinent documents. This material is the crux of the plans for the crossing, and will be examined in more detail later on.

I. COMMAND AND MISSIONS

...

II. INTELLIGENCE

a) At sea: intelligence reports are to be transmitted immediately before and during the operation.

b) Air situation: major air superiority has been gained in the Channel. Nevertheless, surprise attacks by lone British fighters and bombers are to be expected.

c) Situation on enemy coast: coastal artillery fortifications in all landing zones should be assumed. Artillery attacks on advance detachments and towed formations must be expected.

III. GERMAN FORCES

a) Naval: Three groups of five submarines each, all destroyers and torpedo boats west of the western minefields and all MTB east of the eastern minefield.

b) Air: Fighters covering the embarkation harbours and the Channel; fighters and bomber units over the landing zones.

c) Timely reports about own minelaying.

IV. MISSION

Transport of the Ninth and Sixteenth Armies from northern France to the English coast.

V. IMPLEMENTATION

The Commanding Admiral France is to provide transport according to the orders of the Naval War Staff [Skl].

a) Timing: The Führer is to decide the start of the operation. Day 1 of the landing is S Day; time of the landing S Hour. The operation is to be prepared in such a way that its start can be called off with 24 hours' notice. Earliest S Day is 24 September, thus earliest embarkation day is 23 September.

b) Transport fleets, towed formations and escorts are to be loaded with all materials in accordance with orders from Naval War Staff in the embarkation ports. Troops and horses are to embark only after establishment of S Day and S Time, that is, beginning on S minus 3 days.

c) Mine countermeasures and escort forces cannot be accommodated in the embarkation ports due to lack of space. They are to enter these harbours under orders from the unit commander once the already loaded vessels have sailed.

d) Composition and movement of the individual units are to be determined by their commanders after liaising with the Army Command. They are to ensure that the troop units remain together as much as possible after landing.

e) Embarkation times from the individual harbours and routes:

1) *Rotterdam*
Convoy 2 is to assemble in two lines abreast 18 hours before S Time in Assembly Area I: 51°54′ north, 4°0′ east; 52°0′ north, 4°0′ east; 51°54′ north,

3° 50′ east; 52° 0′ north, 3° 50′ east (Qu 8579 AN), thereafter cruising at 8 kn. Mine counter measures by the 4th Minesweeper Flotilla on course Red–Pink, Lilac–Pink. Head of convoy is to reach the sea buoy on Route 1 at S minus 3¼ hours. From there along Route 1 in accordance with the plan (Annex 1) behind Convoy 1 to Zone B.

2) *Hoek van Holland*

4th Minesweeper Flotilla sails in accordance with 1) and protects Convoy 2 beginning at Assembly Area I.

3) *Antwerp*

Convoy 3 is to assemble in two lines abreast at S minus 11 hours in Assembly Area II: 51° 24′ north, 3° 0′ east; 51° 30′ north, 3° 0′ east; 51° 54′ north, 2° 50′ east; 51° 0′ north, 2° 50′ east (Qu 8756 AN), thereafter cruising at 8 knots. Mine countermeasures are to be provided by the 15th Minesweeper Flotilla along the route Lilac–Pink, arriving at the marker buoy on Route 2 at S minus 4½ hours, according to the plan to Zone C. Arrival S plus 2 hours.

4) *Vlissingen*

15th Minesweeper Flotilla to embark in accordance with 3), providing protection for Convoy 3 beginning from Assembly Area 3.

5) *Ostend*

aa)   Tow Unit 2 is to assemble at S minus 14 hours, three convoys abreast at West Diep. It is to sail from Ostend on a new course of 285° until they bisect the Pink Route at 51° 15.6′ north, 2° 47.7′ west, continuing to West Diep. It is to cruise at 5 knots; minesweeping by the 3rd R-boat Flotilla on the Pink Route, arriving at Point 11 at S minus 9.5 hours. It will then join Tow Unit 1 from Dunkirk to sail to Zone B via Route 1, in accordance with the plan. (Embarkation time to be determined in conjunction with Convoy Fleet 1). Assembly Area III = West Diep.

bb)   3rd R-boat Flotilla, 2nd Patrol Flotilla sail in accordance with aa) and sweep the route of Towed Convoy 2 starting at Assembly Area III (West Diep).

cc)   The seven steamers of the VII Corps assigned to Zone C are to embark from Ostend and arrive at Assembly Area II (Qu 8756 AN) at S minus 11 hours in two lines abreast. They are to proceed to Zone C under the command of Captain S. Wesenmann, commander of Convoy 3.

dd)   The eight steamers of the XIII Corps meant for Zone B now form all of Convoy 1, under the command of Captain Wagner. Convoy 1 is to assemble in two lines abreast in the roadstead at S minus 13 hours, proceeding at 8 knots via Qu 8759 on route Pink–Lilac–Pink ahead of

Convoy 2; cleared by the 16th Minesweeping Flotilla. It is to arrive at the marker buoy on Route 1 at S minus 3½ hours. In accordance with the plan, it will then sail to Assembly Area B, arrival S plus 2 hours. Sailing from Ostend to be co-ordinated with Tow Unit 2, arrival at start of Route Lilac with Convoy 2.

ee)   The 16th Minesweeper Flotilla sails as described under dd) and sweeps for Convoy 1 beginning at the Assembly Area.

6)   *Dunkirk*

aa)   Tow Unit 1 embarks so that its head reaches marker buoy on Route 1 three tows abreast at S minus 9½ hours in Assembly Areas IV at 51° 2.5′ north, 1° 3′ east; 51° 0.5′ north, 1° 54′ east; 51° 4.5′ north, 2° 1′ east; 51° 1.5′ north, 2° 3′ east. It then proceeds at a speed of 5 knots with minesweeping by the 3rd Minesweeper Flotilla along Route 1 in accordance with the plan to Zone B.

bb)   The 3rd Minesweeper, 11th R-boat, and 3rd Patrol Flotillas embark according to aa) and sweep for the Tow Unit 1 starting from Assembly Area IV.

7)   *Calais*

aa)   Transport Fleet C embarks at S minus 8½ hours, its head reaching the beginning of Route 2 three tows abreast. It shall then proceed at a speed of 5 knots along Route 2 to Zone C in accordance with the plan, minesweeping being provided by the 4th R-boat Flotilla.
      Assembly Area V is at: 50° 58.6′ north, 1° 50.9′ east; 50° 58.1′ north, 1° 50.0′ east; 51° 0.1′ north, 1° 45.8′ east; 50° 59.1′ north, 1° 43.6′ east; 50° 58.6′ north, 1° 44.3′ east; 50° 59.2′ north, 1° 45.8′ east.

bb)   1st Minesweeper, 32nd Minesweeper, 4th R-boat and the 7th Patrol Flotillas embark according to aa) and sweep the route for Transport Fleet C along Route 2 starting from whistle buoy 1.

8)   *Boulogne*

aa)   Transport Fleet D embarks so that its head arrives at S minus 10 hours 10 nm west of the beginning of Route 3, four tows abreast. It will then sail at 5 knots to Zone D, minesweeping being provided by the 2nd R-boat Flotilla along Route 3 in accordance with the plan. Assembly Area VI is 50° 43.8′ north, 1° 31.8′ east; 50° 45.8′ north, 1° 31.8′ east; 50° 45.8′ north, 1° 34.4′ east; 50° 43.8′ north, 1° 43.8′ north; 1° 33.4′ east; continuing along Route 3.

bb)   The 2nd Minesweeper, 18th Minesweeper, 2nd R-boat, 15th, 16th and 19th Patrol Flotillas will embark as under aa) and provide protection for Transport Fleet D on Route 3. They are to sweep Route 3 from the embarkation point to the assembly area westwards before the transport fleet assembles.

9) *Le Havre*

aa) Convoy 5

1a) Given a favourable strategic situation, it will embark in such a way that it assembles in two lines abreast with its head at Point 20 on the Pink Route 20 (15) hours before S Time. It then sails at 7 knots along the Pink Route to 50° 15' north, 1° 11.6' east, with mine countermeasures being provided by the 14th Minesweeper Flotilla. The hours in parentheses indicate sailing time to Zone D. Should no decision have been taken in regard to landing before departure from Le Havre, times for departure for Zone E are to be observed. Should the order be given to proceed to Zone D, the escort force should sail so that it reaches it 2 hours after S Time, continuing either via 50° 30.4' north, 0° 40' east to either Zone D or E, depending on the strategic situation. (Cruising to Zone E via 50° 39.3' north, 0° 1.3' east.)

Assembly Area is 49° 39.5' north, 0° 0.9' east; 49° 39.5' north, 0° 3.2' east; 49° 31.3' north, 0° 0.9' east; 49° 31.3' north, 0° 3.2' east.

1b) At times of unacceptable enemy threat Convoy 5 will remain loaded in the harbour, and will embark only by special order, from higher authority.

bb) The 14th Minesweeper Flotilla will embark in accordance with aa) 1a) and will sweep for Convoy 5 along the Pink Route from Point 20, or will remain in the harbour in accordance with 1b).

cc) Convoy 4

1a) Given a favourable tactical situation, it will embark in order to assemble in two lines abreast with its head at 49° 35.5' north, 0° 5.2' west at S Time minus 11 hours. It will then sail at 7 knots behind Transport Fleet E directly to Zone E, mine countermeasures being provided by the 12th Minesweeper Flotilla. (In this case, commanded by the senior officer of the 12th Minesweeper Flotilla.)

Assembly area VIII: 49° 36.2' north, 0° 7.5' west; 49° 32.2' north, 0° 3.0' west; 49° 31.4' north, 0° 7.5' west; 49° 31.4' north, 0° 3.' west.

1b) Should the strategic situation not allow this, Convoy 4 will form behind Convoy 5 in a timely manner and accompany it.

1c) As 9.) aa) 1b).

dd) The 12th Minesweeper Flotilla will embark according to cc) 1a) or 1b) and will clear the way for Convoy 4 or remain in the harbour according to 1c).

ee)   Transport Fleet will depart in order to arrive at Assembly Area VIII at S minus 11½ hours. Formation: motor fishing vessels forward, followed by 20 coasters (two columns of 20). The 1st R-boat, 4th, 13th and 20th Patrol Flotillas and five heavy auxiliary gunboats will sail ahead and abreast of this unit to secure its route to Zone E. (Cruising speed 7 knots.)

ff)   The 1st R-boat, 4th, 13th, and 20th Patrol Flotillas and five heavy auxiliary gunboats will embark according to ee) and will sweep for Transport Fleet E starting from Assembly Area VIII. Note: The auxiliary gunboats assigned to the various landing zones are stationed at some distance and will redeploy to or outside of the embarkation ports to provide air defence support before loading.

VI. SPECIAL ORDERS

a) Flags
   1) All naval vessels, auxiliary gunboats, tugs and motorboats are to display the Reich war ensign.
   2) Convoy steamers are to fly the Reich service flag.
   3) Should the barges become separated, they are to display the Reich service flag or none at all.

b) Command of the fleet from the embarkation ports to the landing zones is in the hands of the Navy commanders and their subordinates.

c) Army unit commanders are to be embarked on the Navy commanders' flagships.

d) Bow protection equipment will be used only on minesweeping flotillas.

e) Ships are to carry on if mines are encountered.

f) Ships are to sail at a uniform speed in fog.

g) Artificial smoke is to be employed before the landing only under orders from the individual group commanders after consultation with the Army commander on board. Three minesweepers of each of the 1st to 4th R-boat Flotillas will be fitted with permanent smoke generators.

h) Damaged ships separated from their units which cannot reach the landing zones should anchor and report their position after S Hour and await recovery by units of Naval Commander West.

i) Visual signals for German aircraft: On S minus 2 days, all naval ships in Operation Sealion will repaint their fo'c's'le upper decks red and the aft sector of the ship yellow. Steamers, tugs, barges and motorboats shall follow suit. Paint and brushes to be supplied by the KMDs.

j) Every transport vessel must know the correct identification. Only naval vessels are allowed to show them. Damaged ships may do so of their own accord.

[Signed] Lütjens

The Naval Commander West added a number of directives to make navigation easier.

Aside from the Routes Red, Pink and Lilac, exact details of which will be sent subsequently to the appropriate authorities, Advance Routes 1, 2 and 3 will be designated as follows:

1) Buoy at 51° 1.3′ north, 1° 53.4′ east for approach to Route 1.
2) Buoy at the demarcation line Lcht-Hl-HX TN 1 (Calais) 50° 59.4′ north, 1° 45.8′ east for approach to Route 2.
3) A buoy 50° 45.4′ north, 1° 30.3′ east for approach to Route 3.
4) Buoy at the peacetime position of the whistle buoy at the southern edge of The Ridge [sandbank in the middle of the Channel] 50° 48.9′ north, 1° 16.3′ east (positions marked in the plans). Identification will be communicated in a timely manner.

   b) Lit buoys: Buoys carrying lights will be placed at intervals of 2 nm along Routes 1, 2 and 3 for the towed convoys and escorts. Course change positions will be indicated by dropping two lit buoys at a distance of 30 m to assist the steamers following. The minesweepers anchoring will not affect this.

   c) Light-ships: Course changes for the towed convoys will be marked on Route 1 by a minesweeper (with smoke apparatus) at 51° 0.5′ north, 1° 22.5′ east; on Route 3 by a minesweeper (with smoke) at 50° 43.9′ north, 0° 40.9′ east. Both boats are to show two shrouded red lights. Once the tow formation has passed the boats will weigh anchor and rejoin their flotilla. (The light-ships will no longer be stationed on Routes 1 and 3 for the convoys following the towed formations. Course changes for the escort fleet are marked by two closely spaced lit buoys as in b.)

   d) Placement of buoys according to a) by a buoy tender will be on S minus 2 days under the direction of the *Seebefehlshaber.*

   e) Two minesweepers will position the lit buoys during the approach to the landing zone under the direction of the commander of the transport fleet. The boats are to precede the towed formation sufficiently to allow the buoys to be positioned on time. Once the buoys have been dropped the minesweeper is to anchor at the termination of the particular route and show the 'two red' signal.

Once the unit has changed course the motorboats are to follow the advance detachments.

f)   The tow units and convoys are to pass the buoys to leeward; the windward or leeward side depends on the current, so when the tide shifts the buoys have to be passed on the other (new leeward) side in order to avoid colliding with the buoys.

Nineteen lighthouses on the French and Belgian coast were recommissioned for Operation Sealion. Radio beacons were also set up.

Lütjens was very exacting about the composition and routes of the towed formations. This was essential for an orderly crossing, since the passage of such a vast number of small vessels was completely unprecedented in living memory. Co-ordinating the movements of individual towed units was also difficult.

Map 1 on pages 196–7 shows the routes as established by the Naval Commander West for 14 September 1940. Towed formation 2 from Ostend had to sail 43nm to the beginning of Route 1, where it was added to Tow Unit 1 which had come 19nm from Dunkirk. In order for these forces to rendezvous successfully on the evening of S day minus 1, the vessels from Ostend had to leave on the morning of S day minus 1 and those from Dunkirk that afternoon. Transport Fleets B and C were to cross the Dover Straits by daylight, thus ruling out the chance of a surprise attack; and the British forces would have the advantage of daylight to launch a counter-offensive.

Tidal charts were scrutinised in planning the routes. The tow units would have to sail against the tide for only a short time and after the course change the tide would increase cruising speed by about 1 to 1.5 knots. By the time the tide had changed again the formations would have just about reached the markers for the course change directly into the shore.

Keeping the towed formations together would not be easy. Transport Fleet C had over 100 tows and extended over 14–15 km, half the distance between Calais and Dover; so the transport fleet commanders in the lead could never have been able to see the vessels at the rear of the formation. To improve the situation, six tows were organised under one group leader who was to give directions from a fast motorboat. Transport Fleet D, with its 165 tows, was the largest, and would have stretched at least 20 km. Its commander, Captain Lindenau, chose a four-column formation for sailing about 1,550 m wide, in contrast to the other fleets, which were divided into three and were about 1,000 m wide.

In order to make good the minimum speed of at least 5 knots, only those tugs able to do at least 6 knots were selected. This was all very well in theory, but in practice not all the tugs would have been able to keep up the pace and the flotillas would probably have drifted apart. Captain Kleikamp addressed the problem in

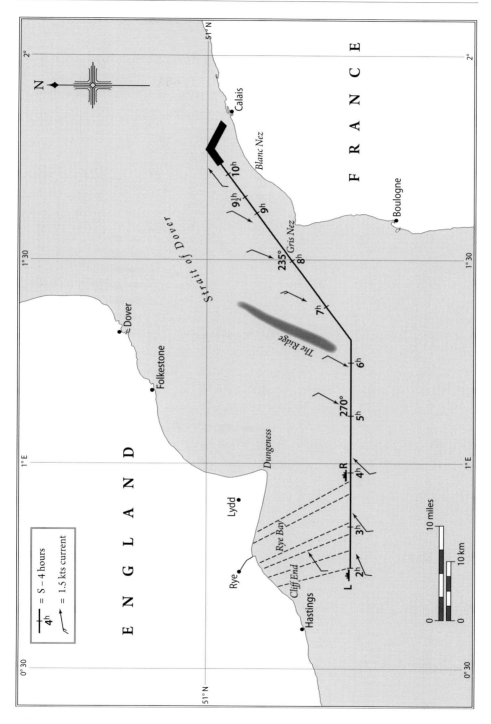

Route of Transport Fleet C, with tides.

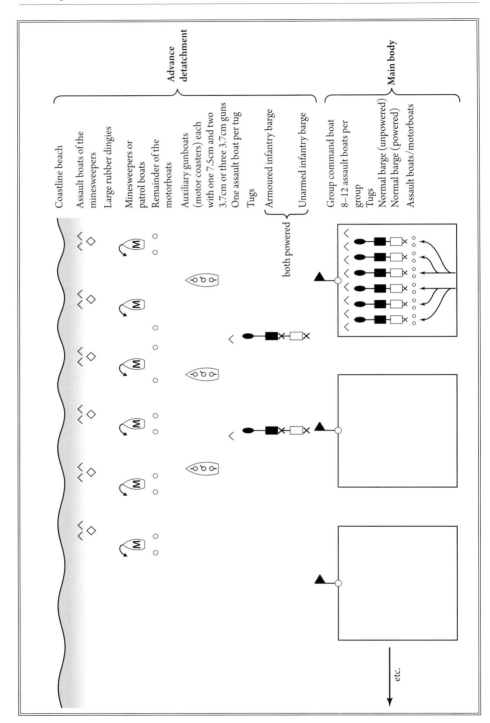

Schematic diagram of the landing formation.

his Transport Fleet C by placing the most powerful tugs at the rear since they could keep up better. In the third of his annexes, he noted:

The following points must be considered in organising the fleet:

1) Shortly before landing, the fleet will turn 90 degrees to the coast. The towed groups must ensure that the Army units remain as closely together as possible…

2) …

3) Minesweeping will be done by R-boats, since they are better suited to this task than the fleet minesweepers, due to their shallower draught.

4) The vessels of the advance detachments are to sail in groups on the landward side of the fleets in order to prevent the other tows from getting in their way after the turn.

5) The R-boats with permanent smoke apparatus cannot carry mine-sweeping gear; one is to be assigned to each advance detachment.

6) Minesweepers and R-boats at the head of the formation belong to the forward (left) advance detachment, those at the rear to the right one.

7) Minesweepers cannot stream their gear at less than 7 knots [because they would have been ineffective]; thus at approximately 8 knots they are to pull ahead, and, on a predetermined signal, turn about and rejoin the formation…

8) …

9) Communications concerning turning are via radio, and are to be passed along by all radio operators on tows, using a 'green blinking' signal with a course change lantern and a verbal signal. Turning within the tow unit is to be treated as a combat manoeuvre (starting from the rear), with the landward side turning first.

In the fifth annex of this order Captain Kleikamp applied himself to the matter of the actual landing and its importance warrants its quotation here in full:

Landing and Return of Empty Transport Vessels

I. The tow formations shall proceed to Areas A, B and D in three or four columns along the routes prescribed for the individual units. Once the minesweeping flotilla reaches the end of its course it is to stow its sweep gear. When the head of the tow formation reaches the end of its course, the Transport Fleet Commander is to give the order via radio for the entire formation to change course toward the coast, in accordance with the plan.

II. After turning, the advance detachments are to assemble forward of the formation in readiness for the landing. The advance detachments are numbered from one to three from left to right. Each advance detachment is to have a commander (the most senior flotilla commander).

The Transport Fleet Commander is in control of the formation until the turn, when he joins the middle advance detachment. The Transport Fleet Commander is to communicate any delay in the landing (S Time) caused by delay in departure of the fleet. The advance detachment will land at S Time, the tow units 20 minutes later. Commanders of the advance detachments will order the use of smoke after liaising with the Army troop commanders on their vessels. They are to give the order to their detachments to open fire, though only in the case of British resistance; otherwise the element of surprise should be exploited. Ceasefire orders are given by the Army.

III.   Tow units

1)   Tows are to advance upon the coast in lines abreast after the turn.

2)   Tow group leaders are to determine when the powered barges are to be released as well as the unpowered ones which are to be beached with the aid of the motorboats.

3)   Tugs and pusher boats are to assemble under the direction of the tow group leaders once the barges have landed; they are to be assigned to the following transports as laid down in the plan in order to land the loaded barges and unload the steamers themselves.

The tow group leaders are thus responsible for ensuring the smooth flow of empty barges to the individual steamers and for their transport to the coast for unloading. Naval beach parties will lend assistance.

4)   Tugs, barges and pusher boats of the individual tow groups are to remain in the landing zone until all the steamers have been unloaded. Return of empty tow flotillas is described under Section VII.

5)   Should the redisposition of tow groups for unloading the steamers be required as a result of the situation, the Transport Fleet Commander is to take this decision for his own particular landing zone.

IV.   Convoys

1)   The convoys following the tow units are to sail in close formation until they reach the centre of the landing zone.

2)   Anchorages for unloading the transports are to be predetermined and distributed over the entire landing zone.

3)   The convoy commander is to give the order for dispersal of the convoys to their moorings. The leading steamers are to anchor at the extreme ends of the route and those at the rear in the centre of the zone, both simultaneously. The steamers should be loaded and positioned within the convoys accordingly.

V.   Transport fleet commanders and the unit commanders who report to them are to remain on their command boats after landing to direct the unloading of the steamers. They are to be recalled by the *Seebefehlshaber*. The minesweepers, R-boats and patrol craft for the advance detachments are at the disposition of the Transport Fleet Commander, once coastal fire support has been provided, for defence and support of unloading operations of the barges and steamers and for the return of the empty vessels.

VI.   Situation reports

Transport Fleet Commanders are to report the following via radio telegraphy:

1) Any unusual occurrences during the crossing (after the landing, if there has been no contact with British forces).

2) Landing of the advance detachments.

3) Landing of the tow formations.

4) Status reports every six hours on the unloading of the convoys.

5) Overall ground situation as far as can be determined.

VII.   Return of the empty transports

1) In each landing zone, after unloading all barges and transports, ten large high-speed motorboats, and if required, tugs and powered barges are to be placed at the disposal of the Army for transport of equipment.

2) Half the number of tugs, barges, and pusher boats are to remain in each landing zone to unload the transports of the second and third echelons and, if necessary, of the Second Wave. They will not withdraw until about half of the south coast of England has been secured for the remaining transports. (Subject to the change by the order of the *Seebefehlshaber*.)

3) Depending on the tactical situation, the remaining transport vessels are continually to return for reloading at ports which are still to be determined; these groups are to comprise at least four steamers and/or ten tows in convoy with the minesweepers, R-boats and patrol craft available in the landing area.

The Naval Commander West did not mention in his operational report how long each landing wave would take. Captain Kleikamp, Commander of Transport Fleet C, on the other hand, decided to commit his thoughts to paper and excerpts of his order No. 2 are quoted here.

C. Unloading

1) Barges (almost all unpowered) towed by the steamers are to be picked up by the tugs as soon as the steamers have anchored and begin unloading operations immediately. The steamers are to remain anchored with engines running.

2) Unloading is to proceed as quickly as possible to allow the two barges to be returned to the steamers without delay.

Landing exercise with a tow group at Le Touquet on 17 October 1940.

3) Once Transport Fleet C has landed, those barges which have not grounded on the receding tide are to return immediately to their assigned steamers for further unloading.

4) In other cases, as soon as barges can be refloated and towed free (at about S plus 8½ hours), they are to be returned to their steamers.

5) Barges loaded from the steamers are to be unloaded only during a falling tide at least 1 hour after high tide. The only exceptions are barges which have to be landed on steeply sloping beaches, for example at Cliff End, and only then if they can be unloaded in half an hour.

6) If possible, six barges per steamer are to be loaded before the second high tide on S Day and to be beached for unloading one to two hours after high tide.

7) The same procedure applies for the first high tide on S Day plus 1 and if required, for the second high tide of that day.

8) In addition to unloading the steamers with the barges, troops are to be brought as close to shore as possible on the tugs and motorboats and unloaded in rubber dinghies.

9) The objective is to unload the steamers of Convoy 3 by the evening of S Day plus 2.

The other transport fleets would probably have followed suit. The time required to unload the transports is surprising for even if each had six barges as lighters, it still would have taken until the morning of S Day plus 2 to offload the transports at an average of twenty-four barge loads per ship.

The following table, based on tides on an unknown day in Rye Bay shows their influence on the landing:

S Day

05.32	*High tide*
07.00	Advance detachments land
07.30	Barges of tows land
09.30	Transports reach anchorages
10.30	Transports' barges land
12.09	*Low tide*
16.00	Barges towed free
17.00	Offloading of transports begins
18.22	*High tide*
19.22	First barges loaded from transports land
00.49	*Low tide*

S Day plus 1

05.00	Barges towed free
06.00	Offloading begins
06.59	*High tide*
08.00	Barges land
13.31	*Low tide*
18.00	Barges towed free
19.50	*High tide*
21.00	Barges land
02.19	*Low tide*

S Day plus 2

06.30	Barges towed free
08.26	*High tide*
09.30	Barges land, first transports unloaded
15.05	*Low tide*
19.00	Barges towed free
21.15	*High tide*
22.15	Barges land. All transport fleet craft are unloaded and turned around, with the exception of some of the tows, which remain to lighten later convoys.

These operations would then be followed by a lull while transports returned back across the Channel to reload. The first smaller tows and transport groups with the remainder of the First and Second Wave could not be handled at the landing zones until S Day plus 4. This lengthy schedule was due to the lack of adequate landing craft able to beach at high tide.

What was supposed to happen with transports later during the operation was not clear, since it was impossible to calculate accurately losses and delays. Undaunted, however, the Sixteenth Army produced projections on cargo capacity on 8 September and the Ninth Army on 21 September which at least give a rough guide to the transports' movements after the initial landing.

According to the Ninth Army, the 175 barges which had sailed from Le Havre to Landing Zone E were to remain there to offload the transports if the tactical situation would allow it. The whole of Transport Fleet D, with its 165 tows, on the other hand, was supposed to return to Boulogne and embark a second time for England on S Day plus 2. A later report, produced in the winter, criticised this plan as being too slow so that it was altered to allow the second echelon also to be sea-lifted from Boulogne in the barges and transports. One hundred and twenty-five tows from these transport fleets were reserved for this 'shuttle service' consisting of the smaller formations. Those tows which had survived the assault were to remain in the landing zones to offload the transports. The transports each from Antwerp and Rotterdam were to unload in Zones B and C, and return to Calais for use by the Ninth Army. The fifty tows from Zone C which had made their way back to Calais were also to be allocated to the Ninth Army. The harbour too was given over to this force. According to this plan, an additional five transports from Rotterdam would have returned to Calais after unloading for the second time.

This redistribution of shipping capacity between the Ninth and Sixteenth Armies was necessary because Sixteenth Army had more cargo space for its four divisions than Ninth for its five, partly because the Army had insisted on a strong left flank (see page 10). In addition, the only embarkation ports for the western sector and the Ninth Army were Le Havre and Boulogne while the Sixteenth Army could use Calais, Dunkirk, Ostend, Antwerp and Rotterdam. The Ninth Army was further hampered by the Navy's insistence that Le Havre be used only for the initial sailing because of its longer, more exposed route; this limitation forced transport vessels from Le Havre to return to Boulogne and Calais to reload. The redistribution of transport capacity was mandatory to prevent the left flank from lagging behind.

In Landing Zones B and C, half of the Sixteenth Army's barges were to stay to be used as lighters. Dunkirk would only get fifty of its barges back – twenty-five were to go to Ostend, since Dunkirk was still largely inoperable after the devastation in May 1940. Those transports which were not turned over to the Ninth Army were to return to their home ports at Ostend, Antwerp and Rotterdam.

The Navy tried to work out realistic plans based on estimated losses and a report of 23 August predicted that losses for the

> ... Blue Route would amount to 30 per cent during the first landing, 15 per cent during the remainder of the second and five per cent of the remaining forces with each new assault. It was projected that the Green Route would sustain losses of around 50 per cent during the initial landing, 30 per cent of the remainder for the second and 5 per cent thereafter. No additional losses were estimated after X plus 8 days.

The Blue Route referred to landing Zones B, C and D, and the Green Route to the landing in Zone E, which the Navy regarded as risky. The Day 'X', later renamed S Day, was the code name for the date of the landing. It should be mentioned that not all these assumptions were accepted by the Army, and the schedules (see pages 202 ff) were drawn up without reference to potential losses. The novelty of the operation produced different difficulties for the various departments involved, and, not surprisingly, mistakes were made.

The embarkation harbours were visited by Dr Agatz, a professor of harbour construction, and Dr Gerdes, a Navy Building Inspector, probably in July, and they worked out suggestions for the accommodation of shipping, based on the Navy's estimates of numbers required at each port. They pointed out that Boulogne and Calais would be overcrowded and suggested that the number of barges be reduced by about 110 in Boulogne, and by around 45 in Calais, but that the numbers at Dunkirk, Nieuport and Ostend be increased by around 85, 26 and 44 respectively. The Navy's planning would not allow these alterations, but eight of the fifteen transports intended for Ostend were moved to the Zeebrugge breakwater.

A large proportion of Sealion discussions related to the employment of fire-support and defensive weapons by the Army on the landing craft. The Navy was concerned that inexperience might lead Army gunners to fire on their own vessels, and expressed strong opposition to this in Appendix 7 of the orders of Naval Commander West (14 September 1940). They proposed that all convoy vessels be allowed to use their weapons only in an extreme emergency (being boarded, for example), or when separated or damaged, and then only when they could clearly identify the enemy. A special staff of the BSW, formed after Sealion had been called off, in order to consolidate the planning experience, regarded the Navy's position as impractical and emphasised this in a report. In fact, they felt that every opportunity should be taken to increase the use of the Army's weapons, by improving communications between the transport convoys. Furthermore, they suggested that the transports carry liaison personnel with gunnery experience.

This staff also doubted the tactical wisdom of such large convoy formations. They felt that it might be safer and more efficient to sail in a sequence of smaller units; because of the inexperience of transport and tug skippers in night convoy sailing, any incident (such as a barge breaking its tow) would cause confusion from which the formation would not recover. The Navy High Command's only response was to insist that the transports had to sail together since they all had to land at the same time. This was a superficial analysis, but the Navy had to consider more serious problems than a landing at this time.

In the Landing Zones

One of the countermeasures which was envisaged for protecting the advance detachments and the landing of the first troops was smoke, which was to be laid by the minesweepers fitted with smoke generators and floats, and by aircraft (generally Henschel Hs 126s).

The two armies tailored the use of smoke in their landing zones to their own requirements. The Sixteenth Army produced 'Guidelines for Smoke Deployment in the Sixteenth Army Landing Zone for Operation Sealion' stating that:

> One flight of ten aircraft is to be assigned for smoke dispensing for each First Wave division. The aircraft are to be deployed in formations of two so that smoke is dispensed in five stages. Judging from the time necessary for the outward-bound and return flights and refuelling, it can be safely assumed that the first formation will again be operational when the fifth has discharged its smoke. The second formation will take off 15 minutes after the order is given to the first formation to cease dispensing smoke and so on. The tactical commander aboard ship is to give the order to begin deployment via radio (using the division's signals troop). The pilots are also to be briefed on the area of coverage, force and direction of the wind.
>
> In case of radio failure the command to lay smoke is to be given via red signal flares from the tactical commander's ship. All units are to be distinctively marked by flags to ensure accurate communications . . .
>
> Two flights of seven aircraft each (seven formations) will be kept in reserve; these are to be deployed in pockets of greatest resistance or where smoke coverage is thin due to aircraft losses.
>
> Unless there are extenuating circumstances – for example, heavy resistance – the formation will dispense smoke from one aircraft at 20 m altitude and the second at 40 m and about 150–200 m apart. The top aircraft is to fly about three to four wing spans from the first. It is important that the smoke be as close to the surface of the water as possible to screen ships from the British coast. On the other hand, it should be high enough so it cannot be seen over from the land.
>
> The tactical situation will dictate whether it is necessary to dispense smoke over the enemy's rear positions, that is, batteries, observation points, etc.).

Commands to the Luftwaffe's operational aircraft to discharge smoke bombs before and during the landing will be issued as required. It is not anticipated that both smoke screens will be co-ordinated by area or time.

The Ninth Army produced a plan for smoke deployment for Transport Fleet E: 'Naval smoke dispensing vessels are to provide coverage during the approach to the coast and the Blues Group during the landing with the 1/KG 11 smoke bomber.'

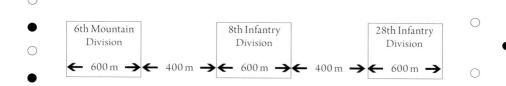

Advance Detachment

6th Mountain Division	8th Infantry Division	28th Infantry Division
← 600 m → ← 400 m →	← 600 m → ← 400 m →	← 600 m →

● = 4 R-boats with smoke equipment for 1 hour of operations.
○ = 4 R-boats with smoke equipment for 8 hours of operations.

VIII Corps	XXXVIII Corps

Colonel Stephan

I/KG 1

1 Staffel: 8 He 111
2 Staffel: 8 He 111
3 Staffel: 8 He 111

Nebelgruppe Bues

1 Staffel: 12 Hs 126
2 Staffel: 12 Hs 126
3 Staffel: 12 Hs 126
4 Staffel: 12 Hs 126

Nebelgruppe Giesse II/KG 1

32 × 50 kg smoke floats or 8 × 250 kg smoke floats per aircraft.
Smokescreen 8–10 km per aircraft.
Smoke duration 3 min per aircraft.
Deployment: in sequence.

Communications for Luftwaffe smoke deployment

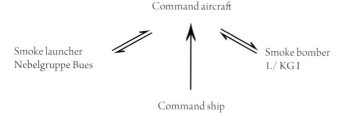

Command aircraft

Smoke launcher
Nebelgruppe Bues

Smoke bomber
1./ KG I

Command ship

No records exist on those Luftwaffe forces put at the disposal of the XXXVIII Corps, but they are probably comparable to those for the VIII Corps. Despite the dearth of information, it is possible to estimate the extent to which smoke would have been used. (The Germans were not alone in using smoke to screen amphibious troops for the Allies used it too in the D-Day invasion.)

Tests using smoke from assault boats went on into late October and were successful, especially so since the smoke dispensing did not hamper the use of these craft for transport.

*

First Wave troops would be most vulnerable during the actual landing, as they would bear the full brunt of the British resistance and the advance detachments were formed to provide the greatest amount of 'punch' in the early stages. Three each of these detachments were to land in Zones B and D and four in C. Almost all German Navy minesweepers and patrol boats were assigned to protect the transport fleets and each of these boats could carry about sixty lightly-armed infantry troops from these detachments. The Type 35 minesweepers carried two assault boats, up to six rubber dinghies and their own pinnace for ship-to-shore movement. In the case of the former trawlers and whalers being used as minesweepers and patrol boats, two assault boats filled the landing role. Any superfluous motor fishing vessels not needed for the following tows were to carry anywhere from six to thirty infantry troops. Boats of around 40 grt were armed with an infantry gun in the bow while those vessels of around 25 grt had an anti-tank gun to support troops as they landed and to be landed later on.

Larger vessels carried one or two assault boats and smaller ones one or two large rubber dinghies.

By using these vessels each advance detachment would have been able to achieve the strength of a reinforced company. The importance of these advance detachments grew over the months of planning for Sealion and each one was thus assigned two tow formations comprising a large armoured Type AS infantry barge and a standard powered barge. The tugs could carry a small twenty-man commando unit which could land in an assault boat and dinghy. The barges also had assault boats and the barge-borne advance detachments were made yet more formidable by having three or four flamethrowing tanks apiece and an optional gun-armed tank.

These tanks had an important role to play in the advance detachments as the submersible and amphibious tanks were assigned to particular landing places which gave them unimpeded travel but which in some instances were several kilometres away from the advance detachments and removed from the action.

Further reinforcements were the ten-man units on the tugs of the following wave who were to move forward to the advance detachments in assault boats. Each advance detachment could also count on two or three light auxiliary gunboats.

The six minesweepers and patrol boats, approximately ten motor fishing vessels, two tows and the tugs from the bulk of the transport fleet were sufficient to lift the 1,600 men of each advance detachment, which was equivalent to four reinforced companies or a reinforced battalion – a larger fighting force than had been originally projected.

The diagram on page 180 illustrates the landing operation, although the composition of the individual transport fleets varied, a particular exception being Transport Fleet E, which in itself was practically an advance detachment.

It is interesting to take a closer look at the role of a transport fleet, and at the Operational Order No. 1 dated 13 October 1940 from Captain Kleikamp of Transport Fleet C, concerning the landing of the advance detachments:

a) After reaching the 6–4 m depth (depending on the ship's draught) the advance detachment's vessels are to heave to.

b) Assault boats and rafts are launched and landed.

c) Tugs with armoured barges release their tows which land under their own power.

d) Minesweepers, patrol craft and R-boats, motor fishing vessels, auxiliary gunboats and heavy pontoon ferry groups on the flanks are to provide fire support (also toward the flanks).

e) Minesweepers, patrol craft and R-boats with troops of the first four advance detachments are to land these troops as quickly as possible under the direction of the commanders.

f) Thereafter, artillery support for the advance detachments in their attempt to gain a bridgehead is to be given the highest priority for these vessels.

g) Once the bridgeheads have been established, and the transport fleet barges have crossed the line of the minesweepers, patrol craft, etc. and no further clearly established land targets have to be shelled, their mission has been accomplished.

The Navy had numbered among the first-echelon troops those which were to form the core of a naval organisation in Britain. These beach parties were divided up into units each of which consisted of two officers (a harbour captain and director of shipping), eight naval NCOs and thirty-two crew. Fourteen of these units were formed, four each for Zones B and E and three each for C and D.

They were to lend technical assistance and advice to the Army and engineer troops in unloading and constructing landing bridges while later on they would form the basis for harbour authorities throughout Britain.

Every naval amphibious unit had folding tables and white, green, and red railway lanterns to mark the landing zones so that they could be seen at night. Zone C, for example, was marked as follows:

Point 29	3 × green
38	3 × green
41	3 × white
49	3 × white
55	3 × red
64	3 × red

Once the first echelon had reached British soil, Captain Degenhardt was to sail for England as a special envoy of the Naval High Command to take command of the beach parties.

Captured British harbours were to be repaired by Bridge Building Battalion 655 of Army Group A, placed under the command of the Navy if necessary. A fictitious engineer deployment was described in a Sixteenth Army wargame of 23 September:

> Three bridge building companies and a light engineer platoon of the Army Corps in the First Wave are still on the Continent. Each First Wave division has transported a 80 m run of auxiliary bridge (16-ton).
>
> An Army engineer battalion without a bridge company and one engineer lorry unit are integrated into the Second Wave.
>
> The following 16-ton landing bridges are being built on the British coast (and will be finished by about 9 October) [assuming a landing on 1 October] at Dymchurch Redoubt; south of Rye and at the shore end of the southern pier at Dover. The pier at Hastings with a capacity of up to 8 tons is also repaired. There is sufficient wood for a 300 m run 16-ton auxiliary bridge at Antwerp for use if required.

On 13 September the Commanding Admiral France, Schuster, reported that construction troops from the Todt and the Teno organisations which were repairing harbours in France would be available to repair damaged British harbours. He noted:

> A harbour construction supervisor should be assigned to all large transshipping ports; to date three motorised construction teams from steel fabrication factories have been assigned from the Todt organisation. The Navy High Command has also commissioned engineering firms to establish shipboard facilities to fabricate loading bridges, dolphins, and do pile driving and small concrete work. These projects would provide provisional

docking facilities for large vessels. These fabrication ships are to be fitted out at Rotterdam and Antwerp, where they will be at the disposal of the Commanding Admiral France.

This information was followed by a note: 'On S Day plus 2 the salvage vessels *Kraft*, *Wille* and *Berger I* will be readied at Dunkirk to clear foreign harbours.' This was a measure against blockships.

*

Führer Directive No. 16 of 16 July 1940 emphasised the importance of secure communications via underwater cables and it added that 'the Navy is tasked with providing' the spare 80 km of the East Prussian cable.

A Special Command for Underwater Cables was set up which would start laying cable on about S Day plus 5 or 7. On 11 November, this Special Command reported:

> The cable layers *Norderney* and *Job* were ready for duty in Nordenham on 6 September. Initially a coaxial cable will be laid from Calais to St Margaret's Bay [near Dover] and back again, which will serve as the operating cable for laying the main one. The *Norderney* will lay the first length of the East Prussian cable (23 Vlr telephone circuits) from Calais to St Margaret's Bay, approximately 50 km.
>
> The cable now in the steamer *Neptun* will be transferred to the *Norderney;* this work should take about two days to complete. The *Septun,* with its second length of cable and military crew are under the command of the OKW and are to remain permanently on call. The OKH is responsible for laying the ground cable to the repeater station and to the terminus of the land cable. The OKH is to transport the repeater. Thereafter the underwater cables are to be checked in the sequence:

Cable 189–190	La Panne–Dumpton
191	La Panne–St Margaret's Bay
280	Calais North–St Margaret's Bay
635	Sandgate–St Margaret's Bay
283–284	Boulogne–Seabrook

Army Operational Plan

The Army High Command issued a directive on 30 August in regard to Sealion which incorporated its narrow-base operational plan.

4) Implementation

a) Destruction of British air forces and defence industry by the Luftwaffe, achievement of air superiority. German Navy sweeps mines and mines the flanks of the transport routes in co-operation with the Luftwaffe.

b) Specially equipped advance forces of the Army's First Wave divisions establish bridgeheads. These are to be immediately broadened into one continuous landing zone, allowing safe unloading of the follow-on forces and an early unified command on British soil. Once there are sufficient forces, the attack on the first operational objective, the Thames estuary and high ground from London to Portsmouth, is to be mounted. Strong British resistance is to be expected against the first German troops; the British will undoubtedly use every means to halt the German advance. Organisation and command of these troops must thus be given high priority.

c) Once the Army has attained the initial operational objective, it must neutralise remaining British armed forces in southern England, occupy London and advance to the line between Maldon (north-east of London) to the mouth of the Severn.
    Other orders will be communicated in a timely manner.
    …

6) Missions of Army Groups and Armies

a) Under the operational command of the OKH, Army Group A is to land between Folkestone and Worthing, securing the coastal corridor for the follow-on forces, also using coastal artillery. British harbours are to be made operational to enable later forces to land more easily. Once Army Group A achieves sufficient strength it is to mount an offensive, capturing territory along the line from the Thames estuary through the southern uplands to Portsmouth. Rapid deployment forces are then to push westward from London, cutting off the city to the south and west, taking crossing points over the Thames for the advance on the Watford–Swindon line.

b) Initial objectives: The Sixteenth Army will load at Rotterdam and Calais and in the harbours in between. It is to land in the zone between Folkestone and Hastings, gaining ground up to a line from the heights halfway between Canterbury and Folkestone–Ashford and the heights 20 km north-west of Hastings. Dover harbour is to be seized quickly. The Ramsgate–Deal coast can only be approached from the sea after the coastal defences have been neutralised, and must be seized as quickly as possible from inland.

The heights north of Dover are to be taken by paratroops at the same time as the seaborne assault.

The Ninth and Sixteenth Armies will land simultaneously between Bexhill and Worthing; the Ninth Army will seize the stretch of coast at least to the line 20 km north of Bexhill to 10 km north of Worthing. The Ninth Army should take note that it will be able to deploy only the first echelon of three divisions of its First Wave directly from Le Havre; the fourth division, later echelons and waves will have to use the Sixteenth Army's more secure corridor from Boulogne, unloading east or west of Eastbourne depending on the tactical situation.

Brighton is to be captured by paratroops. The demarcation between the 16th and 9th Armies is Boulogne (9th)–Hastings (9th)–Reigate (16th).

c) Mission of Army Group B: Army Group B will not participate in the initial landing operation. Given a favourable naval situation, it could make an air or seaborne landing at Lyme Bay from Cherbourg, advancing towards Weymouth and a line from the heights 20 km north of the town to 15 km north of Lyme Regis, from where it will advance to Bristol under the direction of the OKH. Elements of Army Group B could also be used to occupy Devon and Cornwall.

Army Group B and Naval stations are to report on the status of the loading ports; Army Group B is to assemble its landing troops so that they can embark within five days of an order from the Army High Command.

This order was subsequently modified, reflecting the Army High Command's hope for a broader-based landing. This optimism apparently waned, since there were no further significant references to exercises and preparations for a landing operation.

Landing Zone E was shifted in late September from Worthing–Brighton to the east between Brighton and Beachy Head, as a result of the Navy's decision to land reinforcements for the troops in Zone E east of Beachy Head in Zone D under normal conditions. A shift toward Zone E at Beachy Head seemed to be a rational approach, which was supported in an Army High Command report of 21 September: 'The Ninth and Sixteenth Armies are to land between Bexhill and Brighton, gaining the ground to at least a line running from 20 km north-west of Bexhill via Uckfield to the high ground west and south-west of Lewes.'

The plan for a massed airborne attack on Brighton was abandoned in favour of a combined massed assault on Dover.

Map 1 shows the plan of operations in England, which is supplemented by a report of an Army Group A wargame played on 25 September at Roubaix.

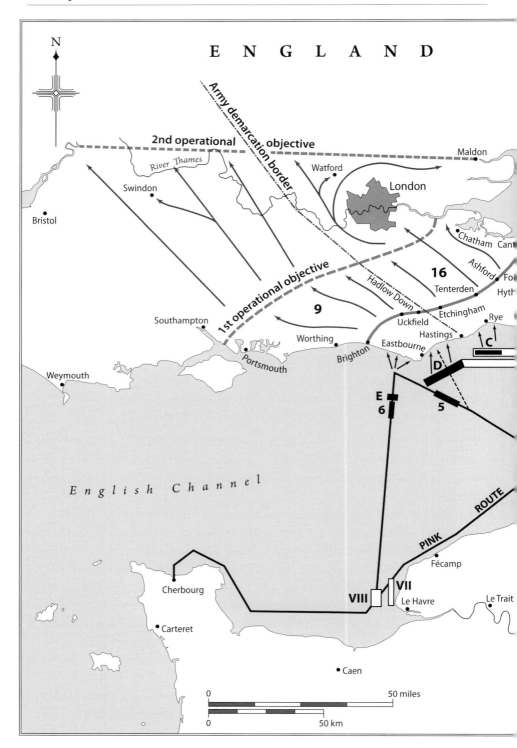

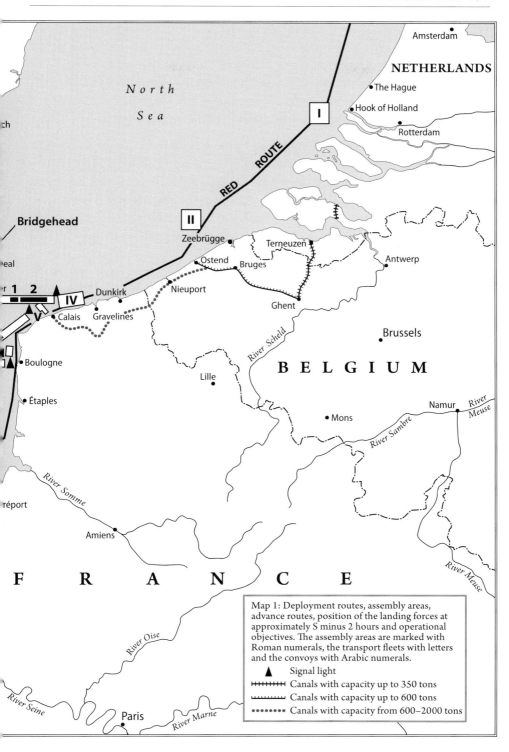

Map 1: Deployment routes, assembly areas, advance routes, position of the landing forces at approximately S minus 2 hours and operational objectives. The assembly areas are marked with Roman numerals, the transport fleets with letters and the convoys with Arabic numerals.

▲ Signal light
┼┼┼┼┼┼┼ Canals with capacity up to 350 tons
⊔⊔⊔⊔⊔⊔⊔ Canals with capacity up to 600 tons
●●●●●●● Canals with capacity from 600–2000 tons

The Ninth and Sixteenth Armies have different roles. The former is to defend the left flank against a possible heavy British attack and the latter will form a bridgehead under more favourable conditions. At the same time, this Army will prepare for the later attack mounted by the middle and the right flank. The left flank (Ninth Army) will remain 'compromised' for a long time and must be given cover by the Luftwaffe and, temporarily, by the Sixteenth Army.

The Ninth Army was also handicapped by the Navy's security measures which resulted in insufficient transport capacity. The Army High Command took a rather dim view of the Navy's narrow-based invasion plan, holding that it reduced Sealion to a mere final stroke against an already-defeated nation. It is interesting to compare the wide front of Sealion with the Normandy invasion. The Allied assault front was only about 80 km long, which corresponded to the German Navy's proposed landing front of Zones B, C and D. With the inclusion of Zone E the front broadened to 110–140 km, though the Army would have had greater manoeuvrability in Zone E than in the others. The rule for landing operations still holds true: the Army must be confined by the capabilities of the Navy and not vice versa. In 1940, however, the German Army had not reached this conclusion.

While the Army's fundamental concept of amphibious operations can be criticised, it is also interesting to examine the Navy's contribution to transport. The Sixteenth Army was fortunate in the location of its harbours and the Navy was able to promise to provide about 115 transports and 630 barges. This led the Army to believe that it could transport almost the entire First Wave – four infantry divisions – in one sortie. It was estimated that only three days would be needed until the key combat elements of the divisions and the Army troops would be fully operational – that is, their readiness to advance was dependent only on the time it took to unload the transports. According to the 35th Infantry Division timetable (see page 226) all first- and second-echelon combat troops should have been operationally ready on the evening of S Day plus 1, while the bulk of the divisions' rear services and supplies would have been unloaded on S plus 2 and S plus 3. The remainder of the rear services were to follow in tows in a kind of 'shuttle service' up to about S plus 10. The Second Wave, the Panzer Divisions, would have been loaded on the returning transports. The five transport 'shifts' would have completed the crossing on S plus 16 and this last estimate obviously took into consideration the likelihood of being able to use British harbours.

Nonetheless, the calculations made in the winter of 1940 showed that the remaining divisional rear services which would need transporting were actually far greater than anticipated. The 17th Infantry Division alone calculated that it would need about 550 barge loads, which would require a total crossing time of two to three months using the shuttle system. It requested room on the transports, but this would have delayed the Second Wave.

The Ninth Army was less fortunate than the Sixteenth in its harbours. Located in the western sector of the embarkation area, they had only 50 transports and about 500 barges, aside from the 300 motor fishing vessels and coasters. Since the Ninth Army had five divisions its transfer would have taken longer than that of the Sixteenth Army. The Ninth Army estimated that it would take seventeen days for the First Wave to cross and this delay would have seriously endangered the left flank.

General Halder decided in mid-September to reach a compromise between the two armies and put Calais and 15 transports and 100 barges at the disposal of the Ninth Army after the first run. This redeployment helped to improve the transport times, with the First Wave taking to S plus 14 and the Second Wave to S plus 24.

On S Day itself, the following elements of the Ninth Army would have landed:

Landing Zone D: the complete first echelons of the 34th and 26th Infantry Divisions, one quarter of the second echelon of the 34th Infantry Division, and one quarter of the XXXVIII Corps.

Landing Zone E: the entire first echelons of the 8th and 28th Infantry Divisions, the 6th Mountain Division, as well as about one third of the second echelons of the 8th and 28th Infantry Divisions and the 6th Mountain Division as well as one third of the Corps troops of the VIII Corps. Apart from those for the Sixteenth Army, all returning transport vessels were to be loaded with the rest of the First Wave. The Second Wave would have been delayed accordingly.

All of these calculations were obviously theoretical and their practicability would not have been put to the test until the actual operation. These times were determined according to a number of basic calculations.

The time needed for crossing, unloading, returning, and reloading a transport was calculated to be six days. It would take two days for loading at the embarkation ports, including reberthing; unloading on the open British coastline would take three. This estimate for unloading was probably realistic as the whole process depended upon the availability of barges and upon the tide. The loading time seems to have been excessive, since exercises had shown that it could be done in six to seven hours. Perhaps this over-estimate is explained by the fact that the Schelde was navigable only by day between Antwerp and Vlissingen, as was the New Waterway off Rotterdam, since lights would have attracted the attention of British bombers. Later on, electric circuits were installed which quickly switched off the lights. Being able to move at night at Antwerp gained the Army almost fifteen hours and would have appreciably shortened turnaround times.

A round trip for a barge was estimated to take four days, including loading and unloading (six hours for each) and a one-way crossing at fifteen hours. The remaining time was for reberthing, waiting for the tide to turn, and assembly of the convoy.

Calculating transport capacity for the men and their equipment was easier, though mistakes were made in this regard too. As a rule of thumb it was calculated that it would take twenty barges to unload one transport. Eighty barges or four transports were deemed sufficient for a division without the corps troops in the first echelon; 360 barges or 18 transports for a similar unit of the second echelon. For the corps troops of a general command and their flak, another 360 barges or 18 transports were estimated. These figures, it should be noted, are based on average-sized transports and barges and in reality their dimensions differed greatly. It should not be forgotten that shipping losses would have delayed the transfer, whereas the availability of landing bridges and harbours would have accelerated it.

The transport which would have been required could be calculated from the numbers of troops which were to be landed but, unfortunately, there are no overall figures for the final Sealion planning; they can, however, be extrapolated from documents relating to the individual units. Ronald Wheatley made such calculations in his book *Operation Sealion*, but overlooked the strengths of the army corps and certain shifts of personnel within the echelons of the individual divisions. The table opposite gives only an approximate idea of the figures, but at least allows a comparison with other landing operations.

The numbers marked with an asterisk are approximations only. The designations 'first echelon' and 'second echelon' do not refer to the organisational units, but to their positions within the landing forces. These coincide only in the case of the Sixteenth Army. The 67,000-man first echelon would probably have been at operational readiness only a few hours after landing, though some of its heavy equipment would have taken longer to unload from the transports. Most of the 71,000 men of the second echelon would have been landed by the evening of S plus 1 but their supplies and rear services would not have been landed until the evening of S plus 3. The landing of the remaining 77,000 troops of the First Wave would have coincided with the transport of the Second Wave, which would have been completed on S plus 10 and on S plus 14 in the case of the Ninth Army.

	First Echelon	Second Echelon	Remaining elements of the First Wave
Sixteenth Army			
35th Infantry Division	7,000	9,000	3,000
17th Infantry Division	7,000	9,000*	3,000*
XIII Corps		3,000*	3,000*
7th Infantry Division	7,000	9,000*	3,000*
1st Mountain Division	7,000*	9,000*	3,000*
VII Corps		3,000*	3,000*
Ninth Army			
34th Infantry Division	10,000		9,000
26th Infantry Division	7,000		12,000
XXXVIII Corps	1,000*		5,000*
6th Mountain Division	4,000	9,000	9,000
8th Infantry Division	4,000	8,000	12,000
28th Infantry Division	4,000	12,000	6,000
VIII Corps	} included in above figures		
X Corps			
Total	67,000	71,000	77,000

The Germans would have been able to land a total of 138,000 men in the first two days of Sealion, achieving a force of about 248,000 by S plus 14 if Wheatley's formula is applied, which includes an infantry and a Panzer division for the Sixteenth Army for the First Wave. It is probable, though, that this figure would have been much higher, since the Sixteenth Army would have landed all its Second Wave by S plus 16. If that were the case, there would have been 300,000 German troops on English soil by S plus 14.

It is interesting to compare these figures with those of the Allied invasion in Normandy. On D-Day, 6 June 1944, one division was landed in each of the four sectors and by 12 June 326,000 Allied troops were in France; by 2 July this figure had swelled to 929,000. Compared with that the Sealion plan had aimed to land a relatively large number of troops in the first two days though the rate would have fallen off due to the long turnaround times for the ships.

All in all, it appears that the German Navy had provided enough transports, even if many risks remained. It seems that time was too short to allow a proper assessment of which risks could be tolerated and which could not. At any rate, the Army rejected the operational plan because it was too narrowly based and there were not enough transports.

A final impression of ship capacity can be gained from the Sixteenth Army's plan of September (*overleaf*), though no comparison with the Ninth Army is possible because of the lack of documents.

1st Transport Sortie	Antwerp		Rotterdam		Ostend		Dunkirk		Calais	
	B	T	B	T	B	T	B	T	B	T
Sixteenth Army	–	45	–	49	50	15	150	–	200	–
VII Corps	–	36	–	–	– 1	–	–	–	–	
1st Mountain Division	–	–	–	–	–	2	–	–	80	–
7th Infantry Division	–	–	–	–	– 2	–	–	80	–	
XIII Corps	–	–	–	46	–	–	–	–	–	–
35th Infantry Division	–	–	–	–	–	2	80	–	–	–
17th Infantry Division	–	–	–	–	40	2	40	–	–	–
VII Corps troops (1st Artillery Detachment Corps Signals unit)	–	6	–	–	–	–	–	–	–	–
XII Corps (ditto)	–	–	–	–	–	6	–	–	–	–
Luftwaffe	–	3	–	3	6	–	18	–	24	–
Losses to heavy pontoon ferries	–	–	–	–	4	–	12	–	16	–
Transferred to Ninth Army	–	5	–	5	⟶				10	

2nd Transport Sortie	Antwerp		Rotterdam		Ostend		Dunkirk	
	B	T	B	T	B	T	B	T
After return	–	40	–	44	50	15	50	–
½ Division V Corps	–	–	–	25	–	–	–	–
½ Panzer Division XLI Corps (combat troops)	–	22	–	–	–	–	–	–
Army troops and rear services	–	–	–	–	–	10	–	–
Advance elements, Army Group A	–	–	–	–	–	1	–	–
Tank Detachment 100	–	1	–	–	–	–	–	–
Artillery Command 106	–	5	–	5	–	–	–	–
Nebelwerfer Regiment 51	–	–	–	–	–	4	–	–
Luftwaffe	–	3	–	3	–	–	–	–
Corps troops VII and XIII Corps	–	7	–	8	–	–	–	–
Senior Quartermaster E	–	2	–	3	–	–	–	–
Divisional Rear Services of the First Wave	–	–	–	–	50	–	50	–
Transferred to Ninth Army				5	⟶		Calais	

B = Barges; T = Transports

3rd Transport Sortie	Antwerp		Rotterdam		Ostend		Dunkirk	
	B	T	B	T	B	T	B	T
After return	–	40	–	39	50	15	50	–
½ Division V Corps	–	–	–	23	–	–	–	–
½ Panzer Division XLI Army Corps (combat troops)	–	29	–	–	–	–	–	–
Army troops and rear services	–	2	–	2	–	6	–	–
Nebelwerfer Regiment 51	–	–	–	–	–	4	–	–
Railway Engineers	–	1	–	–	–	–	–	–
Signals Troops, Army Group A	–	–	–	1	–	–	–	–
Luftwaffe	–	5	–	5	–	5	–	–
Senior Quartermaster E	–	3	–	3	–	–	–	–
Divisional Rear Services of the First Wave	–	–	–	–	50	–	50	–

4th Transport Sortie	Antwerp		Rotterdam		Ostend		Dunkirk	
	B	T	B	T	B	T	B	T
After return	–	40	–	39	50	–	50	–
⅔ Panzer Division XLI Corps	–	31	–	–	–	–	–	–
⅔ Division Corps	–	–	–	30	–	–	–	–
Remainder of Army Group A (Signals Troops)	–	–	–	1	–	–	–	–
Army troops and rear services	–	–	–	–	–	7	–	–
Army artillery	–	–	–	–	–	3	–	–
Railway Engineers	–	1	–	–	–	–	–	–
Luftwaffe	–	5	–	5	–	–	–	–
Senior Quartermaster E	–	3	–	3	–	–	–	–
Divisional Rear Services of the First Wave	–	–	–	–	50	–	50	–

B= Barges; T = Transports

5th Transport Sortie	Antwerp		Rotterdam		Ostend		Dunkirk	
	B	T	B	T	B	T	B	T
After return	–	40	–	39	50	15	50	–
Remainder Panzer Division and ⅓ Motorised Division XLI Corps	–	29	–	–	–	–	–	–
Remainder V Corps combat troops	–	–	–	28	–	–	–	–
Artillery Command 106	–	5	–	5	–	–	–	–
Railway Engineers	–	1	–	1	–	–	–	–
Luftwaffe	–	5	–	5	–	5	–	–
Divisional Rear Services of the First Wave	–	–	–	–	50	–	50	–
Available to the Army	–	–	–	–	–	5	–	–

6th Transport Sortie	Antwerp		Rotterdam		Ostend		Dunkirk	
	B	T	B	T	B	T	B	T
After return	–	40	–	39	50	15	50	–
2/3 Motorised Division and Rear Services	–	33	–	–	–	–	–	–
Großdeutschland Regiment and Rear Services, V Corps	–	–	–	32	–	–	–	–
Railway Engineers	–	2	–	2	–	–	–	–
Luftwaffe	–	5	–	5	–	5	–	–
Available to the Army	–	–	–	–	–	10	–	–

7th Transport Sortie	Antwerp		Rotterdam		Ostend		Dunkirk	
	B	T	B	T	B	T	B	T
After return	–	40	–	39	50	15	50	–
Third Wave	–	28	–	27	50	–	50	–
Remainder Artillery Command 106	–	5	–	5	–	–	–	–
Railway Engineers	–	2	–	2	–	–	–	–
Luftwaffe	–	5	–	5	–	5	–	–
Available to the Army	–	–	–	–	–	10	–	–

B= Barges; T = Transports

Notes to table

The number of barges in the second sortie was reduced because half of them were used as lighters for the transports. Only fifty of the barges which set out from Dunkirk would return and twenty-five additional ones were to be sent to Ostend. The entry 'Loss to heavy pontoon ferries' indicates those barges which could not be taken in tow because of the added ferries and lack of tugs. Tank Detachment 100 had flamethrower tanks. Artillery Command 106 had operational control of the Army batteries which would have been set up in coastal emplacements (see page 281). Further details on Nebelwerfer Regiment 51 are to be found on page 157. Hitler's bodyguard regiment (*Leibstandarte Adolf Hitler*) and the *Großdeutschland* infantry regiment were part of the sixth sortie.

*

It is impossible to assess the German prospects for success without calculating the strength of the British forces which might have opposed them. A Sixteenth Army study of 24 July estimated that of thirty-four British divisions only eleven infantry and one armoured division were at operational readiness. Thirteen infantry and one armoured divisions were still in their home quarters to replace material losses in France, and were not yet available. A further eight divisions of new units were regarded as being at a limited level of readiness and the Germans assumed they would be deployed for coastal defence.

The German General Staff produced its own estimate of British strength in mid-September, citing a force of thirty-nine divisions in Great Britain, of which nineteen were fully operational, and seventeen partially so for limited engagements. Seventeen of these divisions were designated for coastal defence. In his book *Invasion 1940*, Peter Fleming comments that the Germans overestimated British readiness: in reality there were only twenty-nine divisions and eight independent brigades, six of which were armoured. In addition, all of these separate units were under-strength.

The Army made a number of organisational changes during the build-up to Sealion, specifically in the creation of landing staffs to supervise beaching and unloading, to reassemble troops which had missed their landing zones and to direct them to their correct position and to oversee the unloading of supplies. The Sixteenth Army set up a landing staff which would have formed commands at Dover and Hastings under operational conditions, and to which seven landing officers would have been assigned. Reporting to headquarters would have been the Military Police Detachment (mot) S61, a heavy machine-gun platoon, an anti-tank gun platoon and Armoured Ammunition Transport Detachment 610. The Ninth Army was probably similarly organised.

Careful planning was necessary to fix the exact time at which the Army Staff Commands would have followed the landing troops. *Heimatstäbe* (home staff units) were set up to oversee the assembly and loading of all elements of the waves that remained as well as the transport of the Luftwaffe and Navy forces, assembly and loading of supplies; command and supply of all elements remaining on the Continent. They were responsible for receipt and onward transport of wounded and prisoners of war, and damaged equipment.

Sixteenth Army designated XXIII Corps as the 'Mainland Command' (*Befehlsstelle Festland*). Its primary role, under a staff headed by Krantz, was to assemble troops and supplies; reporting to this staff were a traffic control battalion and loading staffs at Calais, Dunkirk, Ostend, Antwerp and Rotterdam. It is worth noting here that in March 1941 the corps was ordered to pull all of the Sealion files from the separate divisional records and store them centrally. These records did not survive the war and all that remains are sparse notes on the landing preparations from the divisions; hence the problems encountered when researching the operation.

The Ninth Army also formed a *Heimatstab*, although it had the same authority as Divisional Command 444 (special duties) in regard to logistics. The loading staffs at Le Havre, Boulogne and Calais reported to the *Heimatstab*.

It is odd that the army groups took as long to consider the necessity of setting up *Heimatstäbe* – as was noted by Halder in a discussion with Army Group A on 10 September. He thought it was foolhardy to believe that the high command staffs would be able to make an early crossing to England as an entity, and immediately relinquish the responsibility for resupply. Halder emphasised that it was the primary task of the command staffs to tackle the problems of the Channel crossing and demanded that they remain on the Continent initially – the high-ranking commanders could cross, but the staffs should stay.

*

A discussion of the Army's preparation would not be complete without mentioning an organisation which, due to the lack of documents concerning it and its earlier 'top secret' designation, had a certain aura of mystery about it: No. 800 Special Purposes Construction Training Battalion 'Brandenburg' (*Baulehrregiment z. b. V. 'Brandenburg*). This unit was originally set up as a company on 15 October 1939 at Brandenburg/Havel under Captain Dr von Hippel. It was trained under the direction of the Abwehr, the German intelligence organisation, for covert commando and sabotage operations, and was made up mostly of ethnic Germans from other countries who had special language skills. In October 1940 it was organised as:

	Headquarters	*Operational Areas*	*Companies*
I. Bau-Lehr-Btl	Brandenburg	East–west	1st–4th
II. Bau-Lehr-Btl	Baden/Vienna	South-west	5th–8th
III. Bau-Lehr-Btl	Düren	West	9th–12th

Amphibious exercises of 11./III. Lehrregiment 'Brandenburg' at Büsum on August 1940.

Unloading light motorcycles during the same exercise.

There were also other commands which belonged to it such as the communication unit in Berlin.

The *Lehrregiment z. b. V.* 800 had already seen some action in the war and was proposed for Sealion. It is difficult enough to find source material on this regiment concerning its general role, but its planned role in Sealion is even more elusive. Only marginal references in books, scanty records of the First Wave divisions, and the recollections of the commander of III Battalion, Captain Rudloff, and those of the former Corporal Röseke of the 11th Company allow us to reconstruct some of the unit's history.

Elements of the I and III Battalions were earmarked for the assault on Britain; the former would have been assigned to the Sixteenth Army and the latter to the 9th. Their dispositions are proof of the fact that their assignments were also subject to change: the III Battalion was allocated first to the Sixth Army and was supposed to mount a lightning raid on the harbour at Weymouth near Lyme Bay before the actual landing. This was to be a seaborne attack involving the entire battalion of about 600 men. This fits in with the Army's plan for an attack on a broad front, which would have straddled Weymouth.

The plans for the III Battalion changed with the shift to an invasion on a narrow front. The 11th Company was given the code name of Engineer Battalion 303 and was to cross with Transport Fleet D. Two commando units of seventy-two and thirty-eight men were assigned to the 26th Infantry Division and one of forty-eight men to the 34th Infantry Division. The men assigned to the 26th Infantry Division were to take out the gun battery at Beachy Head and the radio station to the north of it and it seems reasonable to assume that the two other companies were given similar assignments, possibly in Landing Zone E. The units were to be mounted on light motorcycles and were lightly armed.

The Sixteenth Army's objective was to capture Dover Harbour as quickly as possible in order to speed up unloading. A combat unit named 'Hoffmeister', formed from the 17th and 35th Infantry Division and the 7th Airborne Division, was to reach England on S Day and attempt to capture Dover Harbour by the evening with the support of the 1st Company of the I. Brandenburg. Two platoons of this company were to cross with the 35th Infantry Division, one with the advanced detachment and one with Tank Detachment (U) D. These two platoons would have formed a commando unit under Lieutenant Dr Hartmann with a strength of 2 officers, 15 NCOs and 114 men equipped with 50 motorbikes. Their objective was to neutralise bases on the coast and along the Royal Military Canal and the suspected artillery to the north. A commando with three reconnaissance tanks was to be landed with the 17th Division.

An additional commando unit under Captain Hollmann which contained part of the intelligence unit and the bulk of the 4th Company, was to attack Dover directly. Its first tasks were to prevent the British from sinking blockships in the harbour entrances and then to take out the coastal batteries on the Dover heights. At first it was thought that troops might be landed by glider, but this approach was quickly abandoned because the British had effectively obstructed all the suitable landing areas; the assault had to be from the sea. The references to the idea that this was to be accomplished using tows seem barely credible in view of the massive British coastal batteries. An alternative approach is suggested from a hint outlining a motorboat unit. Commander Strempel, the head of the Navy's Motorboat Section (*Motorbootabteilung der Kriegsmarine*), received a top secret order from Captain Voss, at that time head of the Commando Section (AI) of the Naval Operations Office, to select around twenty-five of the fastest motorboats he had commandeered such as those from Customs authorities and the police, and assemble them at Dordrecht from where they would lead a commando unit in advance of the invasion of Britain. The importance of this mission can be deduced from the fact that such a high-ranking officer was appointed to command it. Commander Strempel was never informed about the objective of his mission, but it was likely to have been Dover.

Apart from some loading exercises, the III Battalion held manoeuvres in August 1940 near Büsum. A voyage to Heligoland and landing trials on the Halligen islands is also recorded.

By no means all of the Brandenburger commandos spoke English; in the 11th Company, for example there were only between fifteen and twenty, and it is doubtful whether they would have gone unrecognised behind enemy lines.

This company was visited at La Chapelle by Major Kewisch of the Abwehr. On leaving his comment to a companion was 'Poor boys'.

Luftwaffe Operational Plan

Very few records remain of the Luftwaffe's operational plans for the combined assault and this lack is compounded by the fact that the Air Force did not actually start planning until quite late (see page 161). Then, too, it is the nature of air forces to change missions and targets to meet rapidly developing events.

The airborne assault units were to operate primarily in Zone B, and their roles are discussed in detail in conjunction with that fleet's disposition (see page 228).

The German Air Force deployed three Air Fleets (*Luftflotten*) for the combined assault on Britain: Luftflotte 5 based at Kristiansand/Norway; Luftflotte 2 in Belgium and in north-east France with headquarters in Brussels; and Luftflotte 3 in north-west France based in Paris. The last was to support the Ninth Army, Luftflotte 2 the Sixteenth Army, and Luftflotte 5 was to operate independently of any Army units and mostly against the British fleet.

The order of battle as shown on pages 163–5 was altered in late August, when the VIII and I Fliegerkorps were interchanged. VIII Fliegerkorps' Stuka dive bombers and fighters were redeployed from Normandy to the Pas de Calais, where they were under the command of Luftflotte 2; I Fliegerkorps remained where it was, but was placed under the command of Luftflotte 3. The changes resulted in Luftflotte 2 having control of VIII Fliegerkorps, II Fliegerkorps with its bomber wings and Jagdfliegerführer 2 with fighter wings.

Luftflotte 3 comprised I, IV and V Fliegerkorps with bombers and Stukas as well as those fighters which had been combined under Jagdfliegerführer 3.

In addition to reconnaissance, the Luftwaffe forces had the following roles for Sealion: to provide direct support for the Army and airborne units; to prevent the British from mobilising strategic reserves; to defend the transport fleet against the Royal Navy; and to neutralise the RAF over the Channel. These missions were assigned to the individual Fliegerkorps. VIII and I Fliegerkorps, for example, were to support the German Army troops mounting an assault on British coastal emplacements by countering British forces in the landing areas. General Freiherr von Richthofen's Stuka wing from the VIII Fliegerkorps was in training to attack point targets on land, even though their Ju 87s were particularly vulnerable to fighter attacks and had to be escorted by German fighters. I Fliegerkorps had only one Stuka wing, but the two bomber wings were probably equal to the task of direct support as well.

Luftwaffe liaison aircraft were to ensure communication between the armies and in order to make this easier the headquarters of VIII Fliegerkorps was moved to St Ingelbert and that of I Fliegerkorps to Le Touquet.

Detailed plans for VIII Fliegerkorps have been preserved. On 11 September the Army Commander-in-Chief met with the Luftwaffe staff and agreed that two Stuka wings would attack Dover and Folkestone, while a Stuka wing would strike the gun battery assumed to be at Dungeness. One and two-thirds Stuka *Gruppen* were to support VII Corps between Hastings and Rye, leaving one Stuka *Gruppe* which would probably be held in reserve for operations against British shipping.

The role of II, V and IV Fliegerkorps was battlefield interdiction, though the latter two were primarily assigned to counter British naval forces. II Fliegerkorps were to halt the movement of reserve forces from London by blocking access routes in and out of towns and bottlenecks on the approach routes if necessary. V and IV Fliegerkorps would also have struck against reserves west of London in the same way. It was anticipated that after the landing the Fliegerkorps would be heavily engaged over the Channel, so that on S Day or before concentrated strikes would be made on British Army camps around Aldershot, Newbury, Salisbury, Portsmouth and Worthing. British rail transport was to be disrupted shortly before the landing by bombing seventeen junctions west of London in areas around Watford, Reading and south-west of London, including Aldershot. I Fliegerkorps was to lend support in the latter area.

The success of Sealion depended largely on defending the transport fleets from seaborne attacks and the eastern and western Channel approaches would have to be closely guarded, as well as the approach routes of the British Home Fleet through the Irish and the North Seas from its northern bases. The North Sea route was the province of Luftflotte 5, whose two bomber wings, KG 30 and 27, had previous experience of attacking naval targets. While there are no files which confirm any intent to use Luftflotte 5 for this purpose, it is logical to assume that it might have been so deployed simply because of its capability. Its strength also led Luftflotte 2 to assume that it would need the support of only the 9th Fliegerdivision to protect the eastern Channel entrance.

However, while this unit was well trained for naval air warfare, having been engaged in mining British coastal waters since the spring of 1940, it consisted of only one bomber wing and one bomber group. In actual combat the Stukas would probably have to have been drawn from VIII Fliegerkorps. In the discussions between the Army and Luftwaffe, the Army Commander-in-Chief proposed that II Fliegerkorps be placed on standby to cover the eastern flank; the western flank would have been protected by V and IV Fliegerkorps, which would have attacked British naval forces in their ports or in the western or central part of the Channel. If the British fleet menaced the western flank of the German flotilla with heavy fighter support, the German fighters would mass to provide cover for their bomber forces. This Korps would have to move to advance airbases, striking rapidly and repeatedly. Luftflotte 3 was disappointed to learn that it would not be supported by the 9th Fliegerdivision though it was agreed that the latter would mine the western sector, especially the Solent, Spithead, Portland and Plymouth.

The Luftwaffe had to prepare for attacks by the RAF. Luftflotte 3 did not set up special units, but planned an offensive which was to concentrate on bombing aircraft on the ground (especially fighters), supply depots and airbases. Luftflotte 2 assigned these duties to II Fliegerkorps which was to destroy the British bomber airbases. German fighters were also assigned escort duties for Luftwaffe bombers, and were to destroy any British fighters around assembly areas, transit routes and landing zones.

The Luftwaffe could not hope to execute all these missions simultaneously and so they were planned in phases. Records of these plans exist only for Luftflotte 2, which issued orders accordingly on 29 September. On about S Day minus 8 VIII Fliegerkorps would attack the British coastal batteries, and 9th Fliegerdivision, II and VIII Fliegerkorps and the Italian Division would attack any harbours with British warships as well as any approaching warships. At around the same time, the 9th Fliegerdivision would begin laying mines, especially in the Downs, to augment the mine barriers laid by the Navy, with reconnaissance by Aufklärungsgruppe 122. On S Day minus 2 operations as part of the *Herbstreise* decoy operation were to be implemented, reconnaissance for which would be provided by Luftflotte 5 and 9th Fliegerdivision. Flank support for this 'landing operation' would be provided by 9th Fliegerdivision, after it had mined British naval ports. On the day before, 9th Fliegerdivision would have made a reconnaissance sortie along the British coast up to the Firth of Forth. That night and during the following ones, Thames docks and any other harbours on the east, south and west coasts would be mined to prevent shipping movements. Any additional bomber units would have attacked and destroyed these harbours the night before the landing and during the next morning II Fliegerkorps would have begun bombing railway lines and advance routes of reserve units to the west and north-west of London. During S Day VIII Fliegerkorps would have provided air support for the amphibious forces and attacked a number of pre-determined targets while II and VIII Fliegerkorps would have warded off any ground attacks on the flanks by suppressing coastal defences to the east between Folkestone and Hythe and in the landing zone around Romney, Dungeness and Rye. They were also to lay smoke and attack British forces on the heights north of the Military Canal in the area around Mersham, Bonnington, Ham Street and Kingsnorth. The British forces were to be continually battered, especially in the east, with conventional and incendiary bombs, with any lulls in the airborne attacks filled with artillery bombardment from the heavy guns of Artillerie Regiment Hohmann which had advanced to the Pas de Calais. This regiment was to thwart any flanking thrusts from Dover with the help of the Italian Division which was to move against British airbases and approach routes. The 9th Fliegerdivision were to support II Fliegerkorps and the Italian Division in their push toward Dover and Folkestone while their reserves were to be held back for assaults against shipping.

The Luftwaffe High Command was well aware of the value of reconnaissance and on 10 September ordered a number of areas to be fully surveyed both before and during the operation. Luftflotte 2 was assigned Sea Area 05 East 4761 to Middlesborough, down the British coast to Sheerness and along the Belgian–Dutch coast up as far as Den Helder. Luftflotte 3's area of responsibility ran from Carnsore Point along the south coast of Ireland to Bantry Bay – 24 West 1949 – across to Brest, around the French coast to Cherbourg and then across the Channel to Brighton.

It was requested that the Luftwaffe reconnaissance units be placed under Navy command. As the Navy was tasked by the Wehrmacht with defending the crossing, it made sense for reconnaissance and operations to be under a single command. Experience in Norway had demonstrated that the Stuka units were only effective when they were coupled with Küstenfliegergruppe 506, a coastal reconnaissance unit.

This proposal sparked off a feud between the Luftwaffe and the Navy which had long been smouldering, and which centred around control of maritime aviation. The Naval Operations Office proposed that the Luftwaffe's long-range reconnaissance aircraft be deployed over the Irish Sea, the north Channel and along a 60 km strip on the east coast of Britain, including Scapa Flow – principally in preparation for *Herbstreise* (in which the Navy anticipated using its highly valuable cruisers), and for the planned break-out of the cruiser *Admiral Hipper* into the Atlantic. On this the Navy took an egotistical stand, and the Luftwaffe had to point out that Sealion should take precedence: after all, the other two operations were only diversions. The Luftwaffe added sarcastically that the Navy might certainly profit from airborne reconnaissance sorties, but would have to rely on the Luftwaffe for help anyway because of its own lack of forces. Thereupon the Naval Operations Office retorted that *Herbstreise* and Sealion could very well lead to the British mining the German Bight, forcing the Skagerrak narrows or even bombarding the southern coast of Norway. This reasoning can be understood only in light of the continual wrangling that went on concerning the role of the maritime air forces, but it also demonstrates the Navy's imperfect thinking, which gave higher priority to the feint manoeuvre than to the central operation. On the other hand, the Navy's insistence on reconnaissance of British naval bases in the north was proved correct in retrospect.

*

The fundamental question is whether the Luftwaffe would have been able to tackle all the missions which were planned for it. Support of the Army units was probably feasible, even though the Luftwaffe would have had to have taken over the artillery's bombardment role before and during the landing, since the Navy would not have been able to give the necessary fire support. One fact remains clear: the English coast was by no means as heavily reinforced as the French one in 1944. The Luftwaffe had arguably achieved air superiority over southern England by early September, but the ultimate goal of absolute air superiority leading to Britain suing for peace was to elude the Luftwaffe's grasp.

It is important, therefore, to realise the basis on which the Luftwaffe agreed so readily to protect the transport fleets, especially as it would experience fierce resistance from the Royal Navy. Little was understood about airborne strikes against shipping before the war, though many of the crews of KG 26 (Bomber Wing 26) were experienced former naval pilots. Their know-how was difficult to apply, however, because the wing flew the Luftwaffe's standard bomber, the He 111, which could only drop its bombs on a horizontal run, which was inaccurate against point targets such as ships. Dive bombers, such as the Ju 88 medium-range bomber, were better suited. KG 30 was the first wing to receive this aircraft and, like KG 26, it was assigned to anti-shipping missions. By 1940 the air-launched torpedo had been developed sufficiently to be used in night attacks on merchant ships and the first successful ones were launched by Küstenfliegergruppe 506 in the autumn of 1940. These torpedoes were of little use in daylight and against warships, however, since their relative fragility meant that they had to be dropped from low altitudes and at low speeds, which made the aircraft easy targets.

At the beginning of the war the Luftwaffe had been optimistic about being able to weaken the British Home Fleet, though attacks by KG 30 and KG 26 on its bases at Scapa Flow and the Firth of Forth as well as at sea were not particularly successful. It was not until the Home Fleet moved into southern Norwegian waters after the German occupation that the Luftwaffe really scored when the Ju 88s of KG 26 and KG 30 sank the destroyer *Gurkha* and damaged a battleship and three cruisers on 9 April 1940. The Allies had also suffered losses when the destroyers *Bison* and *Afridi* were sunk by StG 1 and the anti-aircraft cruiser *Curlew* by KG 30 during the withdrawal from Norway. German air power had played a central part in the Allied failure in Norway and had also seen action against the British Expeditionary Force at Dunkirk when five British destroyers had been sunk and twenty-three damaged from a deployment of forty, primarily by Stuka dive bombers; merchant and auxiliary ships also took a pounding. Despite these losses the British were able to achieve their main objective, the evacuation of their troops, on days when the weather was too poor for flying.

Particular attention is drawn to its record against destroyers, as this type of ship was the most deadly to the invasion fleet; the larger combatants would have presented bigger targets and not been particularly effective in the narrow waters of the Channel. The destroyer, though, was fast and effective and the British had them in considerable numbers (about 200); it was estimated that around 40 were within easy reach of the Channel, together with supporting cruisers. It is unlikely that the Luftwaffe could have eliminated all the British destroyers before the landing or before reserves could have come to their aid and little could be done against destroyers at night or in bad flying weather.

The Luftwaffe, like the Army, set up a special organisation for the landing; Luftflotten 2 and 3 formed *Luftgaustab England*, comprising Luftgaustäbe z. b. V. 16 and 14. The staffs and some of the units under their command were to cross with the First and Second Waves, and the remainder with the Third Wave. Their tasks were mainly reconnoitring and securing and establishing ground support for the air units. Airbases for emergency landings and transport aircraft were to be set up and later on JG 26, StG 77 and a combat unit of LG 2 were to be transferred to England, followed by JG 3, JG 27, JG 53 and StG 1. A Landing Staff E reported to these staffs, which in turn supervised four Unloading Commands. On the Continent, its counterpart, the Loading Staff (LW) was created which oversaw the loading staffs in the mounting ports.

The Transport Fleets

The following section describes the organisation and make-up of the individual transport fleets, the forces they were to move, and their parts in the landing operation.

Transport Fleet B

Transport Fleet B was to link up the eastern embarkation ports with the eastern landing zone, Zone B. The ports were Dunkirk, Ostend and Rotterdam, and they were to be loaded according to the following plan:

	Transports	Barges*	Tugs	Motorboats	Coasters
Rotterdam	49	370 (200)	Remainder	Remainder	Remainder
Ostend	15	155 (20)	25	50	–
Dunkirk	–	200 (50)	75	150	–

* The figures in parentheses refer to the number of barges out of the total, which were to be kept in reserve.

These figures are not quite correct when compared with those of the transport fleet. Possibly they stem from an earlier phase of the planning in which each tug or transport was assigned three barges.

Rotterdam, with its New Waterway, had good access to the sea as there were no locks to be negotiated. However, the new electric lighting system on the New Waterway, which could be switched off during air raids, had not been installed by October. As the previous lights had to be extinguished for safety reasons during the night, this would have meant long turnaround times for the transports. Rotterdam itself had excellent facilities and space for fast loading, which was to be done at four different sites: West at berths 1–30; Middle at berths 31–56; East at berths 57–78 and South at berths 79–85. Barges were to be loaded at Coolhaven and towed to Waalhaven to hook up with the transports. Tugs were to be stationed at Schiedam, Vlaardingen, Maasluis and Hoek van Holland in case of emergencies.

Ostend also presented no difficulties in berthing the landing craft, though there was not enough room for the fifteen transports allocated; eight of them were therefore transferred to Zeebrugge.

Dunkirk was another matter entirely. Though the harbour was large, the heavy air raids in May had taken their toll and it was blocked with sunken ships. At

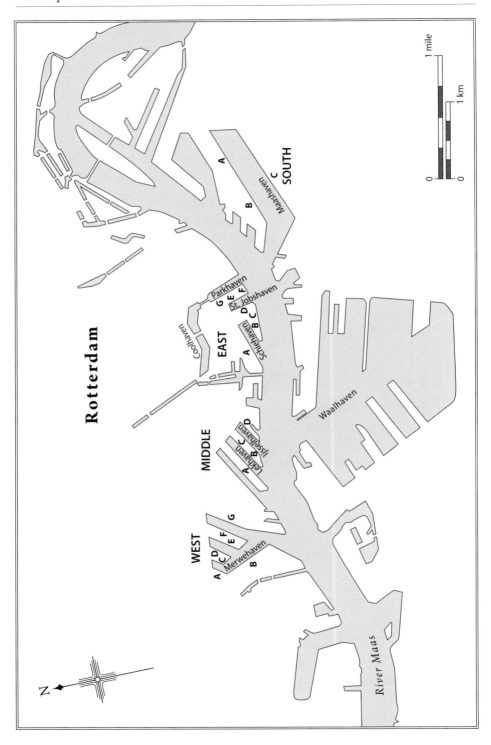

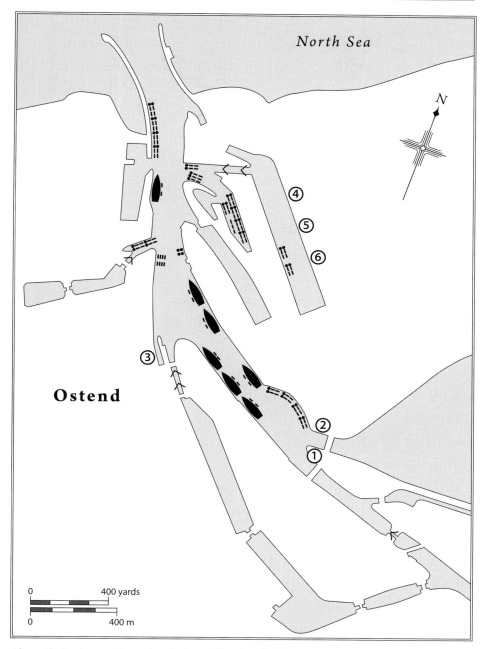

Above: The harbour at Ostend with planned berths. The figures in circles indicate loading ramps.

Left: Berth of Convoy 2 at Rotterdam.

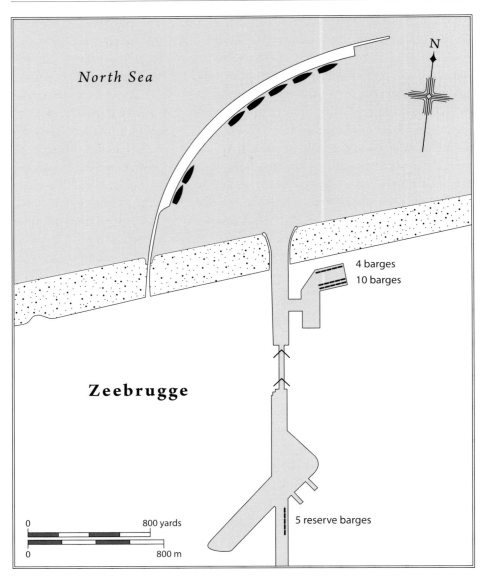

The harbour and mole at Zeebrugge with planned disposition.

first it appeared unusable, but salvage work proceeded apace and by late summer the required number of ships could be berthed there after all. In his report of November 1940, the Commander of the KMD, Captain Bartels, emphasised the difficulties of movement in the partly blocked harbour entrance. A pilot service had helped, though, and a tug in each of the outer and inner harbours was kept in permanent readiness, together with two fire-fighting vessels.

In Rotterdam, loading was to start on S Day minus 6 and end on S Day minus 4. The fleet was to sail on S day minus 2. The escort forces would arrive on S day minus 1. The time for embarkation was estimated to be forty-eight hours for Rotterdam, four hours for the transports at Ostend, and eight hours for the tow formations. Loading of support ships at Dunkirk was set for S Day minus 8 to S Day minus 6. Flak, tanks and the motorised artillery of the 35th Infantry Division would be loaded on S Day minus 5 and the vehicles of the 17th and 35th Infantry Divisions on S Day minus 3 and S Day minus 4. Barges loaded with vehicles would move from the inner harbour to the outer on S Day minus 4. The horses would be loaded on S Day minus 2 and the barges then moved into the outer harbour. The crews would take their places in the barges in the outer harbour and basin during the afternoon and then on S Day minus 1 the tow formation would sail from the outer harbour of Dunkirk, leaving the four tow groups in the basin to put out to sea directly through the open locks at high tide. On the day of departure the entire technical support (Naval Construction, Naval Harbour Construction Office, salvage companies and Teno) were all at the disposal of the Naval Headquarters.

The composition of the transport fleet changed many times during the planning. It was supposed to depart from Calais according to the thinking in August, but this port was later assigned to Transport Fleet C. Escort Fleet I from Ostend with its fifteen transports was originally at the disposal of Transport Fleet B, but then lost half of its strength, seven vessels, to Transport Fleet C. Its final order was:

Tow Formation 1   Dunkirk   (Vice-Admiral von Fischel,
                                    also Transport Fleet Commander)

    75 tows comprising:
        75 fishing trawlers (and tugs)
        150 barges
        150 pusher boats

Tow Formation 2   Ostend   (Captain Hennecke)
    25 tows comprising:
        25 fishing trawlers
        50 barges
        50 pusher boats

Convoy 1   Ostend   (Captain Wagner)
    8 transports
        with 16 barges and 16 pusher boats

Convoy 2   Rotterdam   (Captain Schirlitz)
    49 transports
        with 98 barges, no pusher boats

Loading diagram for XIII Army Corps and its 35th and 17th Divisions.

17. Div.

Raum	DÜNKIRCHEN	OSTENDE	Stärke	Gesamtstärke

1. Staffel

Vorausabteilungen:
1) Meidekopf Korpsstab
2) 3 verst. Batt. ~
3) 2 Pz. Abtlg. u." (ohne 1 Kp.)

R.verst. Batl.

sonst wie bei Ostende!

Panzer-Abt. (ω") B (3 Kpn)

II Gruppe

DÜNKIRCHEN   OSTENDE

II Gruppe

Div. Stab (Führungsstab) ...
2 J.R. ...
½ Sturm-Btl.
1 Flo Kp.
1 Aufkl.-Btl.
16 mb. Btr.
Teile Pi. Bl.
Zuteilungen

2 Div. Stäbe (Führg. Abt.)
4 J.R. (ohne V-Abt.)
2 Art. Abtlg.
1. Nb. W.-Abt.
1 Sturm Btl.
2 Pi. Btl. (unvollst.)
2 Flo-Kp.
2 Aufkl. Abt.
Teile N. Abt.
Zuteilungen

III Gruppe   OSTENDE

III. Gruppe (ohne Korpstruppen)

1 Art. Abt. ohne 1 Btr.
Teile von 2 Pi. Btl. u. N. Abt.
Zuteilungen

1 Art. Abt. (ohne 1 Btr.)
Teile von Pi. Btl.
2. N.-Abt.
Zuteilungen

2. STAFFEL
ROTTERDAM

2. Staffel
(Rotterdam)
(ohne Korpstruppen)
2 Div. Stäbe (Reste)
2 J.R.
2 A.R.
2. Pz. Jgr. Abt.
2 Pi. Btl. u. Teile u. 3 Pi. Btl.
2 N. Abt.
Rückw. Dienste

1 J.R. 2 × ½ Btl.
1 A. Rgt.
Pi. Rgt. St.
o. Pi. Btl.
2 Brüko.
1 Pz Jgr. Abt.
Teile N. Abt.

17

Bemerkungen: sofern noch unterzubringen:
Teile Div. Kdo; (Betriebs-Kol. u. Werkst. Zug)

3. Staffel

OSTENDE   ~~DÜNKIRCHEN~~

Reste der Division
Rückw. Dienste im Baggerbetrieb

Rückw. Dste. u. Rest der Div.

Vice-Admiral Hermann von Fischel, commander of Transport Fleet B.

Nine light auxiliary gunboats would make the crossing with the tow formations. The 3rd Minesweeper Flotilla, the 2nd and 3rd Patrol Flotilla and the 11th R-boat Flotilla would protect these tow formations, while the 4th Minesweeper Flotilla would clear the way for the convoy. The 16th Minesweeper Flotilla had been allocated to Convoy 1.

With its 100 tows, the transport fleet would have been 1,000 m wide and stretched for over 16.5 km. Its theoretical composition, re-created from a number of sources, is shown on Map 3, which also gives the landing zones of the individual units. Map 2 shows the disposition of the 17th and 35th Infantry Divisions as well as the troops of XIII Corps.

Tank Detachment (U) D (minus one company) would support the 35th Infantry Division and (U) B the 17th. Sturmbatterie 666 would have been integrated into the 17th lnfantry Division.

The barges were armed with the small arms and machine guns of the troops on board, and additionally with 7.5 cm guns. The 35th Infantry Division intended to fit twenty of their barges with 7.5 cm guns, fifteen with PAK anti-tank guns, light field or mountain guns, thirteen with 2 cm flak and the remaining twenty-six with machine guns or heavy anti-aircraft machine guns. The 17th Division planned to arm all forward barges in a tow with a 7.5 cm gun and all rear barges with a 2 cm flak or heavy machine gun. Seventeen barges were modified in both Dunkirk and Ostend to accommodate the 7.5 cm guns. Seven transports of the division in Ostend had one of these guns and the fifteen transports from Rotterdam had two guns apiece. Two transports of the 35th Infantry Division, the O 9 and O 11 were each fitted with four 7.5 cm guns. This artillery was to be unloaded and used after landing. Towing vehicles, mostly captured ones, were taken along, where space permitted.

Advance detachment 'Bode' of the 35th Infantry Division had a strength of some 1,200 to 1,400 men, including the staff, communications unit, four rifle companies, four heavy machine-gun platoons with six guns each, four PAK platoons with three guns each, and eight engineer groups. Also included were the coxswains of the assault boats, one company of I./Lehrregiment 'Brandenburg', chemical weapons detection and decontamination troops, airborne liaison troops

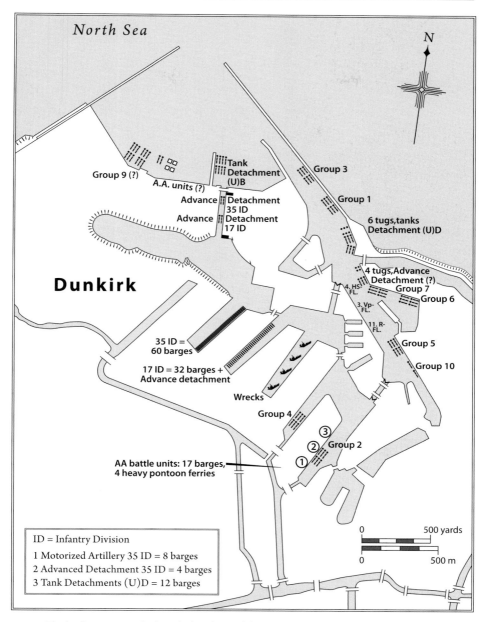

North Sea

N

Group 9 (?)

A.A. units (?)

Tank Detachment (U)B

Group 3

Group 1

Advance Detachment 35 ID

Advance Detachment 17 ID

6 tugs, tanks Detachment (U)D

Dunkirk

4 tugs, Advance Detachment (?)

4. HS-FL.

Group 7

Group 6

3. Vp-FL.

11. R-FL.

35 ID = 60 barges

17 ID = 32 barges + Advance detachment

Group 5

Group 10

Wrecks

Group 4

③

② Group 2

①

AA battle units: 17 barges, 4 heavy pontoon ferries

0   500 yards

0   500 m

ID = Infantry Division

1 Motorized Artillery 35 ID = 8 barges
2 Advanced Detachment 35 ID = 4 barges
3 Tank Detachments (U)D = 12 barges

The harbour at Dunkirk with the planned disposition of tow groups for departure.

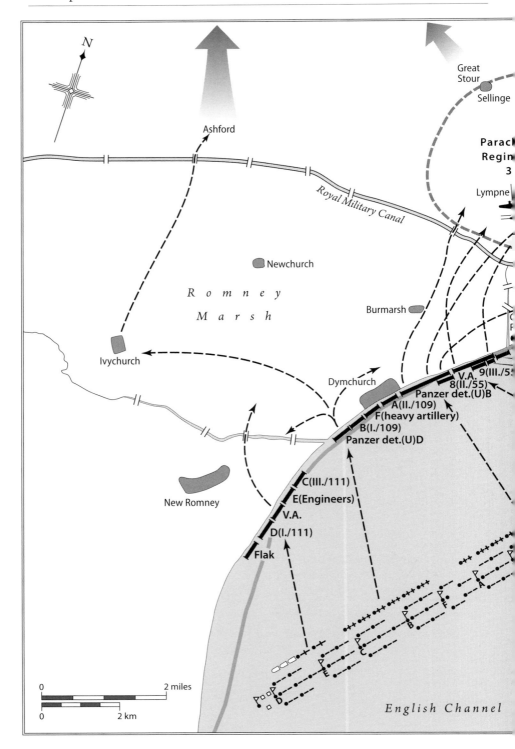

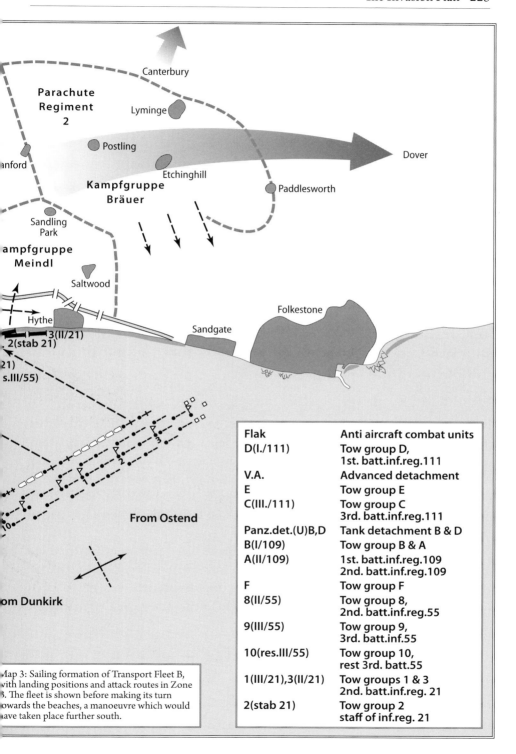

Canterbury

Parachute Regiment 2

Lyminge

Postling

Dover

Etchinghill

Kampfgruppe Bräuer

Paddlesworth

anford

Sandling Park

ampfgruppe Meindl

Saltwood

Folkestone

Hythe

Sandgate

3(II/21)

2(stab 21)

21)

s.III/55)

From Ostend

om Dunkirk

Map 3: Sailing formation of Transport Fleet B, with landing positions and attack routes in Zone B. The fleet is shown before making its turn towards the beaches, a manoeuvre which would have taken place further south.

Flak	Anti aircraft combat units
D(I./111)	Tow group D, 1st. batt.inf.reg.111
V.A.	Advanced detachment
E	Tow group E
C(III./111)	Tow group C 3rd. batt.inf.reg.111
Panz.det.(U)B,D	Tank detachment B & D
B(I/109)	Tow group B & A
A(II/109)	1st. batt.inf.reg.109 2nd. batt.inf.reg.109
F	Tow group F
8(II/55)	Tow group 8, 2nd. batt.inf.reg.55
9(III/55)	Tow group 9, 3rd. batt.inf.55
10(res.III/55)	Tow group 10, rest 3rd. batt.55
1(III/21),3(II/21)	Tow groups 1 & 3 2nd. batt.inf.reg. 21
2(stab 21)	Tow group 2 staff of inf.reg. 21

and four flamethrowing tanks. Half of these men were to travel on naval vessels and motor fishing vessels; four minesweepers or patrol boats were to carry two assault boats and a large rubber dinghy each; the five to eight fishing trawlers carried a large rubber dinghy. The remainder of the men were to be distributed amongst the three tows consisting of one tug pulling one Type AS and one powered barge. Each barge carried eight assault craft and four large rubber dinghies. The guns on the minesweepers and patrol boats, the three light auxiliary gunboats, and one PAK each on the motor fishing vessels were for shore bombardment. The rear barge had a machine gun.

The 17th Infantry Division formed two advance detachments which set off from Ostend and Dunkirk and which were commanded by Major Schuler and Major Pannwitz respectively. The Ostend unit consisted of 992 men, made up of a strengthened battalion and reinforcements with heavy weapons: two mountain guns, three light infantry guns, three PAK, ten heavy mortars, eight heavy machine guns, two smoke launchers, two flamethrowing tanks and a gun tank which was to be used as a command vehicle. These were complemented by nine engineer assault troops, sixteen assault craft crews, twenty dinghy crews, ramp operators for the four barges and a special gas detection unit. The advance detachment was transported in eight patrol boats, eight minesweepers and two tows as described above.

The Dunkirk advance detachment, with a strength of 968 men, was composed in the same manner. Their heavy weapons were two mountain guns, two light infantry guns, three PAK, six heavy mortars, twelve heavy machine guns, two rocket launchers, two flamethrowing tanks, and a conventional tank from Tank Detachment (Fl) 100. The engineers had eleven assault units, a mine detection unit, ramp operators and a special gas detection unit. There were no crews for the assault craft or rubber dinghies in the Dunkirk advance detachment. Their vessels were three minesweepers, four patrol boats and four R-boats as well as two of the tows.

Both advance detachments could count on artillery support at sea from the minesweepers, R-boats, patrol boats and the three light auxiliary gunboats apiece. The diagram on page 180 shows their landing dispositions schematically.

The 35th Infantry Division produced the following timetable for landing the First Wave, assuming an S Time of 0600 hrs:

Time	Landing sequence	Landed forces
	S Day	
6.00	Advanced detachments and Tank Detachment (U) D	
6.15	189 men landed (30 assault boats)	4 rifle coys with engineers.
6.30	Additional 360 men (60 assault boats) landed. Approx. 80 barges of the 2nd and 3rd group land.	Bulk of the motor rifle coys and engineers.
6.45	Further 200 men and equipment land in assault boats and rafts.	⅔ Tank Detachments (U) D and ½ advance detachment.
7.00	Additional 200 men land.	
7.15	Additional 200 men land.	
7.30	Unloading of advance detachment completed. Begin landing barges of the 2nd and 3rd group; transports anchor.	Advance detachment with 1,300 men and all weapons.
8.00	Bulk of men from groups 2 and 3 landed; 18 transports of second echelon Rotterdam anchor.	4,000–5,000 men without heavy weapons and vehicles.
8.30	Vehicles and horses unloaded. Start unloading equipment and supplies. The 4 barges of the Ostend transport landed.	
9.00	Unloading completed of barges of Ostend transports. 36 barges of the second echelon landed.	4 reinforced battalions with 2 mountain batteries, 2 heavy field how. (mot) ready to march.
10.00	Low tide.	3 heavy field how. batteries (mot) ready to march.
18.00	40 barges landed having unloaded transports.	
19.00	Unloading of 40 barges completed. Unloading of the packing of half of the barges of the first echelon (40) completed.	1 light field how. and heavy field how. bn without horses, 1 Panzerjäger bn, staff tank det. U, elements signals bn.
19.30	80 barges available as lighters for unloading 20 transports.	
23.00	Low tide.	
	S Day plus 1	
7.00	80 barges landed. Unloading equipment and supplies from 40 barges of the first echelon completed.	
8.00	80 barges unloaded.	4.7 cm PAK coy, heavy coy Bicycle Btl 35, 1 light field how.bn with horses, 1 PAK coy 34th Inf Reg, bulk of troops, 34th Inf Reg and Eng 296.
11.30	Low tide.	
19.30	Remainder of combat troops, horses, vehicles unloaded.	
20.30	Unloading completed.	All remaining elements of the first and second echelons ready to march.
	S Day plus 2	
20.00	Bulk of rear services and ⅓ of supplies unloaded.	
	S Day plus 3	
20.00	Unloading of all transports and supplies completed.	

It is patently obvious, from this timetable, that the unloading of the packing of the First Wave barges would take so long that they could not be used to lighten the transports after they had been refloated after the first high tide. It is doubtful whether this senseless timescale would have been generally imposed since it would have delayed unloading.

The initial assault of the XIII Corps can been seen on Map 2. Once it had broken through the coastal defences, the 35th Infantry Division was to assault Romney Marsh on a broad front and cross the Royal Military Canal, a relic of a Napoleonic invasion scare. The intermediate objective was the area of woodland directly north and the creation of a bridgehead along a line through Ashford, High Halden and points south of Biddenden and Sissinghurst. Tanks and infantry would work together to gain ground on the Marsh and neutralise bunkers on the Military Canal. The Germans assumed that the British would blow the Canal crossings and lay minefields, and so they anticipated having to use engineers for bridging and mine-clearing. A 'Brandenburger' commando unit was assigned to suppress the British coastal bases, and positions along the Military Canal, as well as the artillery which was assumed to lie north of it. The division was prepared for heavy British attacks, especially armoured ones, once the Germans had crossed the Canal and the basin to the north. Once the bridgehead had been reached, it would be necessary to erect strong field defences, including anti-tank mines, due to the lack of natural obstacles. A strong anti-tank defence and a mobile PAK reserve were needed.

The Germans assumed that the British would use every conceivable kind of mine on the beaches, underwater in the landing zones, in towns and cities, in forests, along roadsides and in ditches, and so they set up mine-clearance squads.

The 17th Infantry Division to the right of the 35th had a tough mission due to the threat to its eastern flank and to the fact that the attack on Dover was to take place at a relatively early stage of the invasion; but they were to be reinforced by airborne troops. The landing at Brighton was thus abandoned and Dover remained the chosen target until mid-September.

Luftwaffe Field Marshal Kesselring met with the Army on 12 September; at this meeting the deployment of an airborne regiment and two battalions, probably glider-borne, of the 7th Airborne Division to the west of Dover was mooted. The attack on Dover itself on S Day was to be a joint operation between this division and the Panzer detachment landing west of Hythe. The Luftwaffe rejected the Army's proposal to use the entire 7th Airborne Division, probably to allow itself to hold part in reserve. But six days later the Luftflottenkommando 2 (Air Fleet Command 2) issued a different directive to the 7th Airborne Division. The gradual obstruction of all open countryside by the British and reinforced air defence around Dover resulted in the proposed landing of the 7th Airborne Division being moved to the north-west of Folkestone. This shift changed the scenario, tasking the 7th Airborne Division with clearing the canal crossing routes west of Hythe for the 7th Infantry Division; securing the maritime assault by blocking all roads leading from Canterbury to Folkestone, and providing some troops to attack Dover as the mission unfolded.

The Army was now uncertain of its ability to make a rapid capture of Dover, the most important harbour in the landing zone on S Day, but was forced to give in to Kesselring. The lack of files on this point is regrettable, as it prevents its critical examination but the impression that the Luftwaffe feared the risks is underlined when it is recalled that in the winter the Luftwaffe believed that air and ground operations around Folkestone were not feasible, and proposed a landing along the line of Dymchurch, Bonnington, Kingsnorth, Woodchurch and New Romney. The assault troops would enable the 35th Infantry Division to cross the Military Canal through the rapid capture of the bridges between Bilsington and Appledore, and a thrust toward Ashford would encompass the bridges over the Great Stour. A further airborne landing near Canterbury to cut off the Great Stour sector was also considered.

The diagram on page 230 shows the composition of the 7th Airborne Division, but little else is known about its strength. Halder had reported on 16 July 1940 that the Luftwaffe had cited the availability of 1,000 transport aircraft, three-quarters of which were operational, and of 150 gliders. These aircraft could have airlifted the bulk of the 7th Airborne Division.

There is also a dearth of material regarding the possible deployment of the 22nd Infantry Division in an airborne role later in the Sixteenth Army's zone, but this can be assumed to have been likely. The lack of transport aircraft prevented a simultaneous landing with the 7th Airborne Division. Unlike a 'true' airborne division such as the 7th, the 22nd could not be landed with parachutes and gliders, but only with the aid of transport aircraft, which, in view of Britain's strong defences, presupposed a bridgehead. Though the Germans had good airborne forces in the autumn of 1940, a massed daylight attack would have been seriously endangered by British anti-aircraft guns and fighters – the Luftwaffe was thus forced to pick its objectives carefully. The Allied forces must have felt themselves in a similar position in Normandy when they dropped their paratroops the night before the actual landing. An undated divisional order of the 17th Infantry Division details co-operation with the 7th Airborne Division for a landing at Folkestone. The first wave of paratroops was to land at the same time as the advance detachments. Kampfgruppe Meindl and Kampfgruppe Stentzler were formed, which both comprised two reinforced battalions. The first combat group was to open up the crossing points of the Military Canal west of Hythe and at Hythe itself, and prevent a flanking manoeuvre by British troops by advancing

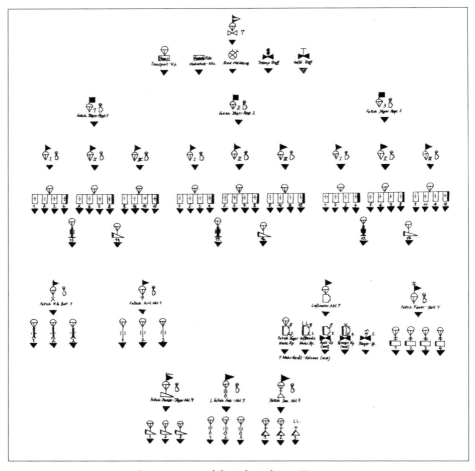

Organisation of the 7th Airborne Division

(*First level*) Transport Company, Logistics Company, Motorcycle Messenger Platoon, Transport Echelon, Reconnaissance Echelon;

(*Second level*) Paratroop Regiments 1, 2 and 3, each of 14 companies, Companies 13 and 14 being Infantry Gun and Anti-Tank Companies respectively;

(*Third level*) Paratroop Machine Gun Battalion 7 (3 companies), Paratroop Artillery Detachment 7 (3 companies), Air Communications Detachment 7 (of 5 specialised communication companies and a motorised intelligence company), Paratroop Engineer Battalion 7 (of 4 companies);

(*Bottom level*) Paratroop Anti-Tank Detachment 7, Paratroop Medical Detachment 7 (each of 3 companies).

This, and the following organisational charts, are copies of original documents. The most important features are pointed out in the captions, but to interpret the details, readers are referred to the key to individual symbols on pages 312–14.

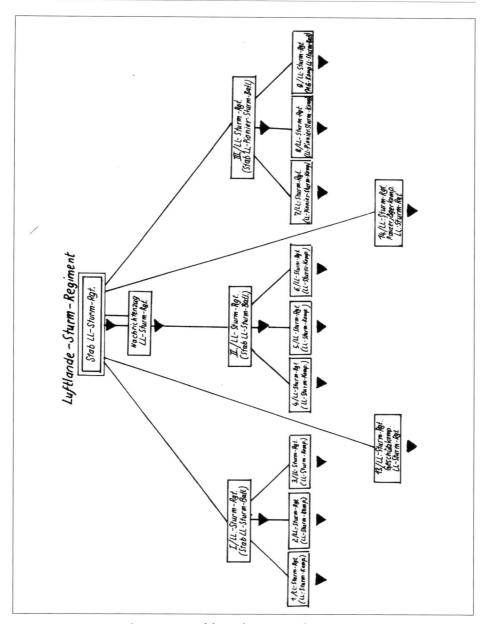

Organisation of the Airborne Assault Regiment

Under the orders of a staff unit and its Communications Platoon were three battalions, each of a staff unit and 3 companies. The first two were Airborne Assault Battalions (Airborne Assault Companies 1–6) and the third an Engineer Battalion (the 7th and 8th were Airborne Engineer Assault Companies and the 9th was a Machine-Gun Company). The 13th (an Infantry Gun Company) and 14th (an Anti-Tank Company) reported directly to the regimental staff.

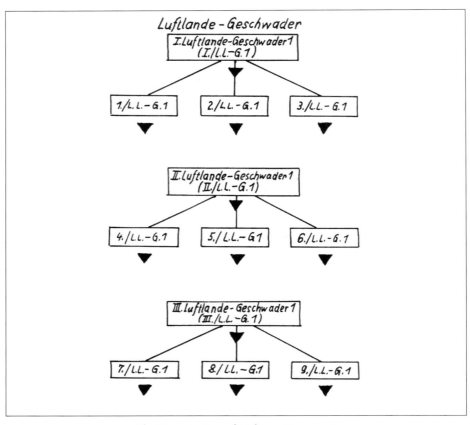

The Organisation of Airborne Transport.
Geschwader I was divided into three *Gruppen,* each of three *Staffeln,*
numbered consecutively from 1 to 9.

toward the line running from Hythe railway station to Saltwood. Kampfgruppe Stentzler was to take the heights to the south-west of Paddlesworth and halt there, keeping back British forces through defensive firepower or by attacking if necessary. Kampfgruppe Bräuer formed the second wave and was to land about an hour later. It consisted of a paratroop battalion, a paratroop engineer battalion and an anti-tank company (the 14th) of Parachute Regiment 1, the whole of Parachute Regiments 2 and 3 as well as a battalion as divisional reserve which would land south of Postling.

Under the leadership of Kampfgruppe Bräuer, Kampfgruppe Stentzler would take Sandgate and secure the heights west of Paddlesworth. Parachute Regiment 2 would assault the Downs north of Postling and counter any attack from the north; Parachute Regiment 3 would secure the western flank, one of its battalions capturing the airfield at Lympne. The development of the operation during the landing would dictate whether additional units with heavy weapons would be needed – probably landing at Lympne – from about S Day plus 5.

The shallow pebble beach would have made a good landing area for the two advance detachments of the 17th Infantry Division, and the submersible tanks of Tank Detachment (U) D would have an easy run-in to their 1.5 km-wide landing zone at Dymchurch, though they would have to deal with man-made barriers and minefields. Advance detachment Schuler was confronted with the old Grand Redoubt (near Dymchurch), a fortress built during the Napoleonic Wars which had been armed with 6 in guns. Once these coastal emplacements had been silenced the advance detachments would regroup along the Hythe–Dungeness railway line, cross the Military Canal and take and hold the high ground in conjunction with the 7th Airborne Division. Part of the tank detachment was to retain its floatation gear to allow it to cross the canal in a single wave with the support of the Meindl group, and begin attacking the high ground to the north. The 21st and 55th Infantry Regiments, which were to land afterwards, were to link up with the advance detachments, supporting the 7th Airborne Division in mopping up the captured territory.

Thereafter, the 21st Infantry Regiment was to prepare either for an offensive on Dover or toward the Great Stour and the 55th Infantry Regiment for an advance on the Great Stour either to each side of Ashford or from a more northerly route. The 17th Bicycle Battalion would reconnoitre and secure the route toward Canterbury for the groups advancing toward Dover and the Great Stour.

A mobile combat unit commanded by Colonel Hoffmeister was to form near Stanford and Sandling Park and push to the north of Sandgate and Folkestone, thence to Dover and so open up the coast to Margate. It was hoped that the group could be formed by the afternoon of S Day from the following:

> Tank Detachment (U) B
> MG Battalion 8
> 1 Company, Lehrregiment 'Brandenburg'
> 1 Company, Anti-tank Detachment 543 (self-propelled)
> 1 Company, Flak Battalion 601
> 1 Company, Anti-tank Detachment 616 (self-propelled)
> 1 Battery, II Battalion, Artillery Regiment 67 (heavy field howitzers – motorised)
> I/Flak Detachment 61 (two heavy, 1½ light batteries) possibly 1 Engineer company (motorised)
> 21st Infantry Regiment depending on strategic situation

To summarise, the 17th Infantry Division was to penetrate British coastal defences between Hythe and Dymchurch, take the heights north of the Military Canal in co-operation with the 7th Airborne Division, and be prepared to form an extended bridgehead on the Great Stour between Chilham and Ashford; parts of the 17th Infantry Division were then to advance on Dover, Deal, Margate, and Canterbury. They had the most formidable mission of all the First Wave divisions.

Transport Fleet C
This fleet was to land in Zone C (Rye Bay), having departed from Antwerp, Calais and Gravelines.

	Transports	Barges*	Tugs	Motorboats	Coasters
Antwerp	50	370 (200)	Remainder	Remainder	Remainder
Gravelines	–	40	20	40	–
Calais	–	200 (50)	100	200	–

* Figures in parentheses refer to the number of barges out of the total that were to be kept in reserve.

Though the harbour at Antwerp had enough berths for all the ships, the departure of the convoy would have been more complicated than from Rotterdam. Half of the transports were in the docks and had to exit through the Kruisschanz lock into the Schelde. This procedure usually took half an hour for four large steamers. Trials had shown that four transports, eight barges and tugs could negotiate the lock in two hours, but the operation could take as much as four to six hours if the wind was unfavourable. The exact time of the departure of the remaining transports from the Schelde quay depended on the tides. During the ebb tide they could sail only with the assistance of two heavy tugs per transport. Moreover, it was necessary to manoeuvre the transports around the first bend in the Schelde and around the second at high tide. KMD Antwerp requested eight tugs of 800–1,000 hp in addition to the three already available (300–400 hp). The barges would be lashed alongside the transports in the Schelde as it made them easier to manoeuvre. The lengthy departure time of the convoy required it to assemble at Vlissingen, where it would have air cover. Weighing anchor, turning and getting under way required further assistance from the tugs. On the other hand, a straight run to Assembly Area II was counter-productive because the convoy's close escort was only the eight trawlers of the 15th Minesweeper Flotilla. The lack of a central switch to turn off the lights along the Schelde prevented any sailing at night. A returning transport, for instance, would reach Hausweerd at 1700 hrs and would have to anchor there because it could not reach Antwerp before dark. It would start again at 0700 hrs the following morning and tie up at the Schelde quay at 1100 hrs. Assuming a loading time of 12 hours, it could not complete the operation before dusk. Loading would continue the next day at 0700 hrs and go on until 1000 hrs. Departure would be at 1100 hrs, and Hausweerd reached at 1400 hrs, that is, 45 hours later. If the Schelde were illuminated, the timetable would be as follows:

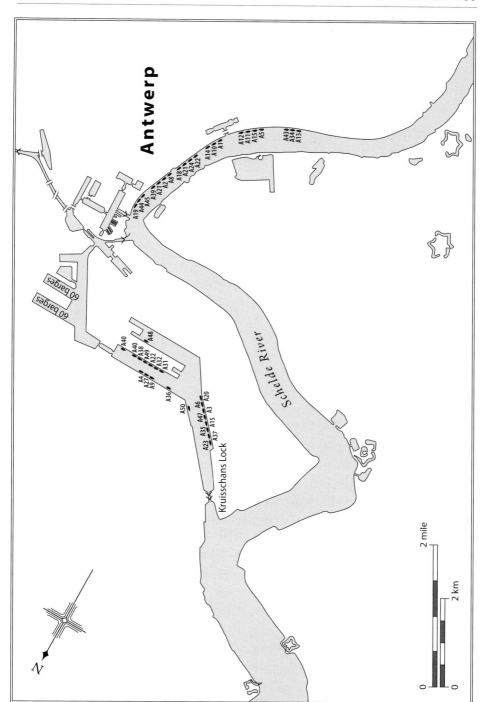

Berthing plan for the transports at Antwerp.

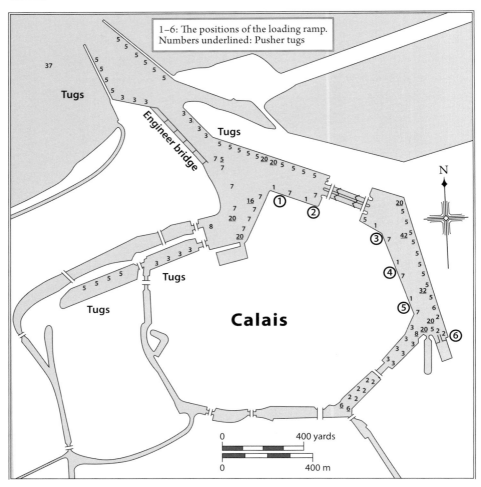

1–6: The positions of the loading ramp.
Numbers underlined: Pusher tugs

Berthing plan for Calais.

Hausweerd passed inward bound	1700 hrs
Antwerp – anchor	2100 hrs
Load on next day	0700–1900 hrs
Depart	2000 hrs
Hausweerd passed outward bound	2300 hrs

This overall time of 30 hours represented a saving of 15 hours, and could have been further improved by loading at night (see page 235).

In the original plan the harbour at Gravelines was only for reserves; in late September, however, it was decided that it should be used for embarkation of the 7th Infantry Division in order to alleviate some of the overcrowding at Calais. Loading time was thus reduced from four to two days. The diagram above shows the distribution of those ships assigned only to Calais before this change.

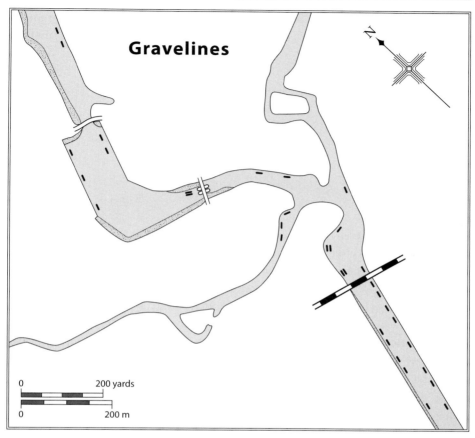

Berthing plan for Gravelines.

Loading of supplies at Antwerp would start on S Day minus 9. From S Day minus 8 to the evening of S Day minus 6 the motor vehicles were loaded; horses and troops were to be loaded on S Day minus 5. The first ships would sail on S Day minus 4 so that all the transports would be assembled on the Schelde by the evening of S Day minus 2. In Calais, where the departure depended on the two locks, the Army supplies were loaded on S Day minus 5. On S Day minus 4 the barges of the 1st Mountain Division would pass through the lock into the outer harbour. Tanks were to be loaded on S Day minus 3; the horses and flak loaded on S Day minus 2 and then the remaining barges would be brought into the outer harbour. Troops embarked on S Day minus 1. Engineer Battalion 665 had erected a 300 m long loading bridge for this purpose. The fleet would sail the same day.

The timetable for Gravelines was similar, where loading of equipment and supplies for the 7th Infantry Division was to take place on S Day minus 5 and S Day minus 3, with S Day minus 4 and S Day minus 2 in reserve. The troops came aboard only two hours before sailing on S Day minus 1.

The commander of Transport Fleet C, Captain Kleikamp, was the only one to issue a detailed order for his fleet, giving historians a good idea of its formation and mission:

Transport Fleet C   Calais   (Captain Kleikamp)
    100 tow formations with:
        100 tugs
        200 barges
        200 pusher boats
Convoy 3   Antwerp (Captain Wesemann)
    57 transports with:
        114 barges and 14 pusher boats

Convoy 3 had varied in strength at different stages of the planning. According to Operational Directive No. 11 of Fleet Commander West, dated 19 September 1940, this convoy was to consist of only fifty transports and one hundred barges, seven transports from Ostend having been added by an order dated 29 September (see page 215), which also had two pusher boats each in order to make up the number of these craft needed in the landing zone.

The number of transports was reduced to forty-seven on 13 October, forty-two of which would be supplied by Antwerp and five from Zeebrugge. This cut was the result of losses which had occurred earlier.

The inventory of Naval Commander West gives due consideration to the commanders of the towed formation and of the convoy, but more closely reflects

a pragmatic approach to their missions. Even though the commander of a convoy was subordinate to the transport fleet commander, he had fairly broad discretionary powers while the fleet was at sea. Captain Kleikamp took due consideration of this in his operational order.

Those documents which have been preserved from Kleikamp's command and from VII Corps attest to the close

Captain Gustav Kleikamp, commander of Transport Fleet C.

co-operation between the Army and the Navy authorities. Kleikamp suggested towing and landing the barges lashed abreast, which would shorten the 14–15 km long transport fleet by one-third and would also eliminate the need for the pusher boats which were generally not up to their job anyway. Kleikamp was also present during the trials of the *Land-Wasser-Schlepper* amphibious tractor.

Map 4 on pages 240–1 shows the composition of Transport Fleet C. The heavy bridge pontoon ferries would proceed under the command of a tow group commander at the head and rear of the fleet and would be on the flanks after the turn off the beaches. Because of their artillery, Kleikamp positioned them slightly toward the south during the crossing as there were hardly any armed vessels in that sector.

The tow groups which had formed in Calais by S Day minus 2 would load their troops and set sail at 1000 hrs on S Day minus 1. In Gravelines this process started at 0500 hrs on S Day minus 1 in order for these tow groups to reach the assembly area off Calais harbour by 0700 hrs. The tows from Calais with flak artillery belonging to Tow Groups IX–XI would join these tow groups, the reason being that the reinforced battalions of the division only filled four tows. (A tow group consisted of six tows so corps flak units would fill the gaps and operate autonomously during the landing.) These tows were to sail to the west of the fleet, in order to provide additional cover. All of the tows and the heavy pontoon ferries were to anchor in the assembly area off Calais on S Day minus 1 at 1700 hrs at the latest. Only the tugs were to drop anchor and the two barges astern would ride on a short hawser. A fishing buoy was to be positioned for each tow group. The transport fleet commander was to board his own command boat at 1300 hrs the next day as the fleet was sailing. At S Day minus 11 hours the 4th R-Boat Flotilla weighed anchor and began sweeping Route 2. Any barrages were to be cleared or else avoided. Two minesweepers followed, dropping lantern buoys. At S Day minus 10¾ hrs the transport would weigh anchor after a radio signal and wait another quarter of an hour until the head of the fleet, led by the command boat, got under way at a speed of 3 knots. The remaining tows with the barges now closed up behind one another were to close up and follow in sequence (see Map 4). After an order via radio an hour later, speed was to be increased to 5 knots. In foggy conditions the aft barges in the tow formations would drop a fog buoy. Lights were to be dimmed, with only those visible from aft lit, though the fleet and group leader boats would have their steaming lights lit dimly if necessary.

Turning the fleet towards the English coast was to proceed after an order from Naval Commander West (see page 171) and once the head of the fleet had reached the R-boat stationed at the end of Route 2 showing two red lights. Unless the fleet had drifted apart, the final tow group would be stationed somewhere near the R-boat at Point R which would be showing two green lights. The change of course

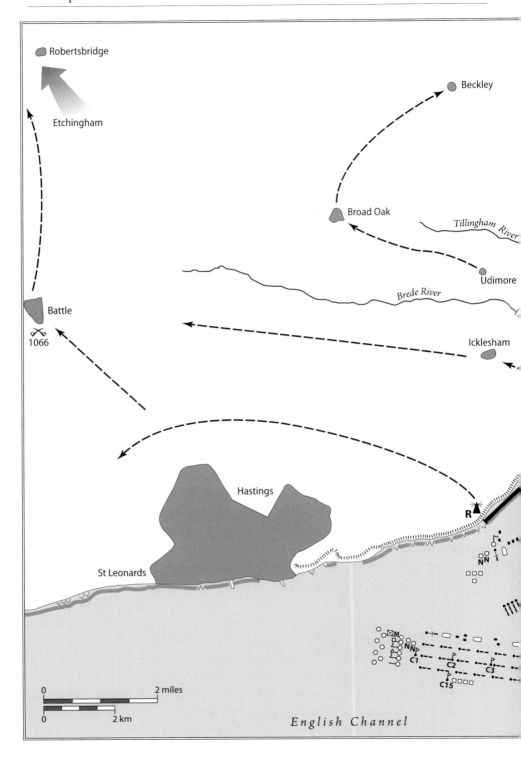

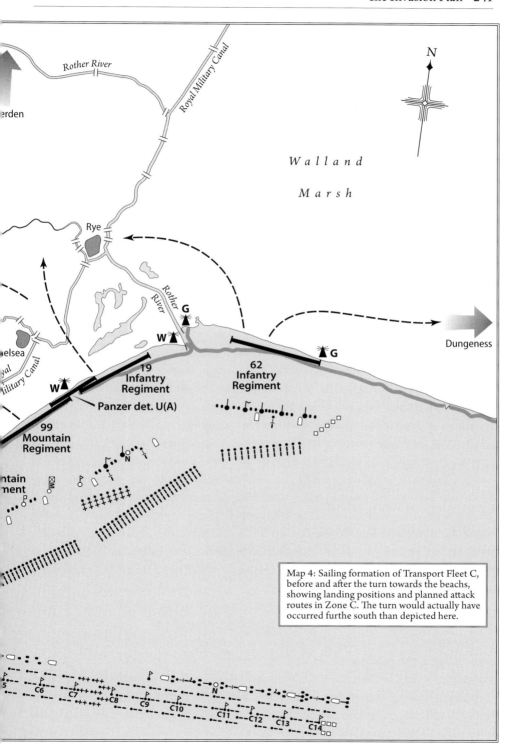

Map 4: Sailing formation of Transport Fleet C, before and after the turn towards the beachs, showing landing positions and planned attack routes in Zone C. The turn would actually have occurred furthe south than depicted here.

within the fleet would be executed as a combat manoeuvre; that is, every ship would turn independently, starting from the rear of the fleet and with the northern line turning first. The two minesweepers serving as markers would then join the advance detachments as smokeboats, followed by the remaining boats of the 4th R-boat and the 1st Minesweeper Flotillas at the head of the fleet. Map 4 shows the disposition of the fleet at that stage. The tows sailing in threes were to draw into a line abreast. The left flank had a much shorter route to the coast than the middle and the right flanks and so would have to heave to for a while. During the landing the naval vessels and the heavy pontoon ferries on the flanks would give fire support to the advance detachments. The tow groups with the 3rd Battalions of 98th and 99th Mountain Regiments were to remain slightly behind the line of the other tows in order to land behind the other battalions. The 62nd Infantry Regiment was unlucky in having a flat beach. The barges which landed there two hours after high water might ground some 800 m from the beach and have a long run through water up to ¾m deep stretching before them. The 19th Regiment was at a similar disadvantage: the barges would ground about 600–700 m offshore. The tank detachment would also land on a sandbank 700–800 m offshore, but they would have no difficulty in negotiating the shallows with the tanks closed down. At Cliff End the situation was better for there the sloping beach allowed the troops to disembark closer to the shore and wade perhaps only 200–300 m to the beach. Kleikamp thought that barges might even be landed here on a rising tide, provided that they were unloaded quickly.

The map opposite shows the anchorage for Convoy 3 at S Time plus two hours. Five of the 1st Minesweeper Flotilla, all of the 15th Minesweeper Flotilla less the convoy commander's vessel and the 7th Patrol Flotilla were to form a picket around the landing zone to guard against British submarines. Depending on the situation, the 4th R-boat Flotilla would be used for anti-submarine or minesweeping duties or for unloading troops from the transports. The motor fishing vessels of the 32nd Minesweeper Flotilla would also be used in the latter capacity and later for minesweeping and anti-submarine duties. Once the transports and the tows had begun their return journey the boats would be withdrawn from these tasks and used as escorts.

Unfortunately, most records from VII Corps, of which 7th Infantry Division and 1st Mountain Division were part, have disappeared.

The organisation of the Corps is shown on pages 244–6. Map 4 shows an overview of the landing zones and the proposed advance routes. The advance detachments of the 98th and 99th Mountain Regiments were each allocated three R-boats, three minesweepers, five motor fishing vessels of 32nd Minesweeper Flotilla and a tow. The advance detachment of 19th Infantry Division was assigned four patrol boats, ten motor fishing vessels and two tows; the advance detachment

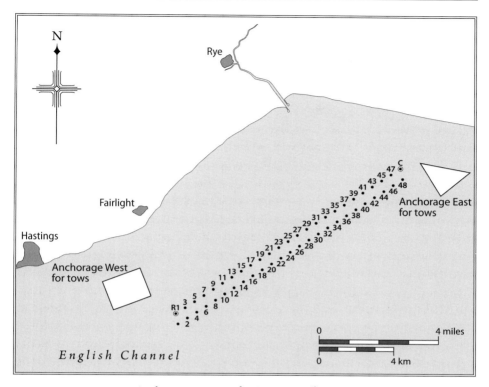

Anchorage positions for Convoy 3 off Zone C.

of 62nd Regiment four patrol boats, ten trawlers and one tow formation. Each of the two advance detachments of 7th Infantry Division would load one barge with three tanks from Tank Detachment (Fl) 100. The 1st Mountain Division's Advance Detachment 3 was also assigned three of these flamethrowing tanks.

In contrast to Transport Fleets B and D, the barges of Tank Detachment (U) D would not sail with the advance detachments, but with the bulk of Transport Fleet C. Therefore, in order to land with the advance detachments, its tow group had to pull ahead of the rest of the fleet. The tanks were to enter the water 3,000 m off the coast, and then travel for half an hour at an underwater speed of 5–7 km/h. If this manoeuvre presented difficulties for the transport fleet, the fall-back plan was to land the barges and unload the tanks directly on to the beach. The tank detachment was to lend ground support in taking the 2 km-long zone, massing subsequently on the coast, where they were to convert for land warfare. They would then be at the disposal of the army corps around Winchelsea.

In the initial assault, the advance detachments of 7th Infantry and 1st Mountain Divisions were to establish local bridgeheads about 2 km deep. The remaining forces in the First Wave were to push forward to the south bank of the River

Organisation of the 7th Infantry Division.
It is marked Secret (*Geheim*) and dated 5 October 1940.

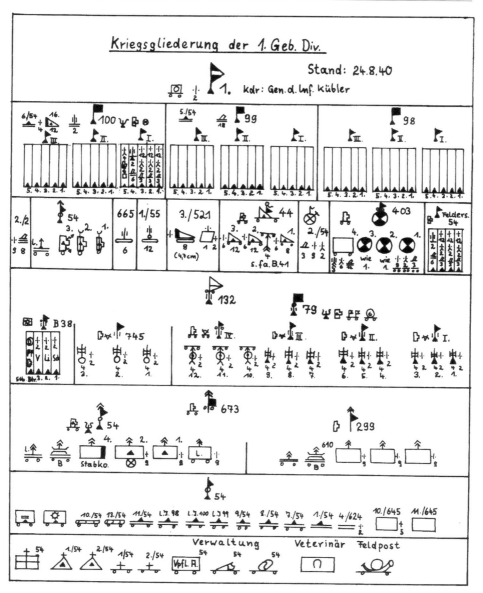

War Organisation of the 1st Mountain Division.
A reconstruction of its state in August 1940 (it was reorganised in the autumn
and units were transferred to the 5th Mountain Division).

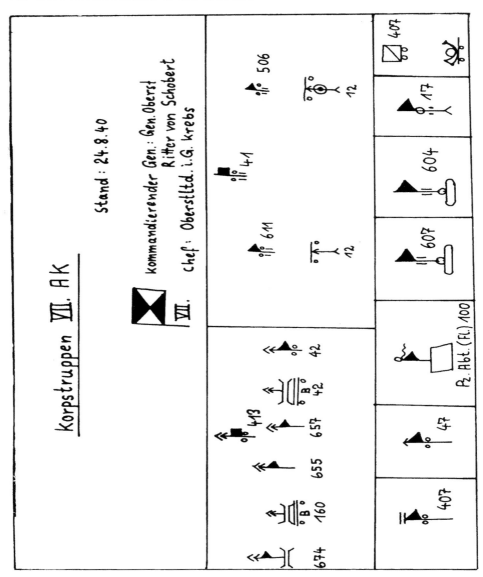

Organisation of the Corps Troops of VIII Army Corps on 24 August 1940.
It included a flamethrowing tank detachment (*Pz Abt (Fl) 100*).

Rother (the first day's minimum objective). Depending on British resistance, the assault would continue to a line along the high ground south of the Sissinghurst, Cranbrook and Flimwell region, west of Burwash which was the desired objective.

The 7th Infantry's orders were to land in Rye Bay and push across the River Rother to the hills north-west of Hawkhurst and south of Sissinghurst and Cranbrook. In theory, a rapid assault along the heights north of Udimore, Broad

Oak and Beckley would penetrate British divisional resistance. Dungeness was to be taken later by rearguard forces advancing from the west.

The 1st Mountain Division would land at Cliff End and Hastings, scale the sheer cliffs and push northward along the hills and to a line between Flimwell and Burwash Common. It was important to achieve a quick success at Hastings and take territory around Battle, scene of another invasion in 1066, and the high ground south-west of Robertsbridge. These lines were to be reinforced by the divisions as much as possible in order to screen the succeeding landing waves and to prepare for the attack on London.

Once most of the unloading had been completed the corps engineer units were to assemble at the various unloading sites. Piers and jetties at Rye Bay would be inspected and forward troops of Bridge Building Battalion 674 would begin constructing a permanent landing bridge at Hastings. The corps command post would be located in the Icklesham area west of Winchelsea.

Transport Fleet D

Transport Fleet D was to take a historical route and follow the ghost of Caesar's fleet which had sailed from Boulogne to invade Britain in 55 BC. Beachy Head had already witnessed the battle between the French fleet under Tourville and the combined British and Dutch fleet under Viscount Torrington. Transport Fleet D was to carry the Ninth Army from Boulogne to Pevensey Bay, including XXXVIII Corps and the 26th and 34th Infantry Divisions. In the absence of other suitable harbours locally, Boulogne was forced to cope with the massed vessels

of Transport Fleet D which included 165 tows each headed by a tug, 330 barges and 330 pusher boats. The harbour was stretched to its limits and not even reserves could be accommodated. (Two orders from XXXVIII Corps dated 2 and 10 September also mention the Canche estuary and the harbour of Etaples as loading points for the 26th Infantry Division, but Navy sources are notably silent about this.)

KMD Boulogne reported on 19 November 1940 that the

Captain Werner Lindenau, commander of Transport Fleet D.

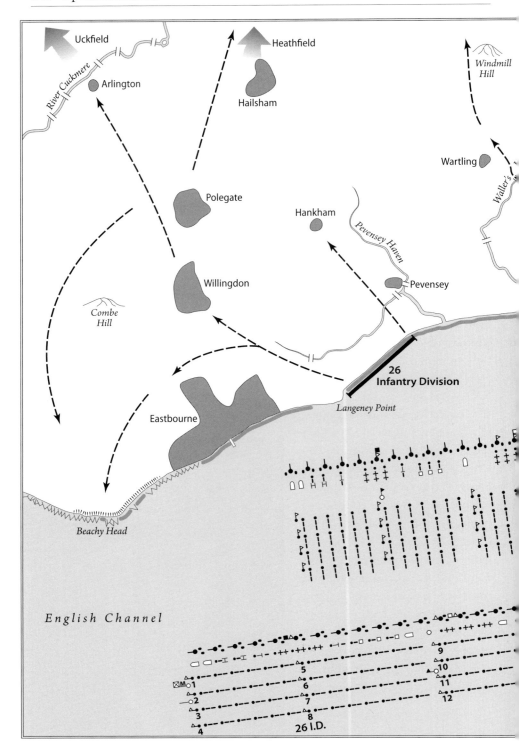

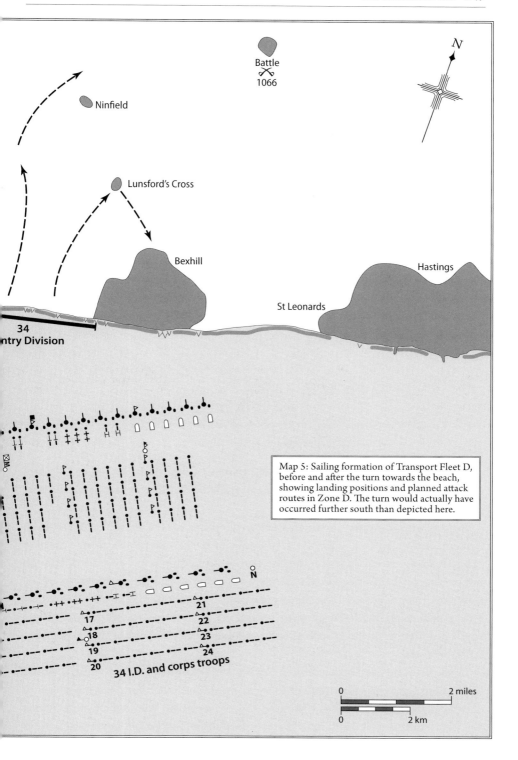

Map 5: Sailing formation of Transport Fleet D, before and after the turn towards the beach, showing landing positions and planned attack routes in Zone D. The turn would actually have occurred further south than depicted here.

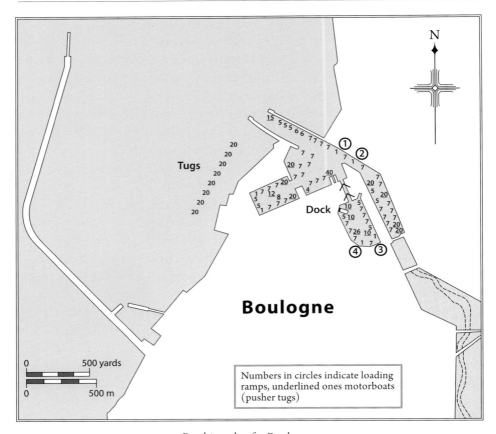

Berthing plan for Boulogne.

docks and the harbour were so crowded that the outer harbour had to be used, weather permitting. All measures were tailored for loading the barges via the bow at the pier.

Pilings were rammed in which were to keep the barges at right-angles to the current and a rail to secure the ramps of the barges was built along the pier. Many loading exercises involving the troops and equipment were held, though not on a large scale since vessels were always arriving and the commander of the transport fleet, Captain Lindenau, added in his report of 30 October 1940 that all the personnel had been extremely cautious during these exercises. As only a small proportion of the craft had been involved, the majority of the crews were still untrained.

Given an estimated rate of fifteen tows leaving the harbour each hour, it would have taken ten hours for the fleet to leave Boulogne. Therefore assembly was to commence on S minus 2 at 1200 hrs. Once assembled, the fleet would depart on S Day minus 1 at 1600 hrs. The tow formation was to be kept in four lines abreast in order to prevent the fleet from becoming too dispersed. To starboard were to be the advance detachments in two lines abreast. In this disposition, the fleet was 2,200 m wide and 20 km long. Commanded by senior officers, lieutenant commanders and staff officers, the tow groups were to sail in columns, which certainly did not make them easy to control. The fleet was divided into three, according to Army requirements, creating a first echelon of 34th Infantry Division, a first echelon of 26th Infantry Division, and half of the second echelon of 34th Infantry Division, corps troops being distributed in each part. Escorting such a gigantic fleet would certainly have been problematical and since 2nd and 18th Minesweeper Flotillas and probably 2nd R-boat Flotilla would have been used to clear the way they would have been unable to fend off attacking British ships and aircraft. The 15th, 16th and 18th Patrol Flotillas would have cruised to starboard of the advance detachments so leaving the port side completely vulnerable. This situation was all the more worrying because the Germans expected the Royal Navy to attack from the west, that is, from the port side. Since the nine light artillery ships were to lend fire support for the advance detachments, would it not be better, Captain Lindenau reasoned, for the heavy pontoon and Herbert ferries and the light auxiliary gunboats to sail on the port side of the formation and close up with the minesweeping craft only after the turn? In contrast to the Sixteenth Army's organisation, the pontoon and Herbert ferries were to be towed along with their barges carrying the light flak guns and the flak combat units' towing vehicles. These would have been cast off after the turn and then travelled under their own power to protect the flanks. Map 5 shows the original plan for Transport Fleet D. KMD Boulogne effectively came to the conclusion that it would be more expedient for the powered and un-powered barges to be towed alongside each other.

The fleet landing in Zone D between Bexhill and Eastbourne would have had an easy run up a flat, gently sloping beach, marred only by the stony ground in the eastern part. The fleet would have been extremely cramped in the western sector with only 27–30 m between the barges and Captain Lindenau contemplated delaying landing some eighty barges to a later stage. He also wanted to avoid Oyster Riff which jutted out and to mark it with buoys. Once on the beach, the German forces would have been confronted with a tank barrier consisting of two rows of concrete 'dragon's teeth', barbed wire, mines and about twenty concrete gun emplacements between Bexhill and Eastbourne, as well as a coastal battery on the promontory at Beachy Head.

XXXVIII Corps, under General von Manstein, wanted to project three advance detachments into Zone D, two from the 34th Infantry Division and one from the 26th. The advanced detachments of the 34th Infantry Division were formed from the 80th and 107th Infantry Regiments and were identical, comprising three so-

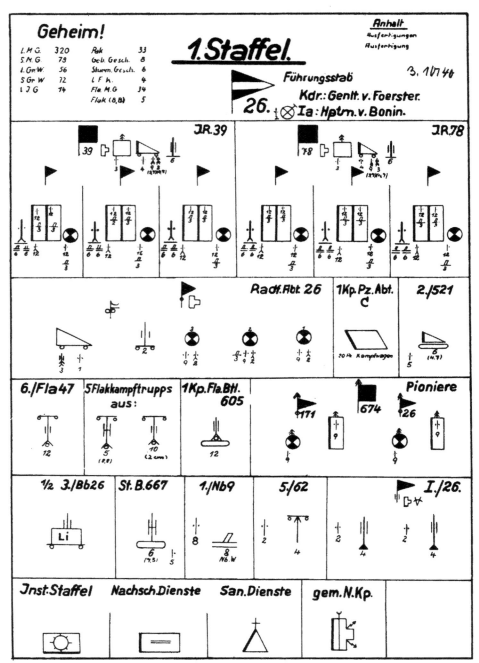

Organisation of the First Echelon of 26th Infantry Division, 3 October 1940
Apart from the 39th and 78th Infantry Regiments, the division also include Bicycle
Detachment 26, 1st Company Tank Detachment C (20 tanks) five Flak units (five 8.8 cm
and ten 2 cm guns) and 1st Company Flak Battalion 605; support units included engineers,
a repair echelon, medical services and a mixed communications company.

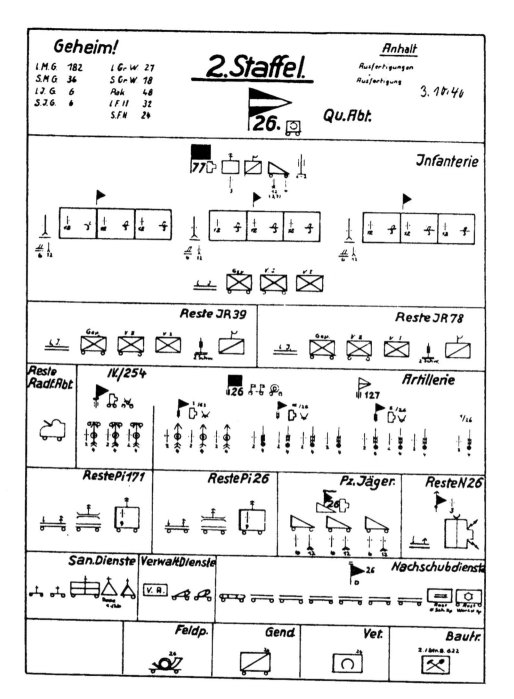

Organisation of the Second Echelon of 26th Infantry Division, 3 October 1940.
This included the remainder of the 39th and 78th Infantry Regiments, the bicycle detachment and the engineer units, plus artillery, anti-tank and support units.

called Assault Companies (*Sturmkompanie*) and three Assault Companies b. The former comprised a command staff with radio and telephone communication troops, a forward reconnaissance mountain battery and three rifle platoons equipped with four heavy mortars, a 3.7 cm PAK and two heavy machine guns. They were augmented by an engineer assault platoon, signals troop and medical personnel. One of these companies also had a *Panzerbüchse* 40 anti-tank rifle, and the second a 4.7 cm PAK in addition to a *Panzerbüchse*. A Sturmkompanie b comprised three heavily armed rifle platoons with four heavy mortars, two heavy machine guns and a 3.7 cm PAK, two engineer groups and a signals troop. Each of the two advance detachments also had two assault guns of assault battery 1/184, two self-propelled PAK from Anti-tank Detachment 521 and two 2 cm flak guns from 1/ Flak Detachment 31. The assault guns and the self-propelled PAK were to be the equivalent of the Sixteenth Army flamethrowing tanks. It is interesting that one company from Tank Detachment (U) C was directly assigned to each advance detachment. The flak guns to be landed on the flanks (five 8.8 cm and ten 2 cm on each) by the heavy pontoon and Herbert ferries or their barges were also assigned to the advance detachments. The advance detachment of 26th Infantry Division was organised like that of the 34th. It comprised six assault companies, three each from 39th and 78th Infantry Regiments. Each company had three rifle platoons, a carrier group and an engineer platoon with a flamethrowing and demolition troop; heavy armament included a light infantry gun, two PAK and two heavy mortars. The 26th Infantry Division's advance detachment had no heavy armour other than a company from Tank Detachment (U) C, though this was compensated for to some extent by the support of the flak troops landing on the flanks.

The orders of battle of 34th and 26th Infantry Divisions and of the corps troops of XXXVIII Corps are given on pages 252 ff. In his planning, General von Manstein focused on the 34th Infantry Division and thus it would have two advance detachments unlike the 26th Infantry Division. After a beachhead had been formed it would be enlarged by a push by the mobile forces of the first echelon. Manstein considered it crucial to take the high ground north of Beachy Head quickly, and he wanted the support of the 6th Mountain Division landing in Zone E, west of Beachy Head, for the troops of XXXVIII Corps pushing northward from Eastbourne. Manstein requested that 6th Mountain Division be placed under his command instead of 26th Infantry Division in order to expand the Army's landing front to the Ouse estuary which was in Zone E. This reorganisation would enable a direct assault on the steep cliffs at Beachy Head, which could only be made by mountain troops. Manstein had a fall-back plan if his request should be turned down which involved the assignment of a reinforced mountain battalion (*Gebirgsjägerbataillon*) under 26th Infantry Division. Army

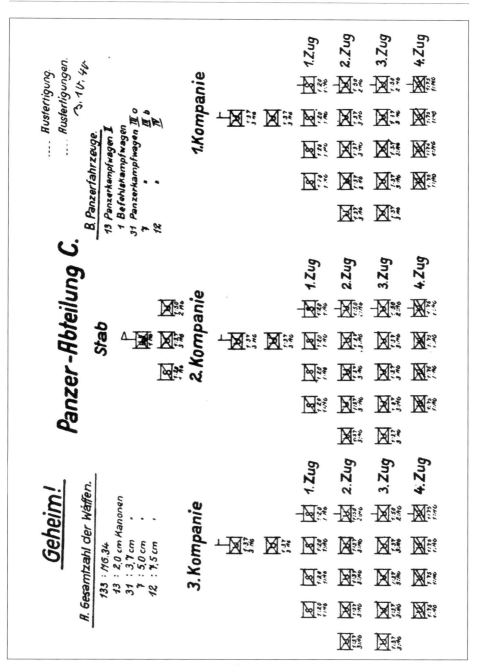

Organisation of Tank Detachment C, 3 October 1940.
'A' gives the total number and calibre of guns, 'B' the number and mark of tank
(*Befehlskampfwagen* is a command tank). The rest of the chart shows the division into staff
and 3 companies, each of 4 platoons (*Zug*), with the weapons assigned.

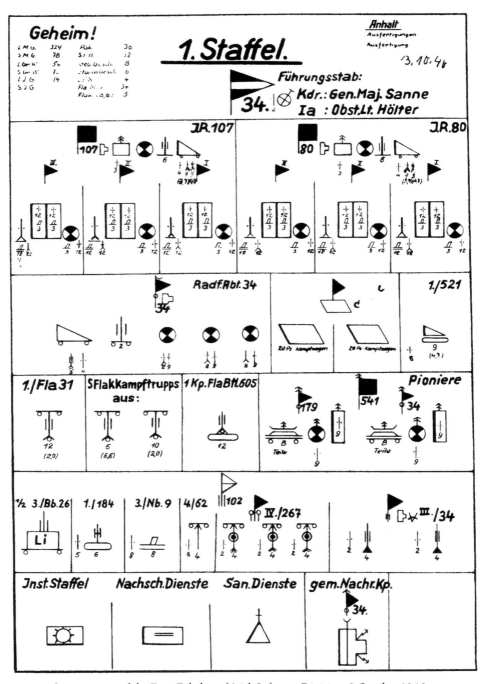

Organisation of the First Echelon of 34th Infantry Division, 3 October 1940.
The principal units were the 107th and 80th Infantry Regiments and apart from having two
20-tank detachments, it was otherwise similar to the first echelon of 26th Infantry Division.

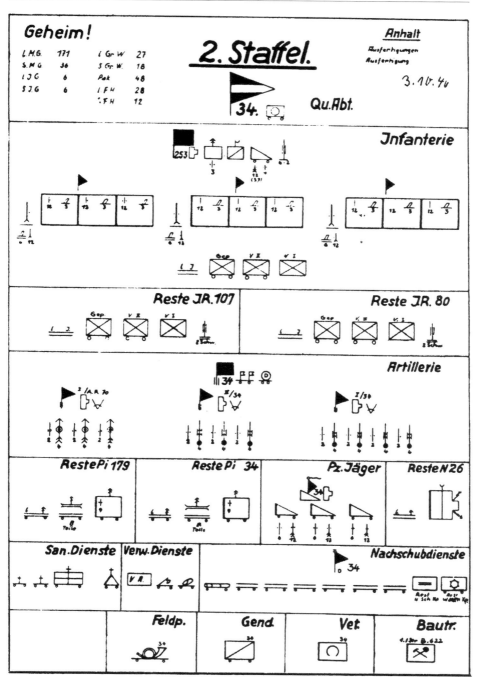

Organisation of the Second Echelon of 34th Infantry Division, 3 October 1940.
As with the second echelon of the 26th, this included the remainder of the first-echelon infantry
regiments and engineer battalions, plus artillery, anti-tank and support units.

records are silent on the answer Manstein received from the High Command and he was thwarted too by the Luftwaffe, which refused to provide paratroops to support the Army's push northward from Beachy Head. The Navy was more co-operative, agreeing to shift a mine barrier planned for an area from Beachy Head to Le Touquet and from Newhaven to Cayeux sur Mer. He made the point that the mine barrage would endanger Transport Fleet D should it drift at all, and that it was too close to the transport fleet's route to preclude shelling by British naval forces. He also pointed out that the attack on Beachy Head would be split in two by the barrier which might prevent the later redisposition of forces. (See also page 283 for a detailed description of the Navy's plan for mining.) Manstein also insisted on the assignment of enough naval forces to open and close gaps in the mine barrage both off the English and Continental coasts. In his requests Manstein demonstrated that type of lateral thinking which is necessary in command of combined operations.

According to the Army Order of 3 October 1940, 34th Infantry Division and its first echelon were to land under cover of smoke along the coast directly south-west of Bexhill and on both sides of the Pevensey Sluice to the estuary at Waller's Haven after neutralising enemy reconnaissance from Bexhill and the heights north-west of it. After they had penetrated the coastal defence they were to make a rapid advance toward the heights at Lunsford's Cross, north of Hooe and near Wartling, taking the first beachhead, expanding on the thrust in a line between west of Bexhill and Lunsford's Cross to the area north of Hooe, Wartling and Rickney, joining up with 26th Infantry Division. As soon as possible the attack would be expanded towards the heights north of Ninfield and Windmill Hill and westwards. Bexhill was to be taken from the rear, allowing the 1st Mountain Division at Combe Haven and 26th Infantry Division north-west of Magham Down to join up.

The 26th Infantry Division was to land with the first echelon between the estuary at Pevensey Haven and Langney Point; a flanking movement from Eastbourne and the heights north of Beachy Head was to be neutralised using smoke and gunfire from warships, auxiliary gunboats, the Herbert ferries and heavy pontoon ferries. British coastal defence was to be penetrated up to the heights at Hankham and west of it as well as at Willingdon in order to establish a beachhead stretching between Rickney, Hankham, Willingdon and to the north-east edge of Eastbourne near Wilmington. As soon as possible, Eastbourne was to be sealed off and the assault extended northward to the Cuckmere River and to a line between Hellingly and Arlington. A commando raid from the 'Brandenburger' special force (see page 206) was to take out the battery at Beachy Head and the radio station north of it. It was hoped that mobile forces would link up with the 6th Mountain Division from Zone E. Eastbourne was to be seized only when the

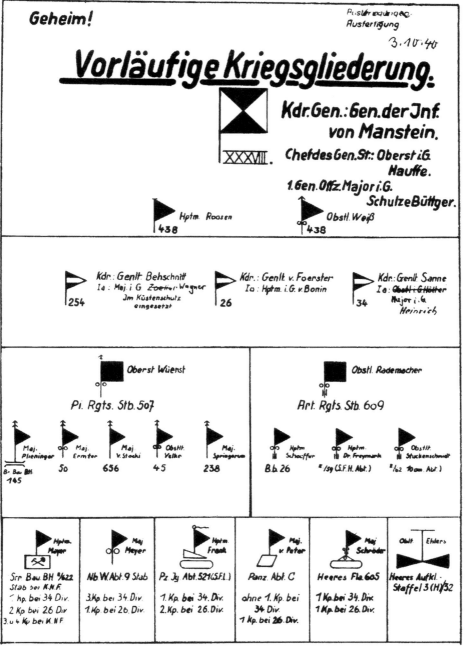

Vorläufige Kriegsgliederung.

Ausfertigung
Ausfertigung

3.10.40.

Kdr.Gen.: Gen.der Inf.
von Manstein.

XXXVIII.

Chef des Gen.St.: Oberst i.G.
Hauffe.
1.Gen.Offz. Major i.G.
SchulzeBüttger.

Hptm. Roosen
438

Obstl. Weiß
438

Kdr.: Genlt. Behschnitt
Ia : Maj. i.G. Zoeller Wagner
Im Küstenschutz
eingesetzt
254

Kdr.: Genlt. v. Foerster
Ia : Hptm. i.G. v. Bonin
26

Kdr.: Genlt. Sanne
Ia : Obstl. i.G.Hötter
Major i.G.
Heinrich
34

Oberst Wüenst
Pi. Rgts. Stb. 507

Obstl. Rademacher
Art. Rgts. Stb. 609

Maj.
Plieninger
Br Bau Btl.
145

Maj.
Ermter
50

Maj.
v. Stochi
656

Obstlt.
Velke
45

Maj.
Springerum
238

Hptm.
Schaeffer
B.b. 26

Hptm.
Dr. Freymark
"/59 (S.F.H. Abt.)

Obstlt.
Stuckenschmidt
"/62 (schw. Abt.)

Hptm.
Mayer
Srr. Bau.Btl. ⁸/622
Stab bei K.N.F.
1. Kp. bei 34 Div.
2 Kp bei 26 Div
3. u 4 Kp bei K.N.F.

Maj.
Meyer
Nb W.Abt. 9 Stab
3.Kp. bei 34.Div.
1.Kp. bei 26.Div.

Hptm.
Frank
Pz.Jg Abt.521(S.Fl.)
1. Kp. bei 34.Div.
2.Kp. bei 26.Div.

Maj.
v. Peter
Panz. Abt. C
ohne 1. Kp. bei
34 Div.
1 Kp. bei 26.Div.

Maj.
Schröder
Heeres Fla.605
1 Kp.bei 34.Div.
1 Kp bei 26.Div.

Obllt.   Ehlers
Heeres Aufkl.-
Staffel 3 (H)/32

Preliminary War Organisation of Corps Troops of XXXVIII Corps, 3 October 1940.
Working down from the General Staff the first level comprises the three divisional commanders,
followed by the staffs of Engineer Regiment 507 and Artillery Regiment 609; the lowest echelon
is formed of Road Building Battalion 8/622, the staff of Rocket Launcher Detachment 9,
Anti-Tank Detachment (Self-propelled) 521, Tank Detachment C, Army Flak Detachment 605,
and Army Air Reconnaissance Staffel 3(H)/32.

lines were firmly in German hands and there were enough forces to do so. Beachy Head was to be taken from the north.

The corps' first operational objective was to secure the line from Heathfield to Uckfield.

Transport Fleet E

Transport Fleet E was to bring VIII and X Corps, with 6th Mountain Division and 8th and 28th Infantry Divisions, from Le Havre to the western landing area, Zone E. The vulnerability of this fleet, which was threatened by the British naval base at Portsmouth, had already been appreciated in the early stages of the planning. Heavily criticised by the German Navy, Transport Fleet E owed its existence to a compromise reached by the OKW. The Navy designated it the Green Route, in contrast to the safer Blue Routes.

This fleet in Le Havre was originally to consist of 50 transports, 200 barges (25 in reserve), 25 tugs, 200 motor fishing vessels and 100 coasters, but the harbour was so cramped that Trouville, Rouen, Caen and Fécamp were later used for loading. KMD Le Havre described these conditions in a report of 17 November 1940:

> It was impossible to load 600 vessels in the time allotted and they could not be redistributed. It was equally impossible to send them through the locks since there was only one lock chamber and one harbour exit available for the large steamers, both of which could be used only at certain times due to the large rise and fall of the tide. Since the locks could be easily put out of action through air raids (which had occurred once), the steamers for the advance detachment and the first echelon (a) were moored in the tidal harbour, though in groups of two to three. After air attacks seven steamers were shifted to Rouen and Caen, and some of the coasters and motor fishing vessels to Fécamp, Honfleur and Trouville. Relocating the ships from Le Havre and transiting the locks into Caen would take two full days, since passing down the Seine estuary and along to Caen is possible only at high tide and in daylight. Up until 15 September there were no tugs at Le Havre for picking up and mooring the steamers; after that there were three. The trawlers the Navy assigned as tugs were inadequate. The lack of tugs was most acutely felt with the arrival of convoys, which could have up to fifteen steamers.
>
> The steamers, trawlers, coasters and motor fishing boats were satisfactorily equipped. The barges were another matter: many were not properly equipped nor degaussed; most of the engines of the powered barges were faulty and the crews were not familiar with the equipment. The harbour master provided training personnel which enabled 175 barges to be made fully operational by mid-October. The crews on the German steamers were satisfactory,

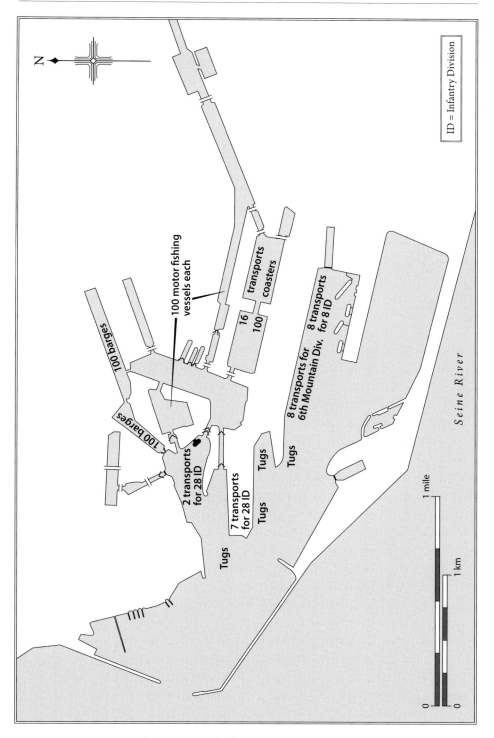

ID = Infantry Division

N

100 barges

100 barges

100 motor fishing vessels each

16 transports
100 coasters

8 transports for 6th Mountain Div.

8 transports for 8 ID

2 transports for 28 ID

7 transports for 28 ID

Tugs

Tugs

Tugs

Tugs

Tugs

Tugs

Seine River

1 mile

1 km

0

0

Berthing plan for the harbour at Le Havre.

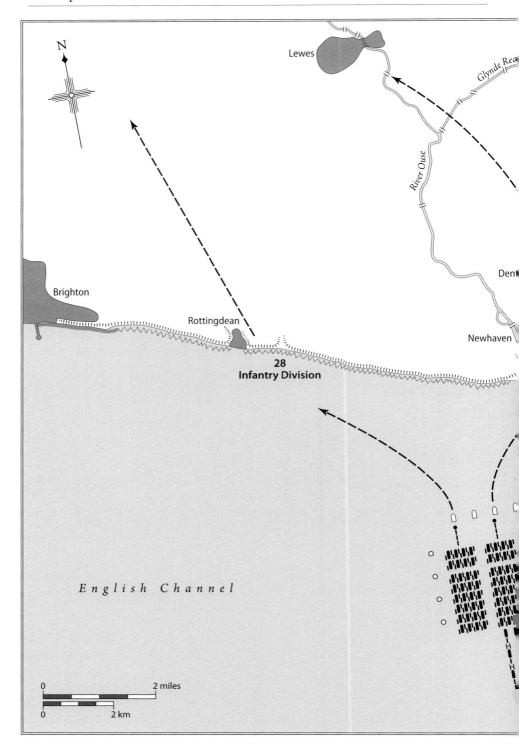

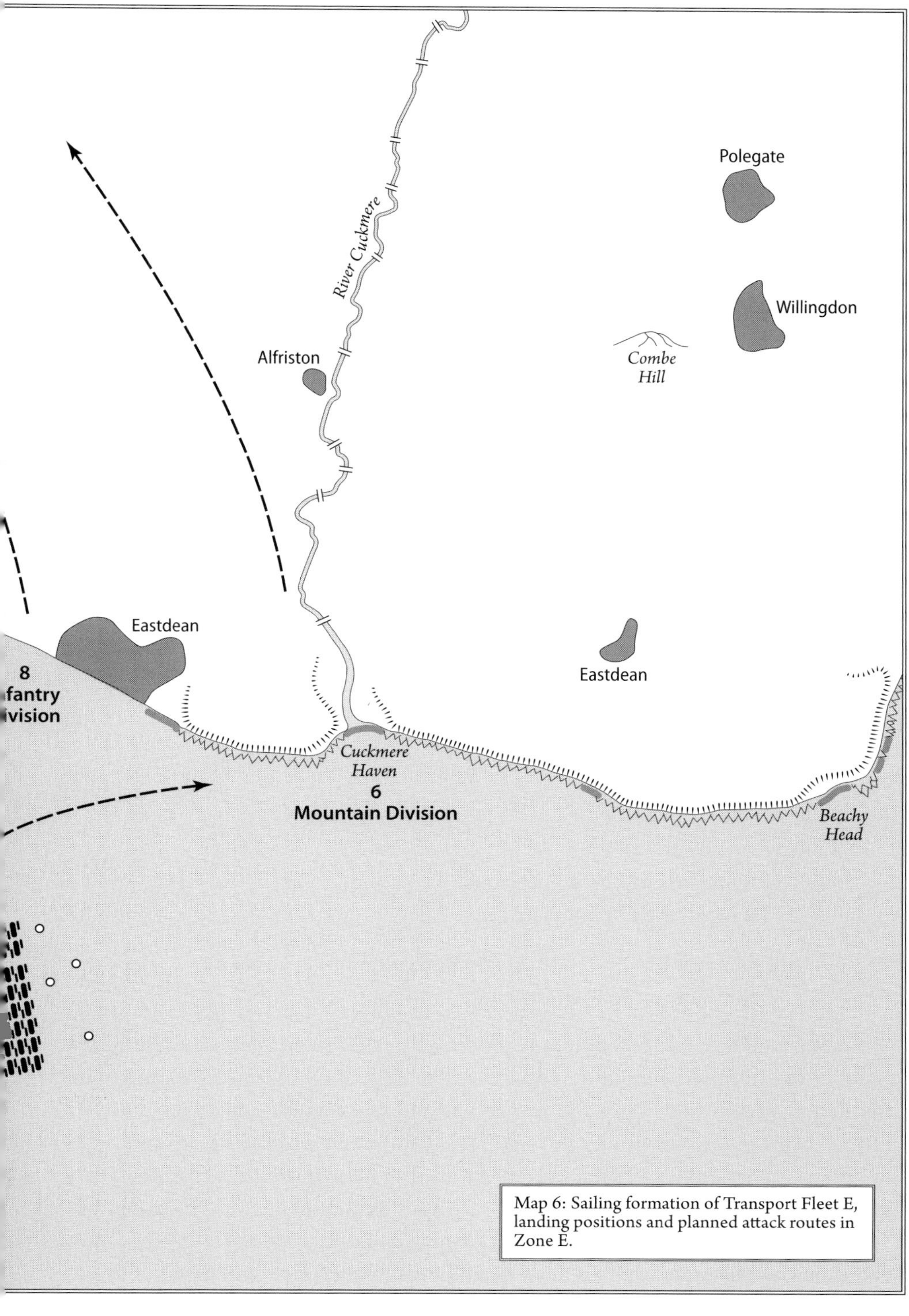

River Cuckmere

Polegate

Willingdon

Combe
Hill

Alfriston

Eastdean

8
Infantry
Division

Eastdean

Cuckmere
Haven

6
Mountain Division

Beachy
Head

Map 6: Sailing formation of Transport Fleet E,
landing positions and planned attack routes in
Zone E.

unlike those of the French vessels; this inadequacy could not be alleviated by assigning 12 dockers to each steamer. Crew discipline aboard the larger vessels such as steamers and trawlers was bad, in contrast to that on the smaller craft. Air raids reduced morale until bomb-proof crew quarters were erected and air defence was strengthened.

The KMD estimated that it would take the advance detachment 55 hours, and the convoys 72 hours to leave Le Havre. VIII Corps planned to load 8th Infantry Division's advance detachment at Le Havre and echelons 1a and 1b partly at Le Havre, and partly at Rouen; 28th Infantry Division would also load its advance detachment at Le Havre and its echelons 1a and 1b at Le Havre and Fécamp. The 6th Mountain Division's advance detachment would load at Caen and its first and second echelons at Trouville and Le Havre.

This arrangement seems all the more peculiar since the harbour at Trouville was small and unsuitable for loading transports. The commander of Transport Fleet E, Captain Scheurlen, divided the incoming coasters and fishing vessels into three flotillas for the advance detachments of the three divisions and anchored them at Fécamp, Le Havre and Trouville, which were far more able to cope with them. The Army sent a few additional coasters and motor fishing vessels to Dieppe, probably for training and testing.

Naval Commander West reported the organisation of Transport Fleet E on 14 September 1940 to be:

> Advance Detachment   (Captain Scheurlen)   Le Havre
> 200 motor fishing vessels (20 each abreast)
> 100 coasters (20 each abreast)
>
> Convoy 4 (Echelon 1a)   (Captain Brocksien)   Le Havre
> 25 transports with 50 empty barges
> 25 trawlers with 75 empty barges
>
> Convoy 5 (Echelon 1b)   (Captain Brocksien)   Le Havre
> 25 transports with 50 empty barges

Transport Fleet E faced different problems to the other fleets because of the rougher seas it might encounter and a possible British naval attack. To minimise the damage from high seas, the transports and twenty-five additional trawlers towed their barges empty which would later be used for unloading. It was hoped to reduce the risk of loss to Royal Navy attacks by distributing the three infantry and mountain division regiments of the advance detachments in 300 small craft. The advance detachments of the other transport fleets consisted of only one or two battalions per division, whereas Transport Fleet E had a full regiment per division;

Captain Ernst Scheurlen, commander
of Transport Fleet E.

with the three divisions being
transported, this resulted in an
advance detachment with the
infantry strength of a division.
On the other hand, they were
very short of heavy armament,
which would have followed
in the convoys, though only
one convoy would sail directly
behind the advance detachment
and even then only if the way
was clear. If not, it was to sail
with the other convoy along
an indirect route behind the
mine barriers to the English
coast. Depending on British
resistance, the convoys could
sail to Zone E or unload in Zone D. If the Army troops landed in Zone D they
would have had to link up with the advance detachment forces overland.

This lack of heavy armament for the advance detachment was recognised and
Transport Fleet E was later reorganised:

Advance Detachment (Captain Scheurlen)
>200 motor fishing vessels
>100 coasters
>10 transports, 6 of which with 2 half-loaded barges each, and 4 each with a
>>Herbert Ferry and its associated barge
>2 fishing trawlers each with 3 empty barges
>4 ocean-going tugs with a total of 4 Type B barges and a Type C barge for
>>1 Company, Tank Detachment (U) D

Echelon 1a (Commander von Jagow)
>15 transports, 11 of which with 2 half loaded barges each
>4 with a Herbert Ferry and associated barge

Echelon 1b (Captain Brocksien)
>25 transports with 2 loaded barges each
>21 fishing trawlers with 3 empty barges each

An exercise with coasters and assault boats near Emden gives an impression of the planned
landing of the advance detachment of Transport Fleet E.

Map 6 shows the planned formation of the motorboats, which was 2,600 m
wide and 2,000 m long. Each division was to have its own flotilla of coasters
and trawlers: the 60th Motorboat Flotilla for 6th Mountain Division, the 80th
for 8th Infantry Division, the 280th for 28th Infantry Division and so on. Each
flotilla would consist of thirty-two auxiliary sailing coasters and sixty-four motor
fishing vessels, which in turn were broken down into four groups each with eight
coasters and sixteen fishing vessels. Two fishing vessels were assigned to every
coaster; fishing vessels with an 'a' after their number were stationed to starboard,
and those with a 'b' to port. Lieutenant Commander (Reserve) Beerman was in
command of the Motorboat Fleet. It was protected by three patrol flotillas and
five heavy auxiliary gunboats, the latter's medium-calibre guns being considered
good for coastal bombardment and a relatively good defence against light British
naval forces. An attempt to counterbalance the lack of heavy armament was also
made by carefully distributing the Herbert ferries, each of which had an 8.8 cm
flak gun.

In addition to the problems at sea, the troops landing in Zone E had a variety
of natural barriers to overcome, among them rocky beaches and sheer cliffs
between Brighton and Beachy Head. The better beaches between Brighton and
Worthing could not be used because they were too far from reinforcements

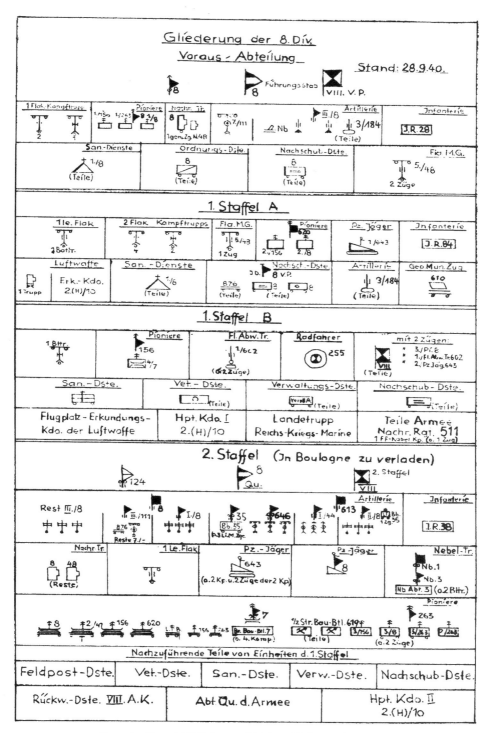

Organisation of 8th Infantry Division, 28 September 1940.

The basic divisions were: Advance Detachment; Echelon 1a; Echelon 1b; Echelon 2 (to be embarked at Boulogne) and finally some elements of the 1st echelon to be shipped later.

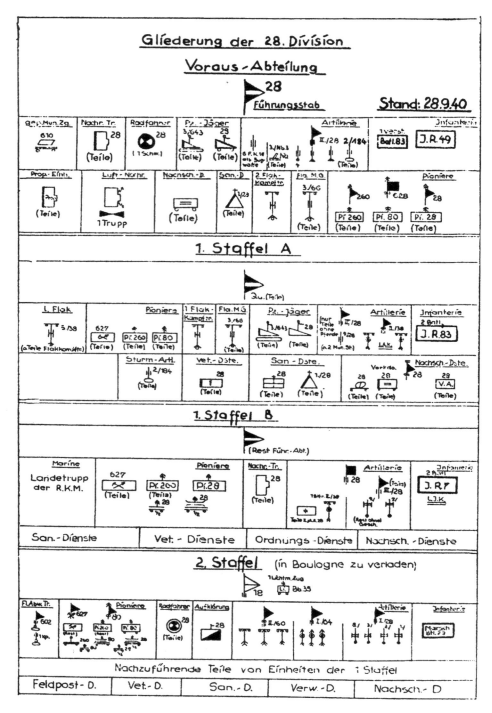

Organisation of 28th Infantry Division, 28 September 1940.
As with 8th Infantry Division, the structure is Advance Detachment, Echelon 1a, Echelon 1b,
Echelon 2 (from Boulogne) and remaining elements of the 1st Echelon to be shipped later.

from neighbouring Zone D, thus forcing them to use the three narrow sectors in the Cuckmere and Ouse estuaries and at Rottingdean, which were the only possibilities in the area. The narrowness of the landing sectors, particularly near Rottingdean, is probably the reason why the reinforcements were to land in Zone D. There was also an old fort at Newhaven which was suspected to be armed with four medium guns, and the western shore of the River Ouse was littered with small emplacements.

The landing zones and the assaults to be carried out by the various divisions are shown on Map 6; the orders of battle of 28th and 8th Infantry Divisions and 6th Mountain Division as well as VIII and X Army Corps are shown on pages 268–72.

The broad-based plan placed 6th Mountain Division and 30th Infantry Division (later dropped) under X Corps; in the plan for Sealion as it finally stood, all three divisions were placed under VIII Corps, with X Corps along with its staff and corps troops assigned to it.

The strength of the advance detachments can be seen from the orders of battle of the divisions. The 8th and 28th Infantry Divisions had four assault guns of their assault batteries 3/184 and 2/184 in the advance detachments and the remainder in echelon 1a. The 6th Mountain Division had a company from Tank Detachment (U) D for the advance detachment. Advance detachments of 8th Infantry Division and 6th Mountain Division each had a flak combat unit on the Herbert ferry and its associated barge, and 28th Infantry Division two units. The 8th Infantry Division integrated two flak combat units in echelon 1a, and the other two divisions one each.

The Luftwaffe had turned down the Army's request (see page 228) for one parachute regiment to land at Brighton and the heights north of Beachy Head. There are no records concerning the role of the divisions after landing, though Map 6 gives a general idea. The second echelon was to sail from Boulogne and had to be prepared to land in Zone D if necessary.

The Second Wave

The operational plan for the Second Wave did not have to be as detailed as for the First, since the bridgehead would already have been established. The Second Wave's objective was to break out from this bridgehead and defeat the British Army throughout rapid armoured attacks. Sixteenth and the Ninth Armies were each assigned one armoured corps (*Panzerkorps*) for this task, consisting of two *Panzer* divisions and a motorised division. In the case of Sixteenth Army these were XLI Corps with 8th and 10th Panzer Divisions, and 29th (Motorised) Infantry Division, in addition to the two motorised regiments *Großdeutschland* and *SS-Leibstandarte Adolf Hitler*, V Corps with 12th and 30th Infantry Divisions was not assigned to the Second Wave until the beginning of September, after it

Gliederung der 6. Geb. Div.

Voraus-Abteilung

Stand: 22.9.40.

Führungsstab 6

Pioniere	Nachrichten-Tr.	Artillerie		II./G.A.R. 118	1./G.A.R.118	Infanterie
2./268 1/91	91 (Teile)	1.Batt. III./142 Nb				Geb.J.R.141

Sanitäts-Dienste	1 Flak-Kampftrupp	Panzer-Truppe
1./169 (Teile)		1 Kompanie

1. Staffel A

gep. Mun.Zg.	Fla-MG	Nachr.Tr.	Pioniere	Pz.Jäger	Artillerie		Infanterie
	2./46	91 1gem.Zg.(Teile) Na.48	268 Pi.51 (Teile)	169	118 III.142	2./G.A.R.118	G.J.R.143

		1 Flak-kampftr.	Luftwaffe	San.-Dienste
			1gem.Zg.	1./169 (Teile)

1. Staffel B

		Fl.Abw.Tr.	Pioniere	Pz.Jäger	Radfahrer	Aufkl.Abt.	Artillerie
		1kp./602	F.Pi. 23 Pi.51 (Teile)	47	402	112	I./752

Sanitäts-Dienste	Ordnungs-Dienste	Verwaltungs-Dienste	Nachschub-Dienste
1./169 (Teile) (Teile)	340	Vpfl.A G.13	91

2. Staffel (in Boulogne zu verladen)

133

Fl.Abw.Tr.	Nachrichten-Tr.		91				Pioniere		Artillerie
1kp / 602	91 (Teile)	3.II./679		268 2.44	4./II 649	3./51 91	91	I./231	I./118 Rest I.u.II./

Nachzuführende Teile von Einheiten der 1. Staffel				
	143	141	L.J.143	L.J.141

Feldpost-D	Veterinär-D.	Sanitäts-D.	Verwaltungs-D.	Nachschub-D.

The Organisation of the 6th Mountain Division, 28 September 1940.
The structure of Advance Detachment and sybsequent echelons is the same as for the infantry divisions.

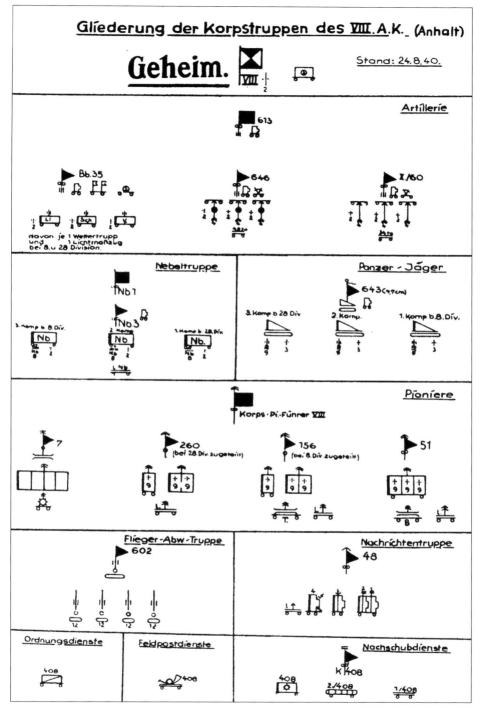

Organisation of Corps Troops of VIII Corps, 24 August 1940.
Headed secret (*Geheim*) and featuring artillery, rocket launcher, anti-tank units, engineer, AA
and communications units, and at bottom military police, field post, and logistics services.

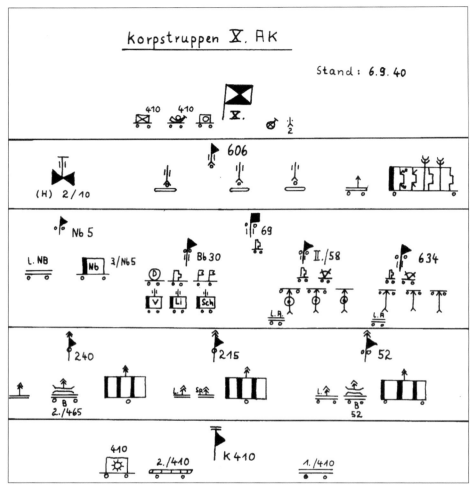

Organisation of Corps Troops of X Army Corps, 6 September 1940.

had been decided to transport the second echelons of VII and XIII Corps' four divisions in the First Wave, in order to have them available immediately as a unified fighting force on British soil.

The Ninth Army had earmarked XV Corps with 4th and 7th Panzer Divisions and 20th (motorised) Infantry Division for the Second Wave.

Only the orders of battle of XLI Army Corps remain from those forces of the Second Wave, and even then those of 10th Panzer Division have gone missing. It is interesting to note that the two élite regiments *Großdeutschland* and *Leibstandarte Adolf Hitler* were both assigned an assault battery.

Protecting the Invasion Fleet

Diversionary Manoeuvres

A considerable amount of planning for Sealion was devoted to diversionary manoeuvres; the Navy in particular was anxious to draw the British Navy off through a feint and ensure the safety of the Sealion fleet. The Navy wanted to send major combatants into the Atlantic and to launch a simulated landing fleet into the North Sea. The Army redeployed troops and held loading and landing exercises, reinforcing these by spreading rumours of invasion in particular areas. From an embarkation zone stretching from Oslo to Bergen, XXXVI Higher Command in Norway was ordered to simulate an invasion of the east coast of Britain between Edinburgh and Newcastle. The XXXVII Higher Command in the Netherlands was to threaten a move against the east coast of Britain south of the Wash and XXXI Higher Command was to prepare a feint attack from the German Bight on the British east coast.

The XXXVI and XXXI High Commands were to work together with the simulated landing fleet; the whole operation was co-ordinated by the XXI Army Command. The XXXVI Army Command's operation was to be implemented by 69th and 214th Infantry Division, corps troops, Tank Detachment 40 and a heavy flak detachment. The ostensible target was Berwick-upon-Tweed, south of the Firth of Forth while the XXXI High Command was to have Blyth as an objective, using the 163rd and another infantry division as well as corps troops.

The feint against the east coast of England between the Wash and Harwich by XXXVII High Command with 197th Infantry Division and the Special Purpose SS Division obviously did not assemble much equipment for this operation, since the Navy in the Netherlands was unable to provide ships for loading exercises, let alone diversionary manoeuvres. The landing preparations of Fourth and Seventh Armies of Army Group B in north-west France were more extensive, having as their objective a simulated invasion of the southern coast of Ireland between Wexford and Dungarvan, called *Fall Grün* (Operation Green). The Fourth Army commanded XI Corps with 211th, 290th and 72nd Infantry Divisions and smaller units and Seventh Army included I Army Corps. Fourth Army was supposedly to jump off from the French coast between Lorient and the Loire estuary. Special orders were given to the engineer units which were to equip small ships between 250 and 500 grt for unloading on an unprepared coast, and build all sorts of rafts and ferries derived from bridging gear.

The diary of the Naval Commander for Western France described the maritime exercise of Seventh Army with the 263rd Infantry Division between 1 and 3 October 1940. On the morning of the 1st, the steamers *Frost* and *Leontios Teryazos* were loaded in Bordeaux with 700 troops, four field howitzers and a number of

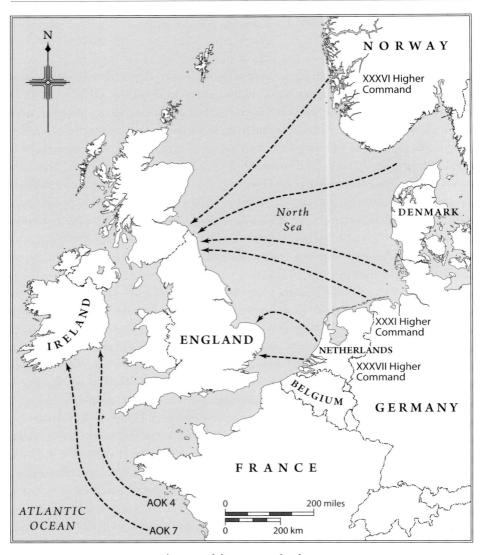

Threatened diversionary landings.

field kitchens. The Greek and Swedish steamer crews protested against 'sailing against England for Germany' and were dismissed and replaced with German Navy crews. The remainder of the troops, 1,600 men, were loaded at 1300 hrs, along with light field howitzers, field kitchens and engineer equipment onto the steamers *Alabama*, *Kolente* and *Cap Hadid* at Le Verdon. At 1930 hrs the convoy and the two ships from Bordeaux departed, with mine countermeasures provided by 2nd Minesweeper Flotilla and *Sperrbrecher 5*. The transports anchored in the Bay Anglaise off La Coubre under cover of darkness. On the morning of the 2nd, a battalion from 485th Infantry Regiment was landed on the coast in dinghies with guns and field kitchens. Later the convoy returned and landed its troops at Le Verdon. The Luftwaffe and the Navy discussed plans for radio deception in support of these operations. Increased frequency of coded radio transmissions on certain channels, broadcast from Brittany – probably from shore stations – were to give the British the idea that the Germans were gearing up for an invasion from there. On the other hand, special radio transmissions on the coast from Vlissingen to Cherbourg were thought to disguise the level of activity from the real landing fleet.

Just before the real invasion, individual aircraft were to imitate an invasion fleet away from the actual zones, drawing off British defences. These three operations were code-named Bluff plus an additional designation. Bluff Alfred, for example, was carried out by an He 111 of the 9th Fliegerdivision, which would take off from the airfield at Gilzen Rijen and sweep the British coast between the estuaries of the Thames and the Humber. In addition to special radio equipment, the He 111 would carry 10 kg bombs in four bays. Bluff Heinz was the code name for the deployment of an He 111 of Luftflotte 3 against the south coast of England; Bluff Erika for a similar run by a FW 200 of KG 40 against the south coast of Ireland. Each of these aircraft also carried a Navy officer and an experienced radio intelligence operator. All these sorties were to take place at S Time minus 30 hours. Before take-off and during flight, British radio broadcasts were to be monitored so that a false message could be transmitted at an appropriate moment. Since the Germans had cracked the RAF code and in part those of auxiliary warships, a false message could, with a little luck, be slipped in by carefully noting the idiosyncrasies of the British broadcasts and the choice of radio code names. Imaginary sightings of German warships, transports or aircraft could be reported; in southern Ireland for instance such a report could be made to seem as if it emanated from an Irish coastal steamer.

In addition to radio deception along the coast, it was also possible to fire rockets at low level, drop small bombs which detonated in the water to simulate artillery fire and deploy tracer bombs, all of which were to point to an imminent landing.

About seven hours before S Time, a German submarine off the southern coast of Ireland was to begin transmitting a message in German code, made more obvious by interrupting any broadcast which might have just started. The transmission was to be repeated on all naval channels, hopefully provoking a lot of radio traffic. The value of these measures should not be overestimated as the main threat to the British south coast was clearly visible. On the other hand, the effort was small and might have caused some confusion.

Herbstreise, Operation Autumn Journey, has already been mentioned. This was a full-scale operation planned for the North Sea, which first saw the light of day

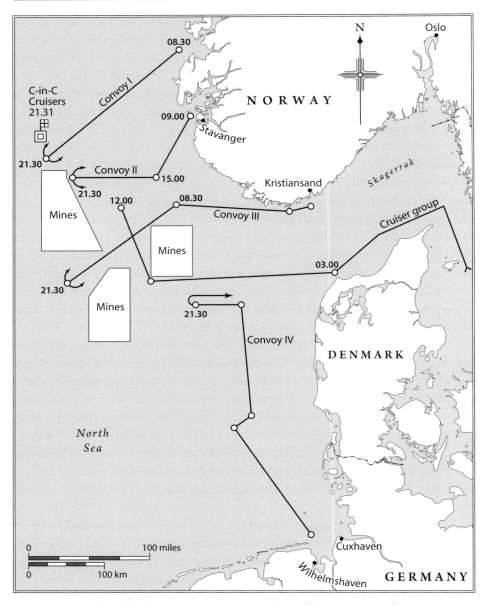

Plan of the diversionary operation *Herbstreise* (Autumn Journey).

in a letter of 1 August 1940 to the Naval Operations Office from General Admiral Carls, *Chef des Marinegruppenkommandos Ost*, whose duties were taken over by Naval Group North. He recommended a feint operation to the north of the actual invasion. This operation would entail troop redeployments in Denmark and Norway and intensive aerial reconnaissance and air strikes on Scotland and the

Orkney and Shetland Islands. Subsequently, in southern Norway, seven to ten freighters of about 2,000 grt were to be assembled and given false funnels and masts in order to make them appear larger. These empty ships were to be escorted and followed by two small hospital ships to give the British the impression of a troop convoy. General Admiral Carls also put forward a landing by a small force of about 600 to 1,000 men on the Shetland Islands as had been done during the occupation and defence of Narvik. The Naval Operations Office did not go along with the latter proposal, though it agreed in principle with the rest.

The Army made a similar proposal on 21 August, recommending a paratroop drop on the Isle of Wight to capture the British coastal batteries and put the naval base at Portsmouth out of action but the Luftwaffe rejected this on the grounds that the troops could not be resupplied.

In the meantime, the German Navy was still on familiar territory with its plans to have the heavy cruiser *Admiral Hipper* and the 'pocket battleship' *Admiral Scheer* sail in conjunction with the deception and actual landing fleets. These ships were to appear suddenly about five or six days before S Day at the British blockade line of the Northern Patrol in the Denmark Strait and between the Faroe Islands and Iceland, attacking auxiliary cruisers on station there. It was hoped that this manoeuvre would draw off considerable numbers of the British Home Fleet, which would then have to return to their home ports to refuel before Sealion. A renewed attack on the Northern Patrol was also feasible on S Day plus 3 in order to divert British attention from Autumn Journey.

After the landing, the ships would operate in the North Atlantic, striking at and, with some luck, destroying the weakly defended Canadian convoys, thereby creating a diversion. In the event, it took longer to refit the *Admiral Scheer* than anticipated, and the operation would have had to count on the *Admiral Hipper* alone. The value of such an operation seems minimal: a nation facing invasion would likely know very well which threat was the more serious.

The *Seekriegsleitung* strongly favoured the diversionary operation, and threw in the liners *Europa*, *Bremen*, *Gneisenau* and *Potsdam* for good measure. The planning for Autumn Journey took on such proportions that it is tempting to wonder whether the Navy was most interested in the diversion or the real operation. Four convoys were set up; troops were to be embarked and then disembarked in darkness not far away; and the ships were then to continue on their journey.

Convoy I comprised the steamers *Stettiner Greif*, *Dr Heinrich Wiegand* and *Pommern*; these would be escorted by two ships from 17th Anti-submarine flotilla (*U-Jagdflotille*), two from 11th Minesweeper Flotilla and *Schiff 47* and *Schiff 7*. On S Day minus 3 the steamers in Bergen were to embark troops of 69th Infantry Division by about 1900 hrs and sail. Unloading of troops would be aided by the six boats of 55th Flotilla of the coastal defence unit at Bekkervig.

Convoy II consisted of the *Steinburg, Bugsee, Ilse L. M. Russ* and *Flottbeck*, protected by two boats each from 17th Anti-submarine Flotilla, 11th Minesweeper Flotilla, 11th Patrol Flotilla and 7th Torpedo Flotilla. The freighters would load troops from 24th Infantry Division at Stavanger by 1900 hrs on S Day minus 3 and unload them by 2400 hrs at Haugesund.

Convoy III was comprised of the *Iller, Sabine, Howaldt* and *Lumme*, protected by two boats of 17th Anti-submarine Flotilla as well as by four old torpedo boats. Troops of 214th Infantry Division would load at Arendal on S Day minus 3 by 1000 hrs, enabling the convoy to be at Kristiansand by 1700 hrs, where the troops would disembark.

Convoy IV comprised the fast steamers *Europa, Bremen, Potsdam* and *Gneisenau*, protected by the light cruiser *Emden*, three old torpedo boats from the Torpedo Training Flotilla and two others. The *Europa* and *Bremen* were to pretend to load at Wesermunde (now Bremerhaven), while the *Potsdam* and the *Gneisenau* would take troops on board at Hamburg, but unload them again at night at Cuxhaven.

Long-range defence was the task of a cruiser group under the command of the C-in-C Cruisers (*Befehlshaber der Kreuzer – Bdk*) aboard the cruiser *Nürnberg*, who was also assigned the light cruiser *Köln*, the gunnery training ship *Bremse*, three fleet escorts (F-boats) and two torpedo boats from the 7th Flotilla.

The courses of these convoys are shown in the map on page 276. Convoys I, II and III were to disperse on S Day minus 2 at about 2100 hrs, the individual ships turning and travelling at maximum speed towards the coast of Norway, where they would then mingle with the coastal traffic once it was daylight. All these units were to remain on alert status for any subsequent operations. Convoy IV, unlike the others, was to keep in formation and return to the Baltic via the Skagerrak. Should the cruiser group encounter British naval forces, they were to attack inferior forces but avoid superior ones, even if this meant sacrificing the convoys.

Radio deception was also planned for the feint. The three steam trawlers *Sachsen, Fritz Hohmann* and *Adolf Vinnen*, stationed to the north-west of Iceland and west of the Norwegian coast, were to report on the movements of large troop transports northward and on the German warships in the Atlantic. If the false landing fleet were not spotted, the Germans would remedy the situation by reporting its sighting via a British aircraft transmitter.

Coastal Artillery

The German High Command, and Hitler in particular, appreciated the importance of an artillery blockade of the Dover Straits which was plausible given that only twenty-one miles separated the English and French coasts.

The Naval Operations Office seems to have regarded a complete artillery blockade of the Dover Straits as possible. The splinter damage from the highly sensitive explosive rounds, even with near-misses, was regarded as formidable. Some also put faith in artillery support of a landing operation from the long-range batteries near Calais. But the Chief of the Naval Ordnance Bureau opposed this on 12 June, on the grounds that only a 38 cm Navy battery and two 28 cm Army railway batteries with the K5 gun, could be used; furthermore, their low rate of fire and large dispersion would have made them unsuitable for fire support of the landing troops. The issue of coastal batteries was brought up at a meeting on 15 July with Hitler at the Berghof in Obersalzberg. It was agreed that shelling from the French coast would not be effective against the Royal Navy, and the German Army thus planned to land motorised batteries in England as quickly as possible to enable a blockade of the Straits of Dover to be made from both sides of the Channel. The order was issued to set up every available Army and Navy heavy artillery piece along the Channel coast. The Navy estimated three months for this work, which would be too late for the landing. The Todt Organisation was lumbered with this almost insoluble problem and began work on 22 July. The battery *Großer Kurfürst* at Pillau was dismantled and re-erected in the Pas de Calais, where three guns were provisionally ready to fire by 31 July. At the beginning of August the four 28 cm traversing turrets of this battery were fully operational, as were all of the Army's railway guns. The latter comprised six 28 cm K5 guns in two batteries and a 21 cm K12 gun with a range of 115 km. These two types were only for land bombardment while the other railway guns could be used – though only to a limited extent because of their slow traversing speeds, long loading times and their ammunition types – against maritime targets. These were the eight 28 cm Kurze Bruno in two batteries; two 28 cm Schwere Bruno; three 28 cm Lange Bruno; three 24 cm Theodor and two 24 cm Theodor Bruno, the latter two of which were set up at Cherbourg. Six 24 cm K3 guns (motorised), six Czech 24 cm guns (motorised) and ten 21 cm K39 guns (motorised) were also positioned in the Pas de Calais. These too were only of limited use against naval targets. The Army guns were placed under Navy command to ensure uniform fire control.

In mid-August three more heavy naval batteries were operational: *Friedrich August* with three 30.5 cm guns which had come from a battery with the same name on the island of Wangerooge, *Prinz Heinrich* with two 28 cm guns and *Oldenburg* with two 24 cm guns. The final one was *Siegfried*, two 38 cm guns, which was ready by mid-September and was later renamed *Todt* to commemorate the great efforts of the eponymous organisation that had employed 9,000 men in setting up these batteries.

The Army and Navy also set up a number of other medium and light batteries totalling 444 barrels, on the Dutch–Belgian–French coast, though these were to protect coastal shipping routes and harbours.

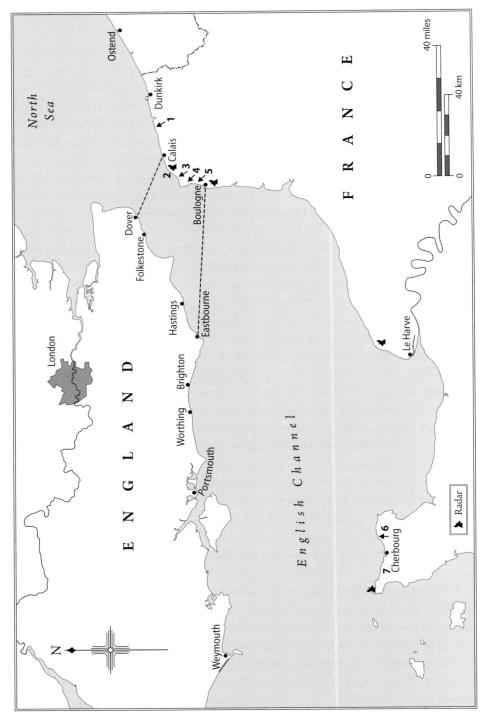

Positions of heavy coastal artillery: 1. Batterie *Oldenburg*; 2. Batterie *Prinz Heinrich*;
3. Batterie *Großer Kurfürst*; 4. Batterie *Siegfried*; 5. Batterie *Friedrich August*;
6. Batterie *Hamburg*; 7. Batterie *Yorck*.

A *DeTeGerät* (fire-control radar for sea targets) was built at Blanc Nez and another one at Cap d'Alprech for the heavy batteries. These were able to reach targets to a range of 40 km, including small British patrol craft inshore off the English coast. The radar at Cap d'Alprech had a range as far as Dungeness and Rye Bay and the one at Blanc Nez as far as the Downs off Deal. By the middle of September these radars were complemented by a *DeTeGerät* at Cap de la Hague and a *Fern DeTeGerät* long-range radar at Cap d'Antifer near Le Havre. The artillery used spotting aircraft in addition to this radar ranging equipment for fire control.

Sixteenth Army placed Artillery Command 106 and its associated units at the head of the Second Wave in order to lend fire support to the transport fleet as early as possible, also from the British side of the Channel (see page 205). They were assigned two 15 cm detachments with a total of twenty-four guns and six 10 cm detachments with seventy-two guns and two reconnaissance detachments. Probably the first third of these could have been in place by the end of the first week. These batteries would have greatly reduced the threat from small British warships such as destroyers from the eastern flank, and were thus set up to cover the routes from Dover to Calais and Hastings to Boulogne. Individual batteries were earmarked for Ninth Army. Naturally, these batteries could not have covered the complete western access to the transport zones, but a large area would have been within range.

On 12 August the heavy artillery in the Pas de Calais experimented with shelling British convoys in the Straits of Dover. The first major shelling of a convoy of thirteen merchant ships and two destroyers was on 22 August and lasted between 1030 hrs and 1300 hrs. Artillery spotter aircraft reported two hits. In the second half of August the British answered German artillery fire with a 14 in (35.6 cm) gun and later also with two 9.2 in (23.4 cm) railway guns, although with only limited effect due to the long range. On 9 September German Army batteries opened up a heavy attack on Dover using Czech 24 cm guns. A total of 226 shells were rained down on a British convoy of twenty ships, forcing it to disperse, with four ships returning to Dover and two going inshore to Deal; smoke poured from one of the ships. According to Churchill, this was the heaviest barrage of this sort. Since the Royal Navy was increasing the number of sorties into the Channel by light cruisers and destroyers to bombard the landing craft of the Sealion fleet in their embarkation harbours, the Germans turned their heavy batteries against this threat as well. The batteries *Oldenburg* and *Prinz Heinrich* shelled a number of British destroyers on 10 September, firing seven 28 cm and twelve 24 cm rounds, though without much success. The order was given on 13 September to use only light and medium artillery against light British naval forces to save barrel wear in the larger guns. On 26 September, for instance, the *DeTeGerät* on the Cap d'Alprech spotted two targets at 0338hrs, which were engaged at 0410 hrs

Ex-Czech 24 cm battery test-firing on 9 September 1940 from near Cap Griz Nez.
(*Dr Zimmermann*)

by three medium coastal batteries in three rapid salvoes. The target veered and gave the valid identification signal. Oddly enough, there were no German naval vessels in this area. On the night of 30 September the British monitor *Erebus* left Dover and fired fifteen rounds on Calais, answered by nine rounds from *Prinz Heinrich* battery after ranging by the *DeTeGerät*. *Erebus* repeated its attacks on 11 October 1940 by firing on Dunkirk and on 10/11 February 1941 on Ostend. The same happened again on 11 October when the British battleship *Revenge* fired on Cherbourg at 0430 hrs. The *Hamburg* 24 cm coastal battery fired without the aid of radar equipment, but had enough straddles to force the British ship to withdraw. Two other batteries which were not linked up with the *DeTeGerät* were unable to fire.

However, the bark of the German coastal batteries was, in the long run, worse than their bite. No British merchantman was sunk by these batteries, and according to Grinnell Milne, it took 1,880 rounds to damage seven British merchant ships in 1940. Only the loss of the old auxiliary minesweeper *Brighton Queen* off Dover on 1 June 1940 could be chalked up to the German coastal batteries. To balance the picture, though, it should be noted that large British merchant ships were unable to pass through the Straits of Dover safely again until the German coastal batteries had been neutralised. These batteries undoubtedly would have taken their toll of heavy ships if Sealion had been launched, though probably not of lighter craft.

Mines

Hitler, the Army High Command and the OKW all attached a great deal of importance to mines for protecting the transport fleets. The Navy regarded mines in a more critical light, being aware that they offered no certain protection and were also effective only if not swept by British ships. Moreover, the strong currents and large rise and fall of the tides in the Dover Straits would reduce the effectiveness of moored mines. The Navy anticipated that most of the mines would lie at too great a depth to endanger British ships if they were moored so as not to float too close to the surface at low tide. With this problem in mind, the EMC tidal mine (*Gezeitenmine*) was specially developed for Operation Sealion. The EMC mine body was suspended by a light snagline at a uniform depth from a small lens-shaped buoy. The disadvantage of this system was the fact that the buoy was easily seen up close and the fact that there had to be a greater distance between them due to the longer lines. Combat effectiveness of the EMG mine was increased by employing 'EMG simulators' consisting of only the buoy, the line and the anchor, which would give the appearance of greater numbers.

A large number of minelayers was needed, since the mine barriers were to be laid at short notice for greater effectiveness. On 3 August the Naval War Staff requested that the railway ferries *Deutschland* and *Schwerin* as well as the Norwegian *Skagerrak* be commandeered as auxiliary minelayers. The *Deutschland* had already served in this role in the First World War, and was reincarnated in the

The auxiliary minelayer *Kaiser* leaving Rotterdam on 9 September 1940. (*H. Christiansen*)

Second as the *Stralsund*. Other minelayers were *Schiff 23* (ex-*Cairo*), *Königin Luise*, *Tannenberg, Preußen, Hansestadt Danzig, Grille, Brummer, Cobra, Togo, Roland* and *Kaiser*. These ships were divided into a Western Group under the command of Captain Bentlage (C-in-C Minelayers), and an Eastern Group under Captain Krastel. In early September these ships deployed to their operational areas and were assigned to their harbours. The Western Group comprised *Tannenberg, Cobra, Schwerin, Togo* and *Schiff 23* at Cherbourg plus the *Stralsund* and *Skagerrak* at Le Havre, while the Eastern Group consisted of the *Grille, Königin Luise, Preußen* and *Roland* at Ostend and the *Hansestadt Danzig, Kaiser* and *Brummer* at Antwerp. All destroyers, torpedo and S-boats in the west were also drafted into minelaying service.

Mining was to begin during the night of S Day minus 9 in order for all the barriers to be in place before the beginning of Sealion. Group West requested a period of 240 hours from the time the order was given to proceed with the operation until S Time. This amount of time would allow a cushion of thirty-six hours before the first minelaying operations began during which the ships would be assembled and loaded. In Cherbourg, minelayers were ready for the order, but the threat of British night air raids on Ostend prevented the same level of readiness there. Mines had to be stored in railway wagons to the south of Ostend, and would be loaded onto the ships only during daylight and under cover of German fighters. The trains themselves were held constantly on alert.

So many mines were required for Sealion that it appeared that German mines would have to be supplemented by stocks from France, but in the end this was unnecessary. Four thousand EMG mines were to be produced and several thousand EMC and EMD moored mines were stockpiled. Four thousand UMA anti-submarine moored mines were held in reserve. So-called snaglines increased the sensitivity of mines directed against submerged submarines and minesweeping measures. Explosive and cable-cutting buoys were dropped on both sides of the mine barriers, which would make minesweeping more difficult by destroying equipment. Details of the mine barriers are shown in the table on page 286 and in the map on page 285.

Barriers A2, C1a, C2, C3 and D2 were to be laid in four rows, the middle two rows consisting of mines and the outer two of explosive and cable-cutting buoys. Barrier C1 was to be in four rows, with the northern row of explosive buoys and the other three rows made up of mines mixed with explosive and cable-cutting buoys. Barriers D1 and A1 were in eight rows, the outside four rows containing protective systems and the middle four the actual mines. Barriers B2 and B3 had to be laid in eighteen rows due to the greater room required for the EMG. Four rows were of protective systems, six rows of EMG simulators and eight rows were of mines.

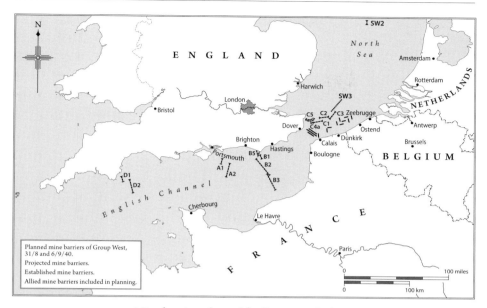

Mine barriers planned for Operation Sealion.

In addition to these measures, coastal waters were to be sown with mines using S-boats; these were areas CD and BS. Mine zones A1 and D1 were to be extended to the coast using protective systems and moored mines. Area BS appears to have been delineated at a time when the landing zone for Transport Fleet E was still planned to run from Worthing to Brighton, and not further east, as was decided later. Presumably, the position of this mine barrier was altered because it would have hindered quick movement between Landing Zones D and E. A gap was to be left between BS and B2 and designated as such.

Mines were to be air-dropped as well by the 9th Fliegerdivision, sealing off the eastern and western accesses to the base at Portsmouth. Ground mines with a six-day delay were to be laid between Start Point and the North Foreland, practically blocking the whole south coast.

Barriers SW0, SW1, SW2 and SW3 which were laid in August were not directly relevant to Sealion, but were considered in the planning. The British destroyers *Esk* and *Ivanhoe* were lost on 31 August in Area SW1, and the destroyer *Express* was severely damaged during anti-invasion minelaying operations. The net effect of these mine barriers is difficult to assess.

Vice-Admiral Prof Ruge, former C-in-C Minesweepers West, commented in a letter to the author in 1976, 'If these barriers had been relatively complete they would have presented a strong obstacle to the British Navy. But even a strong obstacle is not an absolute barrier.'

To be laid on night before	Mine barrier	Length nm	Average distance between mines (m)	Minelayers	Escort	Base	Mines	Explosive buoys	Cable cutting buoys	EMG simulators
S-2	B1	5.2	32	4 destroyers, 4 Type 35 Torpedoboats	MTB	Le Havre	300 EMG	480	28	
S-2	C1	8.2	40	Roland, K. Luise, Preußen, Grille	2 Type 23/24 Torpedoboats, MTB	Ostend	400 EMC/D	800	150	
S-2	C1a	2.0	40	2 Type 23/24, 2 Type 35 Torpedoboats		?	95 EMD	190	20	
S-3	Reserve									
S-4	B2	19.4	30	Togo, Stralsund, Schwerin, Schiff 23, Tannenberg, 6 minesweepers, 4 Type 35, 1 destroyer	Other destroyers and MTB	Le Havre	1,200 EMG	1900	235	500
S4	C3	8.6	40	as C 1	4 Type 23/24, 2 Type 35 Torpedoboats, MTB	Ostend	400 EMC/D	800	150	
S-5	Reserve									
S-6	B3	19.4	30	as B 2	as B 2	Le Havre	1,200 EMG	1900	235	500
S-6	C2	8.6	40	as C 1	as C 3	Ostend	400 EMG	800	150	
S-7	Reserve									
S-8	A1	5.4	40	4 destroyers, 4 Type 35 Torpedoboats	MTB	Cherbourg	250 EMC	300	100	
S-8	A2	16.3	55	Togo, Stralsund, Schwerin, Tannenberg	4 Type 23/24 Torpedoboats, MTB	Cherbourg	550 EMC	700	250	
S-9	D1	5.4	40	as A 1	as A 1	Cherbourg	250 EMC	300	100	
S-9	D2	16.3	55	as A 2	as A 2	Cherbourg	550 EMC	700	250	

The auxiliary minelayer *Stralsund,* the former railway ferry *Deutschland.*

The defence of the minefields against British sweeping efforts could have been decisive. The Soviet fleet at Leningrad was penned up by such measures between 1942 and 1944. Such action at the Sealion barriers was not even considered: German naval forces were regarded as insufficient for the task.

German Naval Forces

The German Navy was the Achilles heel of Operation Sealion, since it was unrealistic to hope that the landing could succeed without the escort of German warships. Night-time and poor visibility hindered aircraft, and coastal artillery and mine barriers were effective only if they could be protected against sweeping. Even though the operation was confined to a small area of coastal water, local control of the sea was crucial and this control could only have been won by German naval forces. What was the German Navy able to contribute on this front?

The Navy had suffered significant losses in the Norway campaign: not only had the cruisers *Blücher, Karlsruhe* and *Königsberg* met their end but ten destroyers as well, a class of ship which was eminently suitable for the narrow confines of the Channel. Other valuable ships had been hit by torpedoes, among them the two battleships *Scharnhorst* and *Gneisenau* and the 'pocket battleship' *Lützow.* The Naval War Staff pressed to have at least one of the two battleships repaired in time for Sealion by late September. But air raids by British bombers prevented work at night and forced the yards to sink the floating docks. Nor could repair on the guns be hurried and it was not until 9 November that the *Gneisenau* was ready, and the *Scharnhorst* ten days later. The *Lützow* was so badly damaged that it had to be taken out of service and in the event repairs were not completed until April 1941, much too late for Sealion.

The new battleship *Bismarck* and the heavy cruiser *Prinz Eugen* entered service in August 1940, running trials and training cruises in September, October and November. *Bismarck* returned to Blohm & Voss in Hamburg in December for final fitting out and *Prinz Eugen* had completed its trials by 18 December. It took until the following April for the crews to be trained and the Naval War Staff did not consider using these two ships, which had not been fully worked up, for Sealion.

Of the other ships, the light cruiser *Leipzig* was docked for repairs after a torpedo hit on 13 December 1939 and the 'pocket battleship' *Admiral Scheer* was undergoing reconstruction. Work on the *Leipzig* was not completed until 30 November, but the ship was only of limited usefulness after that, as its maximum cruising speed remained at 22 knots and it was only used for training thereafter. *Admiral Scheer*, along with *Admiral Hipper*, was scheduled for a decoy operation as part of Sealion (see page 277), but it suffered a machinery breakdown on 20 August and was not ready again until a month after the original date of 10 September. It can be safely assumed that the *Scheer* would have been available for Sealion if it had taken place at the end of September.

Thus, of the major combatants, only the heavy cruiser *Admiral Hipper* and the light cruisers *Nürnberg*, *Köln* and *Emden* were operational and their roles in Sealion were as part of the decoy invasion.

German naval superiority in the Channel would have to be won by the smaller ships, especially the destroyers, which were tailored for this role by virtue of their high speed and heavy armament. But even these light forces were in relatively short supply; in autumn 1940 only seven destroyers were available: *Z 10 Hans Lody*, *Z 20 Karl Galster*, *Z 5 Paul Jacobi*, *Z 6 Theodor Riedel*, *Z 15 Erich Steinbrinck*, *Z 14 Friedrich Ihn*, and *Z 16 Friedrich Eckholdt*. *Z 4 Richard Beitzen* was in dockyard hands until 21 September, *Z 8 Bruno Heinemann* until 4 October and *Z 7 Hermann Schoemann* until 15 October. Even if all of these ships had been available on time, they could not necessarily be counted on, since the type was prone to breakdowns.

Torpedo boats were of limited use as, being only lightly armed, they would have been hard-pressed to stand up against British destroyers. The older torpedo boats of the *Möwe* (Type 23) and *Wolf* (Type 24) classes with their three 10.5 cm guns and solid construction were better suited. *Seeadler*, *Kondor*, *Greif*, *Falke*, *Iltis*, *Wolf* and *Jaguar* of these classes were operational by autumn 1940. *Möwe* was laid up until spring 1941 with hull damage. The Type 35 torpedo boats had only one

10.5 cm gun and a limited combat radius; of this class, *T 1–T 12* were available in autumn 1940, though *T 3* was sunk at Le Havre on 19 September and *T 11* heavily damaged on 18 September. The four torpedo boats captured in Norway, the *Löwe*, *Tiger*, *Leopard* and *Panther*, had three 10 cm guns and were to be used for Autumn Journey (*Herbstreise*), joined by nine old torpedo boats from the First World War which were being used as training and trials ships. There were fifteen of these, but only a few of them had one or two 10.5 cm guns and two torpedo tubes. If any others had been earmarked for use they would have required re-arming. The Autumn Journey landing fleet was to be escorted by three F-Boats. This class of ten was originally conceived for fleet escort and each was armed with two 10.5 cm guns, but they had proved inadequate and had all been converted for various roles such as fleet tenders and torpedo recovery boats. Only some of them retained their weapons.

All three motor torpedo boat flotillas were to be deployed in the eastern part of the Channel. The following were available in late September: *S 10–13, 18–20, 22, 24–28, 30, 31, 33–37, 54* and *55*. On 15 August an explosion ripped through the torpedo magazine at Ostend, damaging *S 23, S 24* and *S 35* badly and *S 37* lightly. An air raid damaged *S 36* severely and *S 37* lightly on the night of 7/8 September. These losses were replaced through new deliveries or the return of repaired boats.

Aside from these surface vessels, all available submarines, including training boats, were to be deployed to the Channel. The Commander-in-Chief, U-boats, Rear-Admiral Dönitz, noted on 6 August 1940:

> Assuming that there are no losses in the next few weeks, the following submarines are available for the operation:
>
> > Seven large Type IX submarines: *U 37, 38, 43, 65, 123, 124, 103*
> > Twelve medium Type VII submarines: *U 28, 29, 31, 32, 34, 46, 47, 48, 51, 99, 100, 101.*
> > Twenty small Type II submarines:
> > Seven front-line boats: *U 56, 57, 58, 59, 60, 61, 62*
> > Thirteen training boats: *U 7, 8, 9, 10, 14, 18, 20, 21, 23, 120, 121, 137, 138.*

These numbers are the highest totals and can be achieved only if none is in for repair, which is not anticipated. *U 2–6, 11, 17, 24* and *29* are not fit for front-line duties due to personnel and machinery. Two of the boats are currently returning due to machinery problems; their date of operational readiness is not known, and they have thus not been included.

During preparations for the operation (fourteen days), during the operation itself, and during the ensuing repairs which will undoubtedly be necessary, training will have to be suspended, with the exception of those boats just entering service. Consequently, ten boats will have to wait for their commanders and an additional fourteen for their crews; their deployment at the front will be delayed proportionally to the time it takes the training boats to be withdrawn from this role. The disadvantages will have to be accepted in light of the scale of this operation.

The submarines will be deployed in the English Channel, forming concentrations off the south coast and in the anticipated approach routes of the British fleet in the western exit of the Channel, along its east coast south of Cross Sand and in the Hoofden. Should there be insufficient room in the Channel, a number of boats will be stationed in the Orkneys in order to attack targets during the deception manoeuvres.

In order to enable redeployment of vessels in the western part of the Channel to the middle section, sufficient gaps must be left in the mine barriers to the west.

Bases having fuels and torpedoes:

West: Lorient and alternative harbours St Nazaire and Brest

Channel: Cherbourg and alternative harbours den Helder and Vlissingen.

Estimated availability of training boats: approximately 14 days.

The disposition of German submarines proposed by Dönitz is shown on the map opposite. On the request of Group West, Dönitz submitted a new plan without the seven large Type IX boats, but otherwise generally the same. It is not possible to explain why the seven boats were withdrawn, but possibly Group West intended the large submarines for a different operation, perhaps a diversion.

If the operational readiness of the German Navy in 1940 is considered, it is easy to see why Naval Commander West managed to cover its deployment in his order of 14 September 1940 in only one sentence: 'Three groups of five submarines each, all destroyers and T-Boats west of the western mine barrier, two groups of three submarines each and all motor torpedo boats east of the mine barrier.'

It is odd that the Navy dismissed the direct cover of a genuine landing operation in one sentence, while Autumn Journey takes up rows of filing cabinets. Deploying all the cruisers for a feint manoeuvre, when they might have acquitted themselves well in the narrow Channel, seems odd. It is possible that, having been forced to accept an operational plan against its will, the Navy High Command decided to protect the German fleet rather than throw it into the fray at any price. The Navy had opposed a landing in Britain from the very beginning, stubbornly insisting upon preconditions such as absolute air superiority, which jeopardised the whole plan. The Navy was aware of its inferiority at sea, and if the British and German navies were compared, the Naval High Command's attitude is more understandable: the disparity was immense.

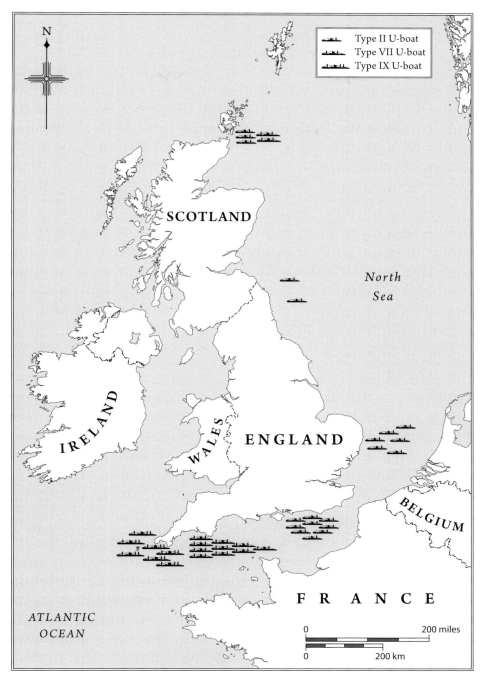

U-boat positions for Operation Sealion.

Was the Naval High Command right? Was Operation Sealion doomed to failure from the very beginning? Would the German transport fleet have been almost helpless against the British destroyer force? These are questions to which there are no answers, and never will be, since the endeavour was never put to the test. The only way to determine whether the Navy High Command was right in its actions is to examine critically the basis upon which the decisions were taken.

On the material side, would it not have been better to devote the resources planned for Autumn Journey to the actual operation? If the operation was to have the best possible chance of succeeding, the answer is surely yes. A decoy manoeuvre would have delayed the arrival of the British fleet in the Channel, but, in view of the almost complete vulnerability of the landing fleet, it would have been irresponsible to send German naval ships into the North Sea and not the Channel. Allowing the light and even heavy cruisers – in addition to the *Admiral Hipper* and *Admiral Scheer* – to enter the mine-infested waters and be at the mercy of the Royal Air Force would have been very risky, as was demonstrated by the losses incurred during the invasion of Norway. On the other hand, the cruisers would have had some scope in the Channel, and a Naval High Command bent on success, as was the case in Norway, should have used these resources to their full extent. Could the training ships and the old, decommissioned ships not have tipped the balance, even if only slightly? To a certain extent they were planned for *Herbstreise*. The gunnery training ship *Bremse* would have reinforced the cruiser squadron with its weapons and high speed. Furthermore, it was planned to use old torpedo boats from the Torpedo Training Flotilla and torpedo recovery units as well as converted F-Boats for escort duties. In early August, the Naval Commander West, Vice-Admiral Lütjens, proposed that the old pre-dreadnought battleships *Schlesien* and *Schleswig-Holstein*, then being used as training ships, should also be included. This suggestion provoked a lively debate in the Naval War Staff. Lütjens found a supporter in Admiral Schniewind, Chief of Staff, who advocated bringing the maximum amount of firepower to bear in the operational area, viewing every additional gun as providing that much greater combat effectiveness, better defence and support for the landing. The Chief of the Operations Division, Vice-Admiral Fricke, did not share this opinion, holding that the old training ships would make very little difference to the outcome. Lütjens had suggested grounding the two battleships on sandbanks in the Dover Straits (on the Varne and the Ridge) or in the landing zones to protect them against underwater attacks, but Fricke pointed out that the ebb tide would create currents which could capsize the ships. Schniewind decided that these two ships would be used only if they could be given more armour. The fate of their sister-ship *Pommern* which had taken a torpedo hit in the battle of Jutland and sunk with all hands was recalled. Test firing against the target ship *Hannover* in 1937–8 had demonstrated that the armour of the old

The two Norwegian coastal defence ships *Harald Haarfargre* and *Tordenskiold* at Horten 1940.

battleships could not withstand rounds from the destroyers' modern 12.7 cm (5 in) guns. It should also be recalled that the medium guns from these two ships had been removed and remounted on various auxiliary cruisers, leaving them with only four heavy 28 cm guns. The lighter guns would have to be refitted on the *Schlesien* and the *Schleswig-Holstein* if they were to take part in Sealion. Blohm & Voss estimated six weeks for improving their armour and Deschimag nine; even then the protection would have been improved only above the waterline as neither yard considered that anything could be done below it. On this basis, Schniewind decided against using the ships, and also turned down a proposal by Group West on 24 August to use them as transports for 1,200 troops each. The vulnerability of these two battleships below the waterline would have made them too risky to use, though it was not so much the loss of the ships themselves that Schniewind feared, but that of their crews and troops. Nevertheless, it is questionable whether it would have been any less risky to let the transports and the thousands of troops on them sail unescorted.

In 1940, there were still a number of old and mostly decommissioned ships whose weapons had been removed which the German Navy did not consider for Sealion. Later on, some of these were used as floating flak batteries. The former small cruisers *Medusa* (1900) and the *Arcona* (1902) of the Kaiser's Navy and later Reichsmarine were converted for this purpose in 1940/41. The small cruiser *Berlin* (1903), used as an accommodation ship, had retained its engines too, but did not see service during the war. In Norway the two ex-coast defence ships *Harald Haarfarge* (1897) and *Tordenskjold* (1897) were taken as war prizes in 1940; despite their advanced age, they were still equipped with two 21 cm guns (their six 12 cm guns had already been removed) and able to cruise at 14 knots, and entered service in 1941 as the heavy AA batteries *Thetis* and *Nymphe*. In the Netherlands the Germans found the coastal defence ships *Vliereede* (ex-*Hertog Hendrik*, 1902) and *Ijmuiden* (ex-*Jacob van Heemskerck*, 1906) which had sunk in shallow water and were still armed with one and two 24 cm guns respectively. These two ships were raised during the summer and autumn of 1940 and entered service as the *Ariadne* and *Undine*. The small cruiser *Gelderland* (1898) which had served as an artillery training ship until 1939 was found without its weapons and being used as an accommodation ship in den Helder. It too was converted into a heavy AA battery. Another former German ship, the light cruiser *Strasbourg* (ex-*Regensburg*, 1915), was found in France, being used as crew quarters, but was not further converted.

The coastal defence ships *Niels Jules* (1918) and *Peder Skram* (1910) were sailing under the Danish flag in 1940, armed with ten 15 cm and two 24 cm and four 15 cm guns respectively. The elderly *Peder Skram* was still capable of cruising at 15.9 knots in 1939 and the *Niels Juel* had been fitted with a modern fire-control system during modification in 1935–6. They entered service with the German Navy in 1943 as the *Adler* (ex-*Peder Skram*) and *Nordland* (ex-*Niels Juel*). It seems probable that Germany could have pressured Denmark into turning these ships over, as in 1941 with the enforced lease of six modern torpedo boats.

Reactivating these ships, some of which had not sailed for five or ten years, would have been challenging to say the least. Much of the dock capacity was taken up for preparing the transports, and modernising the old vessels probably would

Cruiser *Berlin* as a hulk. (*Reinhard Kramer*)

Cruiser *Strasbourg,* ex-*Regensburg,* as a hulk at St Nazaire. (*Reinhard Kramer*)

have halted all new construction and repair work. It was also difficult to locate weapons and fire-control systems for unarmed ships: the *Schlesien* and *Schleswig-Holstein* had had to give up their medium guns to the auxiliary cruisers. During the occupation of France a number of 13 cm and 13.8 cm guns were found in the arsenal at Brest, and the German Navy attempted to repossess twelve 15 cm guns from former German destroyers in Toulon via the Ceasefire Commission. The old coastal defence ships probably would have been useful only if the fire-control system had been modernised; this equipment would have had to have been taken from ships still building or out of commission. Finding and training crews for them was another thorny problem, and some ships were even taken out of service because they could not be manned (see page 153). Crews would have to have been siphoned off from new ships or those in repair.

It can be seen that better protection for the Sealion fleet would have required the entire reserves of the German Navy. But would these reserves have made any substantial difference? Let us compare the British forces they were up against. On 20 September the British could call on three battleships, two battlecruisers, two aircraft carriers, eight heavy and twenty light cruisers, and seventy-six destroyers in their home waters. These were located in Plymouth (the battleship *Revenge,* two light cruisers and six destroyers); in Portsmouth (one light cruiser and sixteen destroyers) and on the south coast (five light cruisers and about twenty destroyers). Most of the major combatants were in Scapa Flow, though the most powerful ones, the battleships *Nelson* and *Rodney* and the battlecruiser *Hood* and two light cruisers and eight destroyers redeployed to the Firth of Forth on 13 September in order to be ready to counter any German invasion attempt. On the other hand, it would have been difficult for the Royal Navy to bring its heavy ships to bear in the Channel, with attacks by Luftwaffe aircraft, mines, submarines and motor torpedo boats posing a decided risk.

The Royal Navy thus decided it would deploy its major forces only if the German Navy did so, not knowing the latter's level of readiness. The Germans had to assume the British would send in three to five light cruisers and about twenty destroyers against each flank of the crossing route. Attacks by Luftwaffe forces would have reduced the threat somewhat, but certainly not completely. The chances of success by submarines and motor torpedo boats against the fast British ships were low, despite the fact that German motor torpedo boats had sunk three British destroyers and damaged another, a further one becoming the victim of a U-boat during the evacuation of the British Expeditionary Force from Dunkirk in May 1940. With their two heavy cruisers, three light cruisers, seven destroyers and about twenty torpedo boats, the Germans would only have been able to engage British Navy ships on one flank. Even the reserves would make little difference: the two old battleships, six coastal defence ships, five old cruisers and approximately twenty old torpedo boats and F-Boat escorts – sensibly placed behind the mine barriers – would have found it heavy going against the Royal Navy, which could have called up its own reserves to replace losses; the Germans could not replace any at all. It is also debatable whether the remains of the Kriegsmarine and the coastal artillery could have kept both coasts and the transport routes open.

Torpedo Training Flotilla at Mürwik with old torpedo boats.

The German Naval High Command at that time was very conservative in its thinking, and unlikely to embark on new ideas like the Army's concept of mobile warfare with armoured thrusts. Naval planners had learnt from the passive role of the German fleet in the First World War that a war against Britain could only be waged on the basis of a war against commerce and adhered to this position throughout the Second World War. Remarkable initiative was shown in the Scandinavian campaign, all the same. The German Navy had successfully avoided the British fleet and occupied Denmark and Norway through surprise and by exploiting the vast seas and the virtual lack of resistance on land. An amphibious landing, which the Navy had not studied seriously, was not necessary in Norway. Britain would be a different matter. But the Navy had such serious doubts about the success of an amphibious landing that they did not pursue it. It should be said in the Navy's defence, however, that no one could see how the strategic situation would develop during the summer of 1940. Even the Army High Command was not optimistic about a quick victory in France, so deeply ingrained were the horrific memories of trench warfare from the First World War. While the *Panzer* units were overrunning France, the Navy's attention was turned to Norway, where German battleships closed in on the Allied supply lines. The campaign in Norway, it seems, had not only drained the Navy of material resources – two battleships, two heavy and two light cruisers and ten destroyers had either been sunk or put out of action – but had robbed it of all capacity for a new initiative at a crucial stage of the war.

On 6 October Group North informed the Naval Operations Office that it was planning an attack on major British warships in Newcastle. Three motor torpedo boats armed with torpedoes and two to four ground mines were to sail to Newcastle escorted by torpedo boats. Under cover of a Luftwaffe attack with flare bombs they would fire the torpedoes at suitable targets and lay mines right next to the British warships. This plan had to be cancelled when it was learnt that the British had moved the ships further north again after the order to halt Sealion had been given. The German Naval High Command had shown no such initiative in autumn 1940.

British Resistance

GERMAN AIRBORNE RECONNAISSANCE in September finally tipped off the British to the German plans for an invasion, but the Royal Navy had been ready for one ever since France had fallen. The British had had a lucky break in cracking the Luftwaffe radio code. The first indication of the German plans was a report that the commanders of 7th Airborne Division had been summoned to a conference on 19 August in Berlin. The meaning of this encoded report was obvious as this airborne unit had already been deployed in the Netherlands during the Western Campaign. German intentions were further confirmed by an order not to bomb British south coast harbours and a report that the Luftwaffe school at Carteret was practising landings using pontoons and ferries made of wine barrels. This report was undoubtedly referring to the trials run by Engineer Battalion 47 (see page 97), although it is puzzling how this ever came to be referred to as a Luftwaffe school and be reported by radio in the first place. The British were also able to intercept a transmission noting that German Navy representatives at a conference had refused to use certain types of ferries. This was undoubtedly a reference to the B ferry, and it is no wonder that the British were aware of the squabbling which had gone on among the armed services about the landing craft before they had even been deployed. The British had also been able to decipher transmissions from Luftgaustab zbV 300, the successor to Luftgaustab zbV 16 which dealt with loading and resupply of Luftwaffe units in Britain. The first hint that the Germans had shelved Sealion in 1940 was a decoded order of 17 September to reduce air loading equipment at Dutch airbases, presumably referring to 7th Airborne Division.

Fearing the strength of the Luftwaffe, the British did not want to rely entirely on their own fleet, and thus began extensive reinforcements of their coastal defences, particularly at Dover, which they felt was at high risk. Before the war, Dover had been armed with two 9.2 in and six 6 in guns; in early September these were supplemented with a 14 in gun, two 6 in and two 4 in guns as well as with two 9.2 in guns on railway mountings. Two 13.5 in guns were removed from the old battleship *Iron Duke*, now serving as a training ship, and placed on railway

British air attack on transports at Boulogne. (*Imperial War Museum*)

mountings, and four 5.5 in guns from the battlecruiser *Hood* were placed nearby. An additional four guns from the *Hood* saw service in coastal batteries at Bognor Regis, Pevensey, Tilbury and Folkestone. Thirteen heavy howitzers were also emplaced along the coast. A total of 153 new batteries was set up during the second half of 1940; they were, however, erected with considerable haste and some were located where they were of no tactical advantage.

The British also laid barriers and mines in the shallow waters off the south coast, and built tank traps along the coastline during the autumn. Flat coastal areas were also littered with all manner of obstructions against the threat of German gliders.

General Sir Edmund Ironside, Commander-in-Chief Home Forces of the British Army since June 1940, was aware of the weakness of the British defence, and ordered a rear defensive line, behind which were stationed the mobile Army reserves which were to make a decisive strike against the German forces. This line of defence was to stretch from Richmond in North Yorkshire to the mouth of the Humber and from there through Cambridge to the Thames at Canvey Island, and south of the Thames through Maidstone and Basingstoke to Bristol. Other lines of defence made of tank traps and small bunkers were thrown up in front of these positionsto slow the German advance. On 20 July General Brooke took over as

Barges sunk at Dunkirk after a British air raid. (*Hansen*)

Commander-in-Chief. He placed his faith in troop mobility and fortified coastal defences and tanks were concentrated closer to the coast.

Britain had already prepared before the war for the use of poison gas. In 1940 1,495 tons of mustard gas were stockpiled and made ready for dispensing from aircraft. Once the German landing fleet began to assemble, the British Navy began to lay mines and bombard the embarkation harbours at night. On the night of 9 September, the light cruisers *Aurora* and *Galatea*, eleven destroyers and five motor torpedo boats shelled Ostend and other Channel harbours. The British claimed that a raid by a motor torpedo boat on the same night was responsible for sinking a number of vessels, but this is not substantiated in German reports.

Shelling continued on subsequent nights. The German coastal batteries kept the British fleet at bay, but inflicted no significant damage. German ships did not attempt to counter the British raids, though German destroyers and torpedo boats did lay several offensive minefields off the southern coast of Britain. In attacking the Isle of Wight, the German 5th Torpedo Boat Flotilla managed to sink the Free French submarine-chasers *CH 6* and *CH 7*. German and British naval forces met during a destroyer operation in the Western exit of the British Channel on 17/18 October. The *Steinbrinck* reported a torpedo hit on a British cruiser, but this was not confirmed by the other side. On 29 November the British destroyer *Javelin* was severely damaged by two torpedoes from a German destroyer.

In addition to aerial reconnaissance, British submarines kept watch on the embarkation harbours in order to have the earliest possible warning of the start of the landing operation. The Royal Air Force was able to score substantial hits on the landing fleet in September. In a night strike on Antwerp on 15 September, the transport *A 26* took a direct hit on the bridge, and the superstructure of the *A 47* was also struck, catching fire amidships, and the engines of the *A 41* took three hits, causing the ship to spring a leak. Bombs exploding next to the *A 30* blew its sides open, flooding the engine room and a number of other compartments. The British were also successful in blowing up an ammunition train.

On the night of 16 September a low-level British strike on Le Havre sank one transport and damaged another, though at the cost of three or four aircraft. The full moon on 18 September was a boon to the Royal Air Force, and the German landing fleet at Dunkirk suffered severe losses: twenty-six barges were sunk or badly damaged, fifty-eight were lightly damaged, and 500 tons of ammunition was blown up. On the following night at Le Havre the torpedo boat *T 3* was sunk and *T 11* took two hits, the transport *H 13* caught fire and had to be towed away, and the *H 37* and *H 49* were damaged in the stern. The *H 6* had shell damage along the waterline and had to be grounded. Aerial mining also took its toll: on 11 September the transport *H 42* struck a ground mine immediately off Le Havre and broke up.

By 21 September British strikes had resulted in the loss of twelve transports, four tugs, and fifty-one barges, putting them out of action temporarily or permanently. Nine transports, one tug and 163 barges were damaged, though they could be replaced with reserves.

The Fate of Operation Sealion

SEALION WAS A LONG TIME IN DYING. Hitler continued to issue orders in regard to this operation until 1944, as if relinquishing it would be the prelude to his downfall. He persisted in giving the impression that it was still a viable proposition, but hindsight tells us that this was indeed only an illusion.

The first sign of the operation's demise began with the continual postponement of the original landing date. On 29 July the Naval Operations Office pointed out that the next deadline in August was unrealistic and would have to be shifted to later in September, since preparations would not be finalised until then. In a conversation with Raeder on 14 August, Hitler stated that the threat should be maintained, even if the actual invasion was not to take place. On 30 August the Naval Operations Office was forced to move the date for completion of preparations from 15 to 20 September. In terms of phases of the moon, the tides and morning light, the days between 19 and 27 September were the best, with the 24th the optimum day; in fixing the landing in this period the Navy was not postponing the invasion. On 10 September Hitler decided not to choose the earliest possible date for issuing the preparation order which would have left ten days' leeway before S Day, but rather fixed the 24th as the first possible day of a landing, leaving only a few days' grace. The air offensive had not resulted in any decisive results up to that time and inclement weather had held up preparations. Raeder reported on 13 September:

1. The present situation in the air battle is not conducive to implementing Operation Sealion, as the risks are too great.
2. Failure of the operation would result in a prestigious victory for the British, which would diminish the effects of the air raids.
3. It is vital that Luftwaffe strikes on Britain, particularly on London, continue unabated. These raids should be intensified given good weather and without regard to Sealion. These attacks could be decisive in achieving a final victory.
4. Operation Sealion must not be cancelled. The British must be kept insecure. Cancellation of the landing would take a great deal of pressure off Britain.

It is astonishing that the Naval Commander-in-Chief had finally adopted the views of Hitler and the Luftwaffe. It is difficult to know whether Raeder really believed in the value of the air raids or whether he was merely trying to do everything possible to distract Hitler from a landing operation. In his memoirs Raeder intimates that his goal was to achieve the second objective.

In a meeting on 14 September Hitler postponed the decision for a Sealion date until 17 September. On that day, he decided to delay issuing the order 'until further notice'; the entire Wehrmacht was under no illusions that this meant anything except 'for good'. On 19 September the order was given to stop the assembly.

Some authorities which had been involved with Sealion at a more practical level tried to keep the operation going, probably recognising the long-term implications of its demise. Captain Degenhardt, Chief of Sea Transport, Special Duties, argued strongly against closing his headquarters in a meeting with his superior, Admiral Schuster, on 9 October, stating that withdrawal of the qualified personnel in the landing fleet would leave only the maritime troops, whom he called 'Santa Clauses' (*Weihnachtsmänner*). He considered it important to keep qualified personnel ready for a relaunching of Sealion in 1941. Degenhardt pressed Schuster to allow him to present the case personally to Raeder, but Schuster turned down the request. The Navy began to dismantle the infrastructure for the operation under orders headed 'Waiting Time' and 'Hibernation'. The content of these orders left little doubt that the operation would continue to slumber. The duties of Naval Group Commander West in regard to Sealion were transferred to a Special Staff at the BSW (*Befehlshaber der Sicherung West*) on 27 October. The Army side of the preparation was subsumed under Naval Headquarters Souverain-Moulain under Captain Gladow. The Special Staff under the BSW was disbanded in spring 1941. Navy Headquarters Souverain-Moulain later became known as Navy Headquarters Schall-Emden, named after its new commander, who was subsequently promoted to *Admiral der Seebefehlsstelle*. His was the only command left which dealt with the practical aspects of Sealion preparations.

Hitler's decision to postpone the operation was followed on 19 September by an order from the OKW at the request of the Naval Operations Office to stop the assembly of forces and disperse the transports lying in the embarkation ports. Thus the transport fleet was never completely assembled. However, in order to keep Britain under the threat of invasion most of the vessels were left at the mounting ports, although some were redistributed to smaller harbours and inland canals to protect them against air raids.

The number of barges at the various harbours was to be kept constant, but only about a quarter of them remained in service, among them the special barges, while the rest were decommissioned and mothballed by the remaining crews. Reserve barges were returned to their owners or sent to various naval headquarters. Some of them were used for Channel Islands transport. Only 130 of the motor fishing vessels were kept, for search and rescue duties on the Channel coast. The pusher boats were kept on a one-to-one basis with the number of barges, including some reserves for resupply.

Ninety-eight Dutch motor fishing vessels would free an equal number of German pusher boats for duties back home. Only sixty-five tugs, mostly foreign ones, remained behind for Sealion. All the fishing trawlers which had been seized as tugs were returned to their owners or were used to replenish the patrol flotillas. Only twenty-four motor coasters stayed at Le Havre or the auxiliary harbours; the rest were returned to their owners. Sixty troop transports, mostly foreign ones, remained on the Channel coast, but most of these were no longer kept in service. Once the operation was totally disbanded these were also returned.

Winter came: Sealion hibernated. Only a few exercises were held in November and December; besides which, the thought of a landing exercise in the icy Channel waters was off-putting. With the arrival of spring, the erstwhile amphibious forces on the occupied Channel coast asked themselves whether it made sense to reawaken Sealion. New orders were issued; exercises were again held. However, the name Sealion had disappeared; now there was a new one: *Haifisch* (Shark). Did this mean a completely new type of operation?

On 1 May the Naval Operations Office issued an order to prepare for a landing in England. The main thrust would come from the coastline between Rotterdam and Cherbourg, and land between Folkestone and Worthing (Operation Shark). Secondary landing operations would be undertaken from between Bergen and Oslo and Jutland (Esbjerg to Aarhus) and land between Berwick and Newcastle; operations from St Malo and Rochefort would land in Lyme Bay. These last two were codenamed *Harpune Nord* and *Harpune Süd* (Harpoon North and South). They were to be feint operations. Enclosed with the orders was a sealed envelope which was to be opened only by the commanding officer of the naval station. Inside was a terse note: '*Haifisch* is also a feint'. These three operations were to draw attention away from other preparations being made for the imminent attack on the Soviet Union.

Nevertheless, Sealion lived on. In Antwerp, the *Fahrenbaukommando I* (sF) of the engineers and *Sonderkomando Fähre* of the Luftwaffe soldiered on with technical innovations, particularly for ferries made of the heavy bridge pontoons. In March/ April the Navy created a Baltic Trials Command (*Erprobungskommando Ostsee*) under Captain Rieve, which was to exploit the know-how from Sealion. By July this command had sixteen motor coasters, five heavy and two light auxiliary gunboats, six command boats, twelve tugs, twelve powered and fourteen unpowered barges, twenty-four assault boats and two smoke boats. The first Navy landing boats, the so-called *Marinefährprähme*, were completed by June. These were modelled on the

Sealion barges, but without their disadvantages such as poor powerplants or none at all, and deep draughts. The Trials Command was to undertake landings on the Baltic Islands of Ösel and Dagö during the German advance on the Soviet Union. For the landings in September and October the Army set up Fährenbataillon 128 with twenty-one heavy pontoon ferries. These were augmented by thirteen Type 39 and 40 engineer landing boats, several assault boats and a *Land-Wasser-Schlepper* amphibious tractor from Pionierlandungskompanie 777. The developments for Sealion and even earlier designs would be put to the test. Despite grumbles about individual shortcomings, the vessels which had been prepared for Sealion did indeed prove themselves, even the motorised barges with their deep draughts. Several hundred of these were used in coastal waters off Norway, in the Baltic, Mediterranean, the Black Sea and many inland waterways.

However, the bulk of the Sealion barges still languished in the embarkation ports under Hitler's orders, to be a 'paper tiger' threat against England. The German wartime economy felt their lack, but it was not until 1942 that Armaments Minister Speer was able to recall them, getting the Naval Headquarters at Antwerp to dismantle them and return them to trade. It proved difficult to remove the concrete bottoms and this work had to be performed at the inland yards.

Sealion lived on, spasmodically, for some time. Führer Directive No. 18 of 12 November 1940 called for improvements to the basic concept of the operation. The three armed services promptly and independently began developing various types of landing craft which were to be used in the different theatres. The Army proved to be the most innovative in this sphere. The amphibious forces always remained a step-child of the Navy, which never quite knew what to do with its creations.

At a meeting on 23 September 1941 Hitler ordered that all material preparations for Sealion were to cease and he set a start-up period of eight to ten months for the operation. This was increased to twelve months in February 1942. It is ironic that Hitler referred to Sealion as late as 24 January 1944, again shifting its materials to other projects. He again set the start-up time as twelve months. These orders had very little impact on the armed forces, since the Wehrmacht had long since ceased making preparations to invade Britain; they merely demonstrate Hitler's delusion that he could recoup a lost opportunity.

Hitler remarked in 1943 to his Naval Adjutant, Rear-Admiral von Puttkamer, that he should never have let the Navy talk him out of Sealion. This indicates that in retrospect he had appreciated the significance of the operation in the strategic situation of autumn 1940, though he had laid the blame on others. The Navy responded by having a report prepared by Vice-Admiral Assmann which was submitted in April 1944. Entitled *Die Seekriegsleitung und die Planung der Invasion in England (Seelöwe) 40/41* (The Naval Operations Office and the Planning of the

Invasion of England (Sealion) 1940/41), this report defended the Navy's reasoning on the basis of the discrepancy between the British and the German navies. It is not known whether Hitler ever read this report, but at any rate, it would hardly have prompted any self-criticism on Hitler's part. It also demonstrated that the Navy had learned very little itself in the meantime, since it had not reassessed its thinking in the light of the amphibious operations in the Pacific, in which only local sea control had been needed.

Epilogue

In 1973 the Royal Military Academy at Sandhurst conducted joint British–German wargames to determine the outcome of Operation Sealion as it had been planned in autumn 1940. It was based on the premise that Hitler had set D-Day for 22 September. The outcome of the games was that the Royal Navy would have foiled the invasion by 25 September by cutting off the German supply lines. But the premise of the games was unfounded, since Sealion was never planned to be implemented. Hitler was clever enough to play off the three armed services against each other in order for Sealion to become what he wanted it to be: merely a threat.

Hitler's ulterior motives did not become clear until after the war. The military files attest to the fact that Hitler often only communicated pretended reasons to his military commanders. His real intentions are to be read in *Mein Kampf*, in which he named France as an enemy which had to be destroyed for the good of the German Reich. He considered that Britain would acquiesce to German hegemony on the Continent, since he believed its interests lay only in its Empire. Hitler did not hold Britain to be an enemy, but a partner. This is the only explanation for his otherwise inexplicable decision in regard to Dunkirk and his attitude toward an invasion of Britain. It would have been absurd, given the strategic situation, if Germany had not prepared for an invasion, and Hitler did so, still hoping for co-operation from Britain. A conquered Britain appeared to be of very little use to Hitler. Hitler gave orders for an invasion, but they were couched in terms that were impossible to fulfil. The Army General Staff and the Operations Branch were to be the prime movers in the preparations. The Luftwaffe generally ignored the possibility of an invasion and offered Hitler a devastating air offensive against Britain instead, which he gratefully accepted as further means to cow the nation. The German Navy, on the other hand, kept putting the brakes on an invasion, thus fitting in nicely with Hitler's thinking. Sealion, in its final form without any naval protection to speak of, was designed so that no military commander in his right mind would have given the order to proceed.

Why was the Naval High Command so pliable in Hitler's hands? Surely this was not due to lack of expertise. The Navy unquestionably gave Sealion no chance of succeeding. It is necessary to delve a little more deeply to understand this attitude in view of the favourable German strategic situation. We have already noted the conservatism of the German Navy at that time. Innovations were accepted reluctantly. The German Navy had never really considered the possibilities of amphibious warfare before the war, either in practical or theoretical terms. Nonetheless, the German Navy should not be judged too harshly, since it differed very little in its thinking from those of other nations at that time. On the other hand, the Army had its *jeune école*. This spirit permeated the Navy in other sectors, one of which was the development of the aircraft carrier, which stagnated during the war in Germany. The German Navy had based its thinking on the classical concepts of wresting sea control from the superior fleet, which could only be achieved through cruiser warfare and submarines attacking merchant fleets. Their thinking extended to the deployment of their few battleships as cruisers, leading in the long run to the loss of the *Bismarck*. The German Navy did not subscribe to the concept of establishing limited sea control for decisive situations. Neither did it think in terms of combined operations as had been used in the Norwegian campaign. The German Navy had been able to slip away easily at that time. It was not used to thinking in terms of fighting a superior force, even in waters such as the English Channel where it could have been at home.

Historians have by and large taken the Navy's side. But Klee, and especially Wheatley, made the mistake of analysing the operation from the point of view of the authorities at the time, and not from the subsequent developments of the war. Neither the failure of the German air offensive nor the bad weather satisfactorily explain why a landing was never attempted. If conditions had been right, the German air superiority over southern England should have sufficed for a landing operation. However, Germany still hoped to bomb Britain into submission, an over-optimistic ambition. But this wisdom was lacking at that time, as was the know-how, particularly in the air and amphibious sectors. The limitations and possibilities of these technologies had not yet been fathomed – the Navy, for instance, believed that the barges were more dependent on good weather than they actually were. But this lack of knowledge is not to the discredit of the Naval and Luftwaffe High Commands.

In the autumn of 1940 the Navy had the chance to end the conflict with Britain with one lightning combined-arms operation. Intellectually as well as materially unprepared for this, the Navy let the chance slip away. While it was able to amass a huge transport fleet in a herculean effort, the Navy considered it impossible to protect. Ansel contradicts this notion, regarding it as conceivable that a British attack on the fleet could have been thwarted given sufficient measures on the part of the Navy and the Luftwaffe. If all the factors are taken into consideration – Luftwaffe attacks on the Royal Navy, mine barriers, coastal artillery and the deployment of the German Navy in its entirety – then Ansel could be right. Sealion was cancelled primarily for political, and not military, reasons.

Yet another aspect of the operation has been largely ignored. Sealion was the first large-scale amphibious operation prepared in modern history. A favourable strategic situation had thrown the opportunity the way of the Wehrmacht, which, with very few exceptions, was largely unprepared for it. It is all the more astonishing, therefore, to see the speed at which the armed forces devised the necessary technology. Those members of all three armed services concerned with the practicalities of the operation co-operated admirably to break new ground; their superiors were found wanting. They were the ones who missed 'the call of history'. When Raeder writes in his memoirs that the energy devoted to Sealion had been squandered, it demonstrates that the Naval High Command had entirely overlooked this aspect. In the further course of the war they made very little use of the knowledge and the material gained from the Sealion preparations, whereas they could have been put to good use. The landing operations in the Baltic islands in 1941, in the Black Sea in 1942 and in the Aegean in 1943 were merely side-shows. Nevertheless, it must be kept in mind that the development of most of modern amphibious technology, be it landing craft, submersible tanks or artificial harbours, stems from Sealion. It must also be noted that it was not until the strategic situation evolved as it did in the autumn of 1940 that the Allies gave thought themselves to enhancing these improvised technologies, as was demonstrated by operations in the Pacific and in Normandy.

Later on, developments in amphibious technology were applied to other fields. The drive for rationalisation in merchant shipping, for instance, led to the development of Ro-Ro (roll-on, roll-off) ferries and barge carriers. Naturally, these ships can be used for military purposes, giving both NATO and Russian or Chinese forces a considerable amphibious potential in case of hostilities.

The decision not to proceed with Sealion was the turning point in the war. Great Britain was no more ready for peace than it had been before the threat of invasion and the German air offensive. Hitler now turned his gaze eastward, attacking the Soviet Union to gain *Lebensraum* for the German nation, with the object of enslaving or destroying the peoples in his path. This was one of Hitler's main military objectives, and one which we know today as impossible to achieve. The German generals who had contemplated a *Putsch* rather than accept the risks of the Western campaign, had been silenced by its success. At the head of the German troops crossing the Bug on 22 July 1941 were the submersible tanks which had been developed for Sealion.

A poem by an unknown author remains on paper, just like Sealion:

Ruber über den Kanal

Auf, Kameraden, eilig nun an Bord,
morgen endlich, endlich geht es fort.
Alle wollen unsern Mann wir stehn,
denken nicht, wann wir uns wiedersehn.
Ob auf dem Land, wie in der Luft,
wir folgen, wenn der Führer ruft.
Im Sturmwind leuchtet das Fanal: Rüber, über den Kanal.

Und sind wir drüben, wir dem Führer melden,
nicht einen Mann wir fanden von den Heiden.
Doch, wie das ging, das bleibt alles gleich,
da hinterließen sie ihre Inselreich.
Ob auf dem Land, wie in der Luft,
wir folgen, wenn der Führer ruft.
Im Sturmwind leuchtet das Fanal: Rüber, über den Kanal.

Across the Channel

Hasten comrades, come aboard,
Tomorrow at long last we sail.
Stout of heart we'll ever be,
Not knowing when we'll meet again.
On land or in the air,
We follow when the Führer calls.
Our banner leads us like a torch
Across the Channel.

Once on shore we tell the Führer
Not one hero did we find,
Though how that was, it does not matter,
They forsook their island kingdom.
On land or in the air,
We follow when the Führer calls.
Our banner leads us like a torch
Across the Channel.

Glossary of German Terms and Abbreviations

Ab, Abteilung – Detachment or Unit
Abteilung Landesverteidigung – Luftwaffe Home Defence Office
AK, Armeekorps – Army Corps
AMA, Allgemeines Marineamt – General Naval Office
AOK, Armeeoberkommando – Army Command
Aufkl, Aufklärung – Reconnaissance
BdK, Befehishaber der Kreuzer – Commander, Cruisers
BRT, Bruttoregistertonne – Gross register tonnage (grt)
Bruckenbaubataillon – Bridge-Building Battalion
BSN, Befehishaber der Sicherung der Nordsee – Commander for North Sea Defence
BSW, Befehishaber der Sicherung West – Commander for Western Defence
Btl, Bataillon – Battalion
Erpr, Erprobungs – Experimental
(F), Fern – Long range
Festungsbaubataillon – Fortress Construction Battalion
Flak, Fliegerabwehrkanone – Anti-aircraft gun
FlaMG, Fliegerabwehrmaschinengewehr – Anti-aircraft machine gun
Fliegerdivision – Airborne Division
Fl, Flotille – Flotilla
FSTA, Flotillenstammabteilung – Fleet Base Units
Gr, Gruppe – Group [air force formation]
(H), Heer – Army co-operation [air force designation]
JG, Jagdgeschwader – Fighter Wing
K III M, Hauptamt kriegsschifbau – Main Naval Construction Office
KG, Kampfgeschwader – Bomber Wing
KMD, Kriegsmarinedienststelle – Naval Base
Kp, Kompanie – Company
KuFlGr, Küstenfliegergruppe – Coastal Reconnaissance Group
LG, Lehrgeschwader – Training Wing

Luftflottenkommando – Air Fleet Command

Luftgaukommando – Area Air Defence Command

LWS, Land-Wasser-Schlepper – Amphibious tractor

Marineoberbaurat – Head of the Naval Construction Office

Mot, motorisiert – Motorised

NJG, Nachtjagdageschwader – Night Fighter Wing

nm, nautical mile(s) – 6,080 ft

ObdH, Oberbefehlshaber des Heeres – Commander-in-Chief of the Army

ObdL, Oberbefehlshaber der Luftwaffe – Commander-in-Chief of the Air Force

ObdM, Oberbefehlshaber der Marine – Commander-in-Chief of the Navy

OKH, Oberkommando des Heeres – Army High Command

OKL, Oberkommando des Luftwaffe – Air Force High Command

OKM, Oberkommando der Marine – Navy High Command

OKW, Oberkommando der Wehrmacht – Supreme Command

PAK, Panzerabwehrkanone – Anti-tank gun

Panzerjäger – Anti-tank

Pionier – Engineer

Pioniersturmboot – Engineer Assault Boat

PkW, Panzerkampfwagen – Tank [Panzer was often used synonymously with tank]

Pz, Panzer – armoured

Reichsluftschutzverband – Reich Air Defence Organisation

R-boat – Raumboot, originally an inshore minesweeper but used for many other naval duties

s S, schwere Schiffsbrücke – Heavy (bridge) pontoon ferry

Schwimmpanzer – Amphibious tank

SKL, Seekriegsleitung – Naval War Staff

Sonderkommando Fähre – Ferry Special Command

StG, Stukageschwader – Dive Bomber Wing

Stab – Staff

Stuka, an abbreviation of Sturzkampfflugzeug (dive bomber) – Familiar name for Ju 87 aircraft

Technisches Amt der Marine – Naval Technical Department

Teno, Technische Nothilfe – Technical Emergency Service

(U), unterwasser – Underwater [as in submersible tank – Pz (U)]

VGAD (K), Verstärkter Grenzanfsichtsdierst (kuste) – Coastal Border Patrol Reserve

Vp, Vorposten – Patrol

ZG, Zerstorergeschwader – Destroyer Wing (heavy fighters)

Key to Symbols

Schlepper
Tug

Prahm
Barge

Prahm Typ AS
Type AS barge

Prahm Typ B oder C
Type B or C barge

Herbert-Fähre
Herbert ferry

s. S.-Fähre
Heavy (bridge) pontoon ferry

Transportfischkutter
Motor fishing vessel

Küstenmotorsegler
Auxiliary sailing coaster

Artillerieträger
Auxiliary gunboat

Transporter
Transport

Gruppenführerboot
Group leader boat

M-Boot
Minesweeper (large)

Vp-Boot
Patrol boat

R-Boot
R-boat (inshore minesweeper)

Nebelboot
Smokescreen vessel

Transportflottenführer
Transport fleet commander

Korpskommandeur
Corps commander

Flottillenchef
Flotilla commander

Regimentskommandeur (auch Führer der Vorausabteilung)
Regimental commander (also commander of advance detachment)

Divisionskommandeur
Divisional commander

Stabschef des Korps
Corps chief of staff

Wattlinie
Shoreline

Felsenküste
Rocky coastline

Leuchtfeur
Beacon

Infanterie
Infantry

MG
Machine gun

sMG
Heavy machine gun

Infanteriegeschütz
Infantry gun

Granatwerfer
Mortar

s. Granatwerfer
Heavy mortar

Radfahrer
Bicycle troops

Gebirgstruppen
Mountain troops

Kavallerie Cavalry		*Nachrichtentruppe* Signals troops	
Artillerie Artillery		*Vermessungseinheiten* Survey units	
Schützenkompanie Infantry company		*Fahrtruppe, Nachschubdienste* Transport troops, supply	
MG Kompanie Machine-gun company		*kl. Kraftwagenkolonne* Small transport column	
Infanteriegeschutzkompanie Infantry gun company		*Veterinärdienste* Veterinary services	
Radfahrerkompanie Bicycle company		*Feldpost* Postal service	
Stab Gebirgsjägerregiment Staff, mountain regiment		*Schlächterei* Abbatoir	
Schwadron Squadron		*Sanitatsdienste* Medical corps	
Stab Art. Abteilung Staff, artillery detachment		*motorisiert* Motorised	
Batterie l. Feldhaubitzen Light field howitzer battery		*Batterie 10 cm Kanonen (mot)* 10 cm gun battery (motorised)	
Batterie s. Feldhaubitzen Heavy field howitzer battery		*Batterie Sturmgeschütz (Sfl)* Battery assault guns (self-propelled)	
Panzer-Einheiten Tank units		*Stab Pz.-Abteilung* Staff, tank battalion	
Panzer-Späh-Einheiten Armoured reconnaissance units		*Pz-Späh-Kompanie* Armoured reconnaissance company	
Panzer-Abwehr-Einheiten Anti-tank units		*Panzer-Abwehr-Kompanie (mot)* Anti-tank company (motorised)	
Kraftradschütze Motorcycle troops		*Kraftradschützenkompanie* Motorcycle rifle company	
Pioniere Engineers		*Pionierkompanie* Engineer company	
Brückenbaukompanie (mot) Bridge-building company (motorised)		*Straßenbaukompanie* Road building company	
Flakartillerie AA units		*Stab einer Flak Abt. (mot)* Staff of a flak [anti-aircraft] battery (motorised)	
l.Flakbatterie 2 cm (mot) Light 2 cm flak [anti-aircraft] battery (motorised)		*s.Flakbatterie 8,8 cm (mot)* Heavy 8.8 cm flak battery (motorised)	
l.Flakbatterie 3,7 cm (mot) Light 3.7 cm flak [anti-aircraft] battery (motorised)		*Aufklärungsstaffel (K)* Reconnaissance squadron	
		I. Nachrichtenkolonne (mot) Signals column (motorised)	

Wettertrupp (mot)
Meteorological detachment
(motorised)

Stab eines Nachschubbatl. (mot)
Staff of a supply battalion (motorised)

kl. LKW-Kolonne für Betriebsstoffe
Small truck column for fuels and
lubricants

Feldgendarmerie
Military police

Bäckerei
Bakery

Krankenkraftwagenzug
Ambulance column

teilmotorisiert
Partially motorised

Sources

A. Unpublished sources

Bundesarchiv-Militärarchiv, Freiburg

RW 4/v. 511 OKW/WFSt.

RW 4/v. 516 OKW/WFA

RW 13/W 10-1/13, H 35/161 Wehrmachtsakademie, Vortrag

RM 6/K 10-2/78 Die Skl. und 'Seelöwe', Forschungsarbeit 1944

RM 6/K 10-2/9, 13 Dokumentation obiger Arbeit

RM 6/92, 93 Handmaterial 'Seelöwe' ObdM

RM 6/127–134, 181–192 Gen. d . Luftw. b. ObdM

RM 6/311, 312 Küsten-u. Hafenüberwachungsstelle

RM 7/109 1. Skl KTB Handelsschiffahrt

RM 7/124 1. Skl KTB Nordsee-Norwegen

RM 7/168 1. Sk1 KTB Luftkrieg

RM 7/876 Seetransportchef z. b. V.

RM 7/881 Landung Island

RM 7 Case GE 385 Seelöwe I, 1; I, 2

        386 Organisation Seelöwe

        387 Hafenanlagen Seelöwe

        388 Nachrichten Seelöwe

        389 Panzerkampfwagen Seelöwe

        390 Landung 40/41

        391 Unterlagen Seelöwe, Heer und Marine

        392–394 Anlagen zu Weisungen Seelöwe

        395 Marschrouten Seelöwe Seelöwe

        396-398 Seelöwe I, 3–5

        399 Seelöwe I, 4, 5 Erfahrungsberichte

RM 7 Case GE 400 Seelöwe I, 8 ObdL, OKH, Seelöwe I, 9 Marine, Luftwaffe

        401 Seelöwe I, 10 Heer

        402 Seelöwe I, 11 operative Absichten

        403 Seelöwe I, 12 Stand der Vorbereitungen

404 Seelöwe I, 13 Denkschrift ObdH
405 Seelöwe I, 14 Landungserfahrungen
406 Seelöwe I, 15, 16 Haifisch
474 Skl, XI, 4, 5
845 Versorgung Seelöwe
RM 35 I/M 205/PG 36766 Gruppe Nord, Herbstreise
RM 35 I/M 206/PG 36768 Gruppe Nord, Herbstreise
RM 35 II/M 377/37875 Gruppe West, Seelöwe
RM 35 II/M 378/37880, 37882 Gruppe West, Seelöwe
RM 35 WM 379/37883-37887 Gruppe West, Seelöwe
RM 35 II/M 380/37891 Gruppe West, Seelöwe
RM 35 II/M 381/37894, 37895 Gruppe West, Seelöwe
RM 45/v. M 297/37303/2 Kdr. Adm. Frankreich, Seelöwe
RM 45/v. M 298/37309, 37310, KTB Kdr. Adm. Frankreich
      37315
RM 45/v. M 299/37328, Kdr. Adm. Frankreich, Seelöwe
RM 45/v. M 300/37340-37349, Kdr. Adm. Frankreich, Seelöwe
RM 61/M 443/38123-38127 BSW, Seelöwe
RM 61/M 443/38136-38138B BSW, Seelöwe
RM 61/M 150/3508, KTB BSN
RM 61/M 484/38464, KTB Mar. Bef. haber Kanalküste
RM 61/M 516/Kr. 7267-7276 Seetransportchef z. b. V., Seelöwe
RM 108/M 832/47704, 47710 KTB KMD Rotterdam 47714, 47728
RM 108/M 837/47750, 47751 KMD Rotterdam, Transporter
RM 108/M 843/47791 KMD Rotterdam
RM 108/M 281/37188-37284 KMD Ostende
RM 108/M 277/37153-37169 KMD Le Havre
RM 108/M 304/37380/5 Umbauvorschrift für Prähme
RM TS/296/57322 S. Zetsche, DeutscheLandungs- fahrzeuge, Manuskript
RM TS/41/26861 Tragflächenboote, Bericht
RM TS/125/9010, 9009 Siebel-Gerät
RM TS/162/21262 Tragflächenboot VS 8
RM TS/210/18220 s. S. -u. Herbert-Fähre
RM TS/255/18542 Tragflächenboote
RM TS/610/6153 Landungsbrücken
RH 2/v. 456, 522 Gen. St. d. H., Op. Abt. (II)
RH 8/v. 1906 Flammanlage Pz. (Fl) III
RH 19 1/60, 156 KTB Heeresgr. A
RH 19 1/57, 61 Anlagen zum KTB Heeresgr. A
RH 19 IV/10 'Seelöwe'-Entwicklungen
RH 20-16/v. 5 AOK 16, Luft
RH 20-16/11301/1-3 KTB 2 Armeepionierführer 16
RH 20-16/13888/5, 8, 9 AOK 16, Seelöwe

RH 20-16/17808/8 AOK 16, Seelöwe

RH 24-7/29-32 KTB VII. AK

RH 24-7/135 Tätigkeitsbericht Ic VI LAK

RH 24-7/154, 155, 169, 170 Anlagen zum KTB VH. AK

RH 24-8/31, 38 KTB VIII. AK

RH 24-8/34, 39, 153, 154, 183 Anlagen zum KTB VIII. AK 186

RH 24-10/42, 65-68, 275- KTB X. AK mit Anlagen 276, 474

RH 24-13/6891/7 Tätigkeitsbericht Korpsintendant XIII. AK

RH 24-23/33, 40 Tätigkeitsbericht Ia(S), XXIII. AK

RH 24-38/8723/3-5 Anlagen zum KTB XXXVIII. AK

RH 26-7/10, 11 Anlagen zum KTB 7. I. D.

RH 26-8/13, 14 Anlagen zum KTB 8. I. D.

RH 26-12/15, 17, 18, 175, 176, Anlagen zum KTB 12. I. D. 184, 185, 188, 190, 192, 194, 254, 275, 276, 286

RH 26-17/3 Anlagen zum KTB 17. I. D.

RH 26-26/1, 2 KTB 26. I. D.

RH 26-34/5, 4, 6 KTB 34. I. D.

RH 26-35/11, 16, 18, 20–23, 25, 27, 29, KTB 35. I. D. mit Anlagen

RH 27-7/29, 30, 33, Anlagen zum KTB 7. Pz. Div.

RH27-10/18, Anlagen zum KTB 10. Pz. Div.

RH 28-1/18, 19, Anlagen zum KTB 1. Geb. Div.

RH 28-6/1, 2, KTB 6. Geb. Div.

RL 7/44, Luftflotte 2, Planspiele

RL 36/33-4, Seelöwe, Sonderkommando Fähre

Hist. Archiv Friedr. Krupp GmbH

WA 70/0-690;WA 70/0-692; WA 70/030-03; WA 70/0-695 (Geschäftsberichte)

Schuster, Karlgeorg: Warum sprang der Seelöwe nicht, unpublished report 1952

B. Published Sources

Ansel, Walter, *Hitler Confronts England* (London, 1960)

Assmann, Kurt, *Deutsche Schicksalsjahre* (Wiesbaden, 1950)

Assmann, Kurt, 'Operation Sealion', *US Naval Institute Proceedings* 76 (Annapolis, 1950)

Buchheit, Gert, *Der deutsche Geheimdienst* (Munich, 1966)

Churchill, Winston, *Der Zweite Weltkrieg* Vol. II (Hamburg, 1949)

Cox, Richard, *Operation Sealion* (San Rafael, CA, 1977)

Eckhardt, Alfred, 'Der Marine-Hafenbau im Kriege', *Nauticus 1944* (Berlin, 1944)

Fleming, Peter, *Invasion 1940* (London, 1957)

Förster, Erich, 'Der Seelöwe im Lichte neuerer Fachliteratur', *Marinerundschau* 57 (Frankfurt, 1960)

Greger, Rene, *Die russische Flotte 1914–1917* (Munich, 1970)

Grinnell-Milne, Duncan, *Der stille Sieg* (Tübingen, 1958)

Gröner, Erich, *Die Deutschen Kriegsschiffe 1815–1945* (Munich, 1966/67)

Irving, David, *Die Tragödie der deutschen Luftwaffe* (Frankfurt/M, 1972)

Jentschura, Hans-Georg, Jung, Dieter, and Mickel, Peter, *Die japanischen Kriegsschiffe 1869–1945* (Munich, 1970)

Kieser, Egbert, *Unternehmen Seelöwe* (Esslingen, 1987)

Klee, Karl, *Das Unternehmen Seelöwe* (Göttingen, 1958)

Klee, Karl, *Dokumente zum Unternehmen Seelöwe* (Göttingen, 1959)

Koch, Adalbert, *Die Geschichte der deutschen Flakartillerie 1935–1945* (Bad Nauheim, 1954)

Kramer, W., Kramer, R. and Foerster, H. D., *Die Schiffe der Königslinie* (Rostock, 1981)

Kugler, Randolf, *Chronik der Landungspioniere 1939–1945* (Self-published, 1971)

Ledebur, G. von, *Die Seemine* (Munich, 1977)

Lenton, Colledge, *Warships of World War II* (London, 1972)

Lewin, Ronald, *Entschied Ultra den Krieg?* (Koblenz/Bonn, 1981)

Longmate, Norman, *If Britain Had Fallen* (London, 1972)

Loose, Bernd, 'Die Entwicklung der Landungsfahrzeuge', in: *Marinekalender der DDR 1984* (Berlin, 1983)

Mordal, Jacques, *25 Centuries of Sea Warfare* (London, 1970)

Petter, Dietrich, *Pioniere* (Darmstadt, 1963)

Raeder, Erich, *Mein Leben*, Vol. II (Tübingen 1957)

Rohwer, Jürgen, and Hümmelchen, Gerhard, *Chronik des Seekriegs 1939–1945* (Oldenburg/Hamburg, n. d.)

Salewski, M., *Die deutsche Seekriegsleitung 1935–1945*, 3 vols (Munich, 1970–5)

Schmelzkopf, R., *Die deutsche Handelsschiffahrt 1919–1939*, (Oldenburg/Hamburg, n.d.)

Schmidt, Kludas, *Die deutschen Lazarettschiffe im Zweiten Weltkrieg* (Stuttgart, 1978)

Senger und Etterlin, F. von, *Die deutschen Panzer 1926–1945* (Munich, 1973)

Silverstone, Paul, *US Warships of World War II* (London, 1977)

Steensen, R. S., *Vore Panserskibe 1863–1943* (Kopenhagen, 1968)

Tessin, G., *Truppen und Verbände der Deutschen Wehrmacht und Waffen SS 1939–1945* (Osnabrück, 1977/80)

Vasseur, André-Georges, *Boulogne 1940* (Boulogne, 1989)

Wheatley, Ronald, *Operation Sea Lion* (Oxford, 1958)

Index